The
Columbia
River

· A Historical Travel Guide ·

The
Columbia
River

· A Historical Travel Guide ·

JoAnn Roe

CAXTON PRESS
Caldwell, Idaho
2013

ISBN 978-0-87004-538-7

Photos by JoAnn Roe unless otherwise indicated

Library of Congress Cataloging-in-Publication Data

Roe, JoAnn
  The Columbia River : a historical travel guide / by JoAnn Roe.
      pages cm
  Includes bibliographical references and index.
  ISBN 978-0-87004-538-7
  1. Columbia River--History. 2. Columbia River--Guidebooks. 3. Columbia River Region--History. 4. Columbia River Region--Guidebooks. I. Title.

  F853.R64 2013
  917.9704'44--dc23

                            2013014548

Printed in the United States of America by
CAXTON PRESS
184123

Contents

Acknowledgments

Essential to this book was access to libraries and museums throughout the Northwest. A big thanks to the reference librarians at Bellingham Public Library: Gayle Helgoe, Jane Lowrey, Margaret Zieeler, Bruce Radtke and Linda Hodge. The Wilson Library at Western Washington University has an astonishing collection of historical books and manuscripts, some very old and obscure. I appreciate the collections and services of: Selkirk College Library, Castlegar; David Thompson Library, Nelson; Columbia Basin College Library, Pasco; Mid-Columbia Regional Library, Kennewick; and Astor Public Library, Astoria.

Historical societies and museums along the length of the Columbia River were most helpful, several double-checking my first drafts. My gratitude to Windermere Valley Museum, Invermere; Golden District Museum, Golden; Revelstoke Museum, Revelstoke; Arrow Lakes Historical Society, Nakusp; Doukhobor Historical Village; Rossland Museum; Stevens County Historical Museum, Colville; the Grand Coulee Pioneers; North Central Washington Regional Museum, Wenatchee; archives and historians of Colville Federated Tribes at Nespelem and Coulee Dam and of Yakima Indian Nation, Toppenish; Skamania County Museum, Stevenson; Cascade Locks Historical Museum; Oregon Historical Society, Portland; U.S. Army Corps of Engineers, Portland; Clark County Historical Museum, Vancouver; Cowlitz County Museum, Kelso; Ilwaco Heritage Museum, Ilwaco; Heritage Center Museum, Astoria; Columbia River Maritime Museum, Astoria; Fort Stevens Museum on Clatsop Spit.

I am grateful to the more than 250 people I interviewed but cannot list here, but particularly thank: Derryll White, Carol Seable, Don Yanko, Winifred Weir, Ian Weir, Ian Jack of Kootenay National Park, Peter Schlunneger, Philip Hein, John Buffery, Marg and Jim Sproat, Ruby Nobbs, Gordon Bell, Margaret McMahon, Al McAskill, Jack Harris, Joe Biagoni, John Charters, Adelin Fredin, Andy Joseph, Wyn Self, Jim Black, Edith Lael, Craig Sprankle, Chic Phillips, Bill Brauner, Keith Murray, Brycene Neaman, Hu Blonk (who checked the Grand Coulee Dam info), Wilfred Woods, Irene Van Doren, Debby Hall, Virginia Wyena, Robert Ruby for consultations about Indian history, Tom Moak, Marilyn Druby of Westinghouse

Hanford, Rich Steele, Captain Keith Rodenbough, Christof Cook, Walt Smith, Gus Norwood, Jim Barbouletos, Cliff Crawford, Dick Montgomery, Fay Nelson, Carl Floten, Gladys Seufert, Irene Sidwell, Henry and Jean Reents, Sam McKintrey, Irene Martin, Stanley Everman, Noreen Robinson, Captain John Roe, Jim Suomela, Don Marshall, Ross McDonald, Darrell Murrdy, Lt. Bill Harper, Steve Felkins, Bob Petersoo, Jerry Ostermiiler, Bruce Berney. Thank you to visitors centers all along the river who double checked information for the travel segment. A special thanks to my husband, Ernie Burkhart, who endured my frequent absences on research. Above all, thanks to editor Mae Reid-Bills who kept me straight on everything.

JoAnn Roe
Bellingham, Washington

Preface

During my extensive travels in the Northwest researching other books and articles, I often drove along the Columbia River or crossed its broad waters. Its variable moods and the diverse terrain through which it flows caused me to speculate on its effect on historical events and people. When a celebration was planned to commemorate Robert Gray's discovery of the Columbia River, the first known entry by a nonnative person, I wanted to write the river's story. I wanted to discover and share with travelers to the river and armchair historians, too, "what happened around here, anyway."

Upon a skeletal framework of the political and scholarly history of the Columbia River's immediate environs I have told about the people who used the river, fought it, narrowly escaped death on it, some of them ordinary, others renowned. The river is the star of the saga. During 1990 and 1991, I spent one third of my time on or along the river; the other two-thirds of the time I delved into scholarly histories, accounts by individuals who have had direct experiences on the river, historical society accounts by people who lived or worked on the Columbia, and talked with hundreds of people about the river and its influence on their lives and works. As a result, I have fallen in love with the river more than ever. I am filled with awe at the sheer force of so much water in motion. In one book on a vast river, I confined my text to the river itself and its immediate environs. Remember, however, that the Columbia River watershed takes in a vast area from east central British Columbia to Nevada, the Rocky Mountains to the Pacific Ocean, except for certain portions west of the coastal Cascades Mountains.

To help the stranger visiting the Columbia River, I also share information about places along the river. The listings are not intended as a complete directory, only some of my own choices.

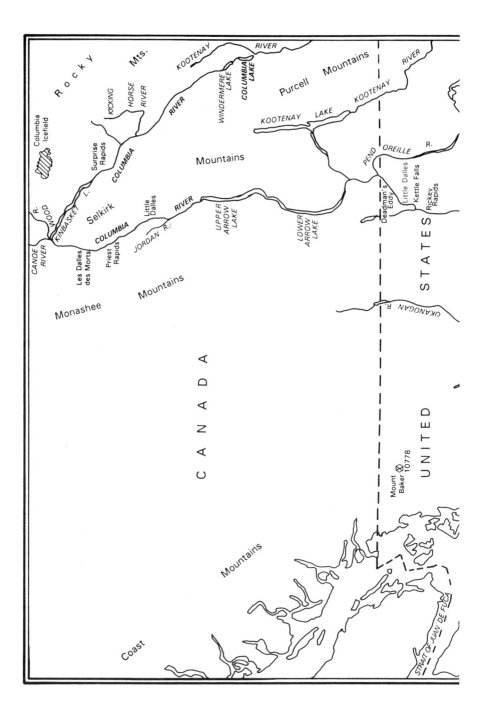

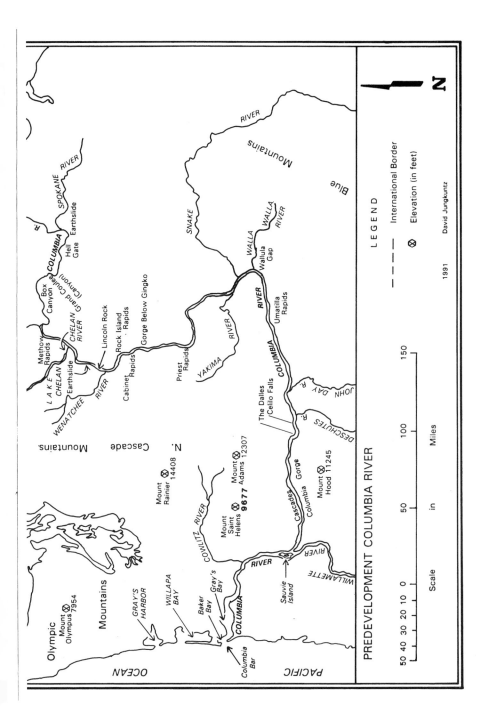

PREDEVELOPMENT COLUMBIA RIVER

Scale   in   Miles

50 40 30 20 10 0   50   100   150

LEGEND

– – – International Border

⊗ Elevation (in feet)

1991   David Jungkuntz

OCEAN

PACIFIC

Olympic
Mount
Olympus 7954 ⊗

Mountains

GRAY'S HARBOR

WILLAPA BAY

Baker Bay

Gray's Bay

COLUMBIA

Columbia Bar

Sauvie Island

WILLAMETTE

RIVER

COWLITZ RIVER

Mount Saint Helens ⊗ 9677

Mount Adams 12307 ⊗

Mount Rainier ⊗ 14408

N.

Cascade   Mountains.

Mount Hood 11245 ⊗

Columbia Gorge

Cascades

The Dalles
Celilo Falls

COLUMBIA RIVER

DESCHUTES R.

JOHN DAY R.

Umatilla Rapids

Wallula Gap

WALLA WALLA RIVER

YAKIMA RIVER

Priest Rapids

Gorge Below Gingko

Rock Island Rapids

Lincoln Rock

Cabinet Rapids

CHELAN RIVER

Earthslide

LAKE CHELAN

WENATCHEE RIVER

Methow Rapids

R.

Box Canyon

Grand Coulee (Canyon)

COLUMBIA

Hell Gate

Earthslide

SPOKANE RIVER

SNAKE   RIVER

Blue   Mountains

N

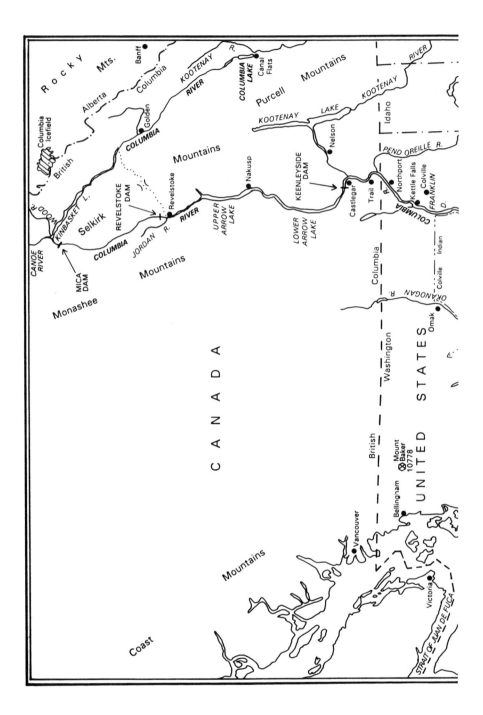

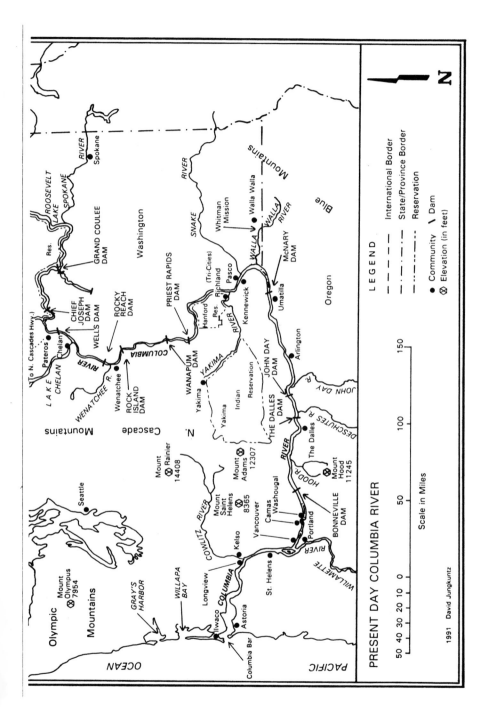

PRESENT DAY COLUMBIA RIVER

LEGEND

International Border
State/Province Border
Reservation
● Community   ⟍ Dam
⊗ Elevation (in feet)

Scale in Miles

50 40 30 20 10 0   50   100   150

1991 David Jungkuntz

Chapter 1

Discovery

On May 11, 1792, Captain Robert Gray on the American ship *Columbia Rediviva* courageously tackled the formidable entrance to the Columbia River from the north Pacific Ocean and came into a quiet inner bay. It seemed to be an anchoring of little consequence, but it changed North American history.

For three hundred years after Columbus' voyage of 1492, Europeans intruded into Mexico and the eastern and southern coasts of today's United States. The Pacific Northwest coast and the lands west of the Mississippi River were known only to the native people and a handful of wandering trappers—most of them Hudson's Bay Company people who worked from scattered posts across the northerly forests (Canada now). In the lands that became Alaska, the Russians established colonies at Kodiak (1784) and Sitka (1799). Before Gray's discovery of the Columbia River, both Britain and Russia had better claims to the Northwest lands than the United States.

In addition to plying a profitable fur trade, British captains sought a northwest passage, hoping for a benign strait that would make it unnecessary to challenge the hoary sea gods of Cape Horn, with their towering waves and gales.

Other European explorers searched, too. In 1775, Don Bruno de Heceta of Spain came ashore at 47 degrees 30 minutes north latitude on the Washington coast to get fresh water and take possession of the area for Spain; but his landing party was killed by local Indians. Returning southward, Heceta was intrigued by muddy stains far at sea. He guessed there was a mighty river, perhaps even the fabled passage, north of 46 degrees latitude and duly noted it in his logs and charts as "Bahia de Asuncion Entry." Captain James Cook of the British navy passed by the Columbia and Strait of Juan de Fuca in 1778, and found Nootka Sound on the west coast of Vancouver Island. But the tantalizing possibility of a passage remained in the back of mariners' minds. In 1787, an enterprising New England merchant, Charles Bulfinch, put together a combine of six investors under a general manager, Joseph Barrell, to launch a trading voyage to the fabled

Northwest. The *Columbia Rediviva,* 83 feet 6 inches long, was placed under the command of John Kendrick, a well-experienced but aging officer; her companion, *Lady Washington,* a 90-ton sloop probably 64 feet long, was given to a younger man, Captain Robert Gray. The plan was to obtain furs from Northwest Indians in exchange for gewgaws, then sail for China and barter or sell them for teas and silks sought after in New England. The two ships left Boston on October 1, 1787.

Captain Kendrick proved to be a strange fellow, procrastinating in every port as if reluctant to face the dangers ahead. He antagonized members of his crew, causing First Mate Simeon Woodruff to request discharge in the Cape Verde Islands, where ships bound for the Pacific stocked up with food and water. Another capable officer, Robert Haswell, requested transfer to Gray's ship. (Haswell wrote a valuable log of the two voyages of the *Columbia.*)

In the ocean wilderness of the South Pacific, the two ships became separated, Gray continuing to the rendezvous at Nootka Sound. En route he landed for supplies, since his men had scurvy, at Tillamook Bay, just south of the Columbia River bar. After several days of friendly trading, local Indians turned aggressive, and Gray's ship barely escaped the bay, which he called Murderer's Harbour (Tillamook Bay). He sped northward to Clayoquot Sound and then Nootka Sound.

After arriving at Nootka, over a month behind the *Lady Washington,* Kendrick assigned Gray to gather furs along the southeast Alaska coast. When a full load of furs was ready for transport to the Orient, Kendrick inexplicably wanted to trade commands with Gray. Thus, Gray sailed off for Macao and Whampoa (port for Canton) as commander of the *Columbia,* returning to Boston via the Cape of Good Hope in August 1790.

The Snake Indians watching white men float down the Columbia River in makeshift rafts. From an original oil painting by Frederick L. Hubbard entitled "White Men on the Columbia." Used by permission.

The financiers of the voyage were disturbed at Kendrick's meanderings, and neither he nor the *Lady Washington* figured again in history significantly. Kendrick was shot dead in 1794.

In Boston, however, general manager Barrell determined to send the *Columbia* back to the Northwest under Gray. Two of the shareholders sold their shares, some to Captain Gray.

On September 28, 1790, Gray sailed off into history, making the trip to Clayoquot Sound near Nootka in eight months, rather than the eleven spent on the first voyage. Ever since learning of Heceta's report, Gray had hoped to explore Heceta's "Bahia de Asuncion Entry," perhaps on this voyage. First, though, he had to discharge his trading duties for Barrell's investors.

Gray's crew built the sloop *Adventure* to ply local waters for fur-trading, the first American vessel built on the west coast. Under command of Robert Haswell, she headed northward.

The *Columbia* turned south on April 12, 1792, as much to explore as to gather furs. At 46 degrees 10 minutes north latitude, the water was as muddy as observed on an earlier passage, but turbulent waters raised by gale-force winds kept Gray from entering the Columbia River, even though he cruised offshore for nearly two weeks. On April 28, anchored off the entrance to the Quillayute River (La Push), he met Captain George Vancouver, H.M.S. *Discovery*, and Lieutenant William R. Broughton, tender *Chatham,* on an exploring mission. The two parties compared notes, and Vancouver was said to scoff at the existence of a big river. Broughton, however, was listening hard to Gray.

After a foray into the Strait of Juan de Fuca, Gray again stood southward on May 5, in calmer weather. This time he spied an opening in the coast, sent a pinnace ahead, and entered Gray's Harbor (which he called Bulfinch's Harbor). On May 10, 1792, he sailed past Willapa Bay in the dark, possibly considering it a large cove, and at 46 degrees 7 minutes saw an opening in the line of breakers, quieter than before. Under short sail he slowly entered the Columbia, partially blocked by two large sand bars. Following the calls of a competent leadsman, he moved smartly up the river to find anchorage on the north side about six miles from the bar (Gray's Bay). Gray estimated the river to be about four miles wide and named it "Columbia's River." Later historians speculated whether it was to honor Gray's ship or the United States, affectionately referred to as "Columbia."

Astounded to see a white-winged ship within their river, the Chinook Indians led by one-eyed Chief Comcomly met one-eyed Captain Gray. The friendly people brought otter skins to trade for copper, iron spikes and other articles.

For nine days, until May 20, the ship's crew enjoyed a respite from the stormy Pacific. They explored upriver seven or eight miles, patched up their ship, explored ashore, and traded.

After leaving the river, Gray in the *Columbia* returned to fur-trading, both in company and separately with the sloop *Adventure,* among the island-studded waters of today's British Columbia and Southeast Alaska, coping with natives friendly one moment, hostile the next. When he had a full load of furs, Gray sold the *Adventure* to the Spaniards at Neah Bay and returned home to Boston via the Orient.

Thereafter the ship *Columbia* was sold; later, she succumbed to shipworms and was sold for scrap in 1801. Given command of the brig *Alert,* Gray and his crew sailed for the Pacific once more in 1798, the time of an undeclared naval war between France and the United States. Off South America the French frigate *Republican* seized the *Alert,* retained the chief mate and a boy, and sent her to the Spanish port of Montevideo, Uruguay, under a prize crew. Gray and the remaining crewmen were confined on the *Republican.* Several months later they were released at Montevideo when the French ship put in for supplies and managed to escape in the American schooner *James* that had been seized and moored at Montevideo. The Americans sailed home to Boston in the leaky vessel, and Gray received command of a different ship. His activities thereafter were unremarkable, and in 1806, the good captain died of yellow fever contracted at Charleston, South Carolina.

Meanwhile, with the door opened to Columbia's River, the next craft to enter was the small British fur-trading schooner *Jenny,* anchoring in the bay named for her master, James Baker, in the autumn of 1792. Discovering her at anchor was the Englishman, Lieutenant W. R. Broughton, who in October successfully made it over the turbulent entrance in the *Chatham* (leaving Vancouver standing out to sea in a gale). In a small boat, Broughton proceeded to explore upstream with a cutter and launch to the mouth of the Sandy River above Portland, crossing to the Washougal River. This excursion formed a partial basis for British claims that they had discovered the river and had a right to adjacent lands.

The Columbia River did not prove to be the Northwest Passage, but it did form an avenue for exploration and settlement of Oregon, Washington and British Columbia. Later a portion of the river became the boundary between Oregon and Washington states.

Let's return to that discovery year of 1792. What might a Pegasus explorer have reported, silently galloping through space above the wildly romantic Columbia's River? (Modern place names are used to provide orientation.)

Between the Purcell and Rocky Mountains of British Columbia in a mountain valley as lovely as a new mother, the Columbia River is born with a murmur. It flows northward purposefully from Columbia Lake to Lake Windermere, then spreads its arms to embrace lazily the entire upper Columbia Valley, often a mile wide with shallow channels between reeds and marsh grass.

North of Golden it narrows and, with little warning, plunges through Surprise Rapids to emerge, once more tranquil, in Kinbasket Lake. The broad river sweeps northwesterly, then sharply veers southwesterly, descending swiftly now in a series of wicked rapids that extend over a hundred miles. It flows tranquilly as the incomparably beautiful Arrow Lakes for 134 miles, only to become a brute again.

The river speeds through the narrow canyons by Castlegar, amplified by the cacophony of rushing water as the giant Kootenay River comes in. Through the steep-walled bluffs it tears, caroming off boulders and foaming around obstructions to form eddies or giant whirlpools many feet in diameter, whirlpools that have claimed countless lives over the centuries.

Churning between high sand bluffs, topped by ragged, boulder-strewn hills, it is joined by the Pend Oreille River with a rush that sends three-foot waves across its width. The Columbia surges into the United States past Northport into the Little Dalles, where the eroded walls of the river bounce the waters back and forth, building frightening waves in the center. It plunges over 20-foot Kettle Falls, where Indians caught fish, and moves on through rock-strewn Rickey Rapids and terrible Box Canyon with their dangerous eddies.

The Columbia passes the primeval Grand Coulee, once the river's bed, an awesome, desolate side canyon. Joined by the Okanogan River in a serene marriage, the Columbia slows to reflect the dry, high benchlands through which its monster ancestor river tore its way.

Blocked by the North Cascades Mountains, the river is shunted southward for over a hundred miles, rippling through rapids less terrible than those above. It loops southeasterly, punctuated by a midstream pinnacle standing starkly like a sentinel, through valleys and canyons parched and deserted. Beyond the Tri-Cities the mighty Columbia turns westward toward its rendezvous with the Pacific, widened by the swift waters of the Snake River.

The river runs straight now, intent on reaching its goal. Over roaring Celilo Falls and the eight-mile rapids of the Dalles it charges and rushes swiftly through the grand cascades of the Columbia gorge. It becomes a broad flow that will carry singing Hudson's Bay voyageurs by canoe to Fort Vancouver, and anxious settlers by makeshift flatboat to the Willamette of Oregon.

The ever-broadening river seeks myriad channels around islands as it makes a double curve north and west past Longview. Still the hypnotic eddies swirl as the swift current separates and reforms.

Finally the goal is in sight. Occasionally more than six miles wide, the mighty Columbia River carrying the drainage from 259,000 square miles of Northwest lands forces its way into the north Pacific Ocean. The seething clash between fresh and salt water, between opposing currents, throws up plumes of foam and creates huge breakers. Vicious patternless waves bounce off each other to form peaks of water like the mountains of the Columbia's birth. Into its maw will go feeble boats and ships crossing the Columbia Bar, a shifting strand of sand and rock.

Staining the water with silt for miles into the Pacific Ocean, the 1,214-mile Columbia River rests at last, relinquishing its flow to the mightier ocean.

The River in Canada

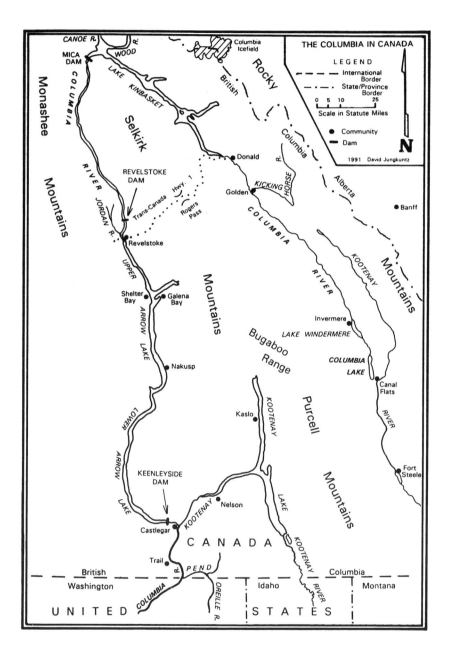

THE COLUMBIA IN CANADA

LEGEND

- - - - International Border
- · - · - State/Province Border

0   5   10   25
Scale in Statute Miles

● Community
▬ Dam

1991   David Jungkuntz

N

Chapter 2

The Headwaters

In a mountain valley of spellbinding beauty 2,601 feet high, hemmed in by the Purcell Range to the west and the Rocky Mountains to the east, the Columbia River—only a few feet across—flows northward from Columbia Lake. The lake is fed by springs and Dutch Creek, and no one can be truly sure which is the exact birth site. A scant mile and a half across a gravelly barrier 11 feet high, the Kootenay River flows southward from its birthplace west of Banff. The two will meet again thirty miles north of the international border after distant meanderings.

The Columbia River follows the deep Rocky Mountain Trench, mirroring the towering crags of the mountain ranges. Interesting to geologists is that, on the west, the largely granite Purcell and Selkirk ranges were raised perhaps 160 million years before the Rocky Mountains of limestone/sandstone base on the east. On September 4, 1845, Father Pierre J. deSmet contemplated with admiration "those rugged and gigantic mountains where the Great River escapes-majestic, but impetuous and in its vagrant course it is undoubtedly the most dangerous river on the western side of the American hemisphere." (J. Monroe Thorington, "The Historical Geography of the Columbia-Kootenay Valley," p. 18, pamphlet, 1933, at David Thompson Library, Canadian International College, Nelson, British Columbia.)

During the Pleistocene Age, glaciers formed and receded, scouring the valleys deeper and leaving gravel behind. As the earth warmed, stubborn ice-filled depressions resisted melting to form Lake Windermere and Columbia Lake. North of Windermere still another large ice block finally melted through to carve out the Big Bend channel. In this young Rocky Mountain/Selkirk region, little erosion has yet taken place to form tillable areas. South of Columbia Lake, the Kootenay River, however, overflowed to create vast, fertile deltas.

In ancient times Kootenay Indians from the south and Shuswap Indians from the north periodically traveled into the Columbia Valley to hunt and fish. Around 1800, a band of fifty or sixty Shuswap Indians, mostly the extended family of Chief Kenpe'sket (or Kinbasket), settled permanently in the upper

Columbia's valleys. Another band, of uncertain ethnographic origin, settled near the Arrow Lakes. Indian camps, probably seasonal, were found on the Slocan River, at Arrowhead, and north of the Columbia-Kootenay junction. Early settlers reported Indian sweat houses around Arrow Lakes, and told of meeting American Indians coming north to fish. Sir George Simpson called the people "Sinachicks," a version of their own word, "sngaytskstx." In 1909 writings, ethnographer James Teit estimated that the Arrow Lakes band included twenty-six members.

Early explorers commented that the local Indians were honest and handsome. They used underground homes in winter (except for the Arrow Lakes bands), building circular underground cellars to preserve fish and other perishables. ("Dimples" from these are visible near Columbia Lake.) They were superb canoeists, using a curious shovel-nosed or sturgeon-nosed canoe unlike others in North America and thought to be directly related to Siberian-style canoes.

In summer the Indians used transportable Plains-style tepees. The men wore decorated skin shirts fastened with thongs at the shoulder, and breechcloths with leggings. Women's garments were loose and fastened with a fancy belt. Shuswaps were more lively than their Kootenay cousins, who were reported as serious and steadfast.

Both were excellent fishermen, using dip nets, fish spears, lines with bone hooks or large nets similar to today's gill nets. They built fish weirs or traps near outlets of streams and lakes, the remains of one visible in the early 1900s near the mouth of the Kootenay River at Robson. To capture deer they used unusual corrals built into the water with only one escape gate, closed by a watchful attendant when the deer were inside drinking.

Heavy snows and bitter cold discouraged settlement around the Big Bend and Revelstoke. These areas usually were shared (somewhat uneasily at times) for hunting and fishing by the Shuswap and Kootetray, as well as Stony and Piegan parties.

In those years salmon migrated all the way from the Pacific Ocean to Columbia Lake, especially favoring gravel beds at Athalmer in the Columbia River channel where it left Lake Windermere. At spawning time, so far from the ocean, the fish began to deteriorate in the upper reaches and were usable only after being smoked or dried. The hunting was good. The marshy river formed one of the best wetlands cradles for wildlife and birds that exists in North America. Intense populations of osprey, eagles, brants, mallards and geese still thrive there, building nests in the dense brush of the marshy islets, heavy with the sweet smell of clover. Between Fairmont and Invermere is a sanctuary for the rare blue heron. Transient species rest in the valley, part of the Pacific Flyway. Profuse numbers of humming birds winter in the valley, and locals have a persistent theory that when summer comes, these tiny birds migrate southward by clinging to the underfeathers of the stronger Canadian geese. A charming story, but wildlife experts are skeptical.

In winter thousands of Townsend's solitaire feed on juniper berries. Western tanager and slate-colored junko dart about, as well as one of the highest populations of blackcap, boreal and mountain chickadees in the Pacific Northwest. Year-round residents include robins, ravens and Canada jays or whiskeyjacks.

The spongy channels are a natural home for Columbia ground squirrels, muskrats and beaver, early attracting trappers. Higher on the pleasant terraces formed by past glacial melts, elk and whitetail deer winter; in summer they gravitate farther to the upland fastnesses to join bighorn sheep, mountain goats, black and grizzly bears. Curiously, bighorn sheep are almost unknown in the Purcells, preferring the warmer, grassier, westerly facing slopes of the Rockies. As late as 1922, numerous wolves as large as one hundred pounds prowled the Selkirks around Slocan Lake, killing deer but not bothering humans.

In the shadow of the Purcells and Selkirks, rainfall is moderate. Prevailing southwest winds are blunted. High above the valley, those same winds rage wildly as they confront the Rocky Mountain barrier, often creating exciting flight conditions for light aircraft.

Signaling turbulent conditions aloft, lightning storms play over the sky-piercing peaks . Thor's legendary thunderbolts reverberate through the valley. Curious phenomena occur among the peaks. In the fall of 1946, among the icy pinnacles of Mount Trident, a family saw the replica of the three sharp peaks of the mountain, suspended in the sky like a phantom. The phenomenon is known as "The Spectre of the Brocken" and is formed when the sun, low in the slry, shines on a bank of clouds, mainly ice crystals, in high mountain areas.

A Swiss guide, Herr Carl Sulzer, had an odd experience at a height west of Mount Tupper. He was sketching the scenery when a thundercloud enveloped him. Suddenly, two stone slabs facing each other nearby began to make a humming noise, and the metal holder of his sketching pencil buzzed. When a mist set in, his dampened fingers buzzed. He related that he realized the potential danger but convinced himself it was not lethal.

During an expedition ordered by the North West Company, explorer David Thompson told of watching a storm form over the steep sides of the Rockies above the Columbia River. He said: "Its first direction was from the Pacific Ocean, eastward up the valley of the lower Columbia River, and McGilliway's River [Kootenay]. ... the Sun was shining on these steep Rocks when the clouds of the Storm entered about 2,000 feet above ... in large revolving circles, . . . circle within circle for nearly twenty miles along these high hills until the clouds closed on me, it all was obscurity: it was a grand sight, and deeply riveted my attention." (J.B.Tyrrell, editor, *David Thompson's Narrative*. [Toronto: The Champlain Society, 1916], 404.)

After Gray's discovery of the mouth of the Columbia River, searchers eagerly sought for its headwaters. Lacking in geographical knowledge, some people thought the river flowed from Lake Superior to the Pacific. Between 1783 and 1793, Alexander Mackenzie searched too far north and found not the Columbia, but the grand Mackenzie, the Peace and the Fraser rivers. The mysterious Columbia had been called the River of the West, the Thegayo and the Rio de los Reyes.

Trying to outflank its rival Hudson's Bay Company, the North West Company sent David Thompson in 1807 to locate the source of the Columbia and establish posts in today's British Columbia and Washington.

A well-educated, moral and intensely energetic man, David Thompson was a surveyor formerly employed by Hudson's Bay Company. He had switched allegiance to the North West Company in 1797. On June 30, 1807, he crossed the Rocky Mountains and came down the Blaeberry River to the Columbia River about twenty miles north of today's Golden. (He referred to today's Columbia as the Kootanie using various spellings.) Tracing the river upstream to Columbia Lake, he discovered the second river, McGillivray's River (Kootenay), a south-flowing stream. Although he felt intuitively that the "Kootanie" River might be the Columbia River, he had no time then to explore. First he established a trading post, the *Kootenae* House, on Lake Windermere, then worked from there to establish other posts along McGillivray's River in what is now Idaho and Montana.

In early September 1810, he was running late on his return trip from Rainy Lake to the Columbia Valley. Winter threatened as his party approached the Rockies and the Blaeberry trail. Wisely he left his family at Fort Augustus (Edmonton). Twenty miles from the Rockies with an advance hunting party Thompson learned that his four trading canoes had been stopped by Piegan Indians, angered that the North West Company was selling guns to the Flatheads, traditional enemies. After a brief skirmish the canoe brigade retreated with injuries. Thompson's hunting party circled around the Indian camp and rejoined the canoeists; luckily a snowstorm obliterated their tracks.

Determined to return to Kootenae House, Thompson obtained horses to follow an old Assiniboine footpath toward Athabasca Pass. By December 29, in the dead of winter, he began the formidable crossing with dogs and sleds.

On January 10, 1811, the party was in Athabasca Pass (elevation 5,735 feet). To the right lay a huge glacier perhaps 2,000 feet high "of a clean fine green color." But the men "were not at their ease," drily remarked Thompson. No wonder. They were enduring temperatures to -32° F., slogging along on snowshoes—hard work on sternly rationed food. Thompson moved down the western slope, steep and ragged, where storms lashed the men and melted the snow, crusting to ice. Dogs and sleds often came to rest on opposite sides of trees.

Lacking three men, who had deserted in the heights of Athabasca Pass, Thompson's party came down the Wood River to its junction with the Columbia and the Canoe River. On the delta there, a point he called Boat Encampment, he wisely chose to stop. In a cedar cabin twelve feet by twelve feet the men spent a cramped winter.

Thompson mentioned the immense trees—white cedars of 15 to 36 feet girth, pines from 18 to 42 feet in girth with no branches for the first 200 feet of trunk.

He also noted that the different species did not intermix, growing in plots adjacent to one another.

Boat Encampment later became the regular transfer point from canoe to horse for fur traders traveling east to their company's headquarters. This does not mean that the trail became improved. In 1817, Ross Cox said that, to cross the Wood River at a point called the "grande traverse," owing to its great depth and breadth, the men had to hold hands and, even then, slightly built men were often swept off their feet by the force of the current.

In 1989 a young mountaineer, Phil Hein, who has a business in the Waputik Range adjacent to Yoho National Park, was asked by the Ministry of Forests to trace Thompson's Athabasca trail on the western slopes. (The pass portion lies within Jasper National Parkand is maintained.) The trail was listed as a Heritage Trail in 1973, protecting the path itself plus a short distance to each side, but little of it had been found. The Ministry feared the trail might be obliterated if subjected to heavy logging machinery. This had happened earlier to the Blaeberry Trail.

Hein and his friend, Jim Oseychuk, set out into the wilderness. Since explorer Walter Moberly brought 250 horses over the trail in 1873, no record existed of its use.

"It was a thrilling project, as I love the history of the Columbia River," said Hein. "We read everything we could find about Thompson's travels to give us clues, and in 1980, the Ministry of Forests had located a few bits of trail."

The men climbed the Grand Côte, the steeply ascending ridge dividing the Wood River from Pacific Creek. They found two faint, discolored blazes in a regrowth forest, some on dead trees, and signs of a horse trail across a rocky section. In a luxuriant, overgrown forest near what appeared to be an old campsite, Phil excitedly yelled to his partner, "Look!"

Several feet above ground there were odd circles with blister-like protrusions, as if an old wound had been repaired. There, inside each bared circle lay ancient blazes on the trees.

Able now to follow the trail, though with difficulty, Hein and Oseychuk found other items, animal traps placed by twentieth century trappers, and best of all, the carved name of "F. Moberly," who must have been with his brother Walter when he came west.

With a strong sense of history Phil Hein, Jim Oseychuk and three young helpers cleared 12 to 15 kilometers of trail, finishing at the Committee Punchbowl promontory one evening. There they watched the setting sun send shafts of orange and pink over the Columbia River Valley. The ghost of David Thompson was strong.

Returning to Thompson's story, in the spring of 1811, as soon as winter's grip eased, Thompson and his men started for Kootenae House, dragging their canoe over ice in Kinbasket Lake. South of that, the river was open, and they reached their post. On May 14, Thompson went by canoe and horse to Spokane House, where Finan McDonald was stationed. Hardly pausing, Thompson moved swiftly to a point below Kettle Falls and ran down the Columbia River to its mouth, arriving on July 15. He found Americans in firm possession of newly built Fort Astoria.

Old and friendly competitors (as individuals), the Americans outfitted Thompson for his return trip, but both parties realized their nations had conflicting claims to this territory. Subsequently, during the War of 1812, the Americans sold Fort Astoria to the North West Company, which merged into Hudson's Bay Company in 1821.

Thompson shortly returned upriver and, entering the Snake River, obtained horses to travel to Spokane. Soon he came back to the Columbia, built another canoe above the falls, and made his way up river to Boat Encampment. He had proven to himself and the world that this was, indeed, the Columbia River, the great river of the West.

Chapter 3

The Upper Columbia Valley

T he Upper Columbia Valley remained pristine for a decade after Thompson's discovery, except for the transient visits of George Simpson, James Sinclair, Father deSmet and other explorers. Francois Morigeau from St. Martin's, Quebec, came with his family in 1819 to become the valley's first permanent settler. He moved near Fort Colville, Washington, in 1845, but his son Baptiste returned as an adult to farm, to scout for Major A. B. Rogers of the Canadian Pacific Railway and to operate a store at Golden from 1883 to 1885.

This remote alpine valley burst into the news when gold was discovered in 1864 on Wild Horse Creek, about sixty miles south of Windermere. Prospectors swarmed through the area—many struggling through the bewildering northern Moyie River swamps, others coming over old Rocky Mountain trails to the Columbia or Kootenay river, then south to Wild Horse. That year John Galbraith started a ferry service across the Kootetroy, around which arose a small permanent settlement, Galbraith's Ferry. The rush subsided as quickly as it began, many prospectors moving on to the Big Bend of the Columbia above Revelstoke—the next promised land. By 1882, only eleven white settlers remained in the headwaters region.

Then came THE RAILROAD. As early as 1857, the British Crown sent explorers to assess the wisdom of building a railway to the Pacific. When British Columbia Colony was promised a railroad as an inducement to join the Confederation of Canada, the surveys became more urgent. Back East many schemes for railways were mere promotions that lined the pockets of real estate developers or amplified the importance of politicians. Yet surveyors sent out West did return with valuable information, especially the expeditions of Captain John Palliser in 1857 to 1859 and Walter Moberly from 1865 to 1874.

Palliser was accompanied by the eminent geologist, Sir James Hector. Near the crest of the Rocky Mountains, Palliser led one group of men into the Columbia Valley by the Kananaskis River, arriving near Canal Flats. Hector led another to travel the Bow River to the Vermillion, then the Beaverfoot to the Kicking Horse River—named thus because a packhorse gave Hector a good smack there.

Palliser met with Walter Moberly, who was then working in Victoria, British Columbia, to express his pessimism over the wisdom of an east-west railroad. A road surveyor during the Barkerville gold rush, Moberly was intrigued, not daunted, by Palliser's report. After his own inspections, Moberly recommended building the railroad directly along the Columbia's Big Bend from Golden to Revelstoke, then westerly through Eagle Pass, a narrow opening twelve miles west (Three Valley Gap).

As it turned out, Major A. B. Rogers, Engineer in Charge of the Mountain Division for Canadian Pacific Railway (CPR), located and surveyed the present route between 1881 and 1884, crossing the Selkirk Range. Crews working from east and west joined the rails at Craigellachie in 1885.

A supply center, Golden got its name when surveyor F. W. Aylmer was told by the mail carrier that Carlin's Camp east in the Rockies had named itself "Silver City," whereupon Aylmer, not to be outdone, said, "Well, then, we'll call our camp Golden City," later shortened to Golden. By 1888, Golden was still a railroad and mining town, a tough place to let off steam at a couple of taverns. In 1890, a tourist found there only a dozen wood and canvas shacks plus the Queen's Hotel built of logs. Golden's chief importance was as an exchange point from rail to Columbia River steamboat or stagecoach.

A member of the Aylmer surveying party, Frank P. Armstrong, quit the CPR in 1884 to preempt 320 acres of land east of Columbia Lake and raise potatoes. He rowed all the way to Golden to sell them to the railroad. With boundless energy but minimal carpentry skills, Armstrong then fashioned a stern-wheeler in 1886 to transport passengers and freight from Golden to Columbia Lake. The *Duchess*, a laughably ugly craft of lumber varying in thickness and sizes, drew only fourteen inches fully loaded, making her admirably suited for the Columbia's shallow channels. Low-hanging trees, fallen trees, shifting channels and occasional rapids made travel a challenge. Frequently, passengers were pressed into cutting wood for the insatiable boiler.

Armstrong's inept maritime efforts were visionary, however. With easier access by rail, prospectors again thronged to new finds at Wild Horse Creek, many going to Golden and then south on his boat.

There was also a stage of sorts from Golden to Galbraith's Ferry, uncomfortable and hazardous. Stage stops like the one at the Hog Ranch south of Golden, named because patrons lay around drunk as hogs, or at Brisco operated by Harry "Shorty" Achison, a man addicted to spitting tobacco juice anywhere in the house-well, they did not constitute gracious overnight traveling. In one incident, a stage fell through a bridge into the cold waters of the river. Yes, the best path to the diggings was on Armstrong's crude craft.

Trouble started brewing in 1884, when two men were murdered near Golden (Deadman's Creek today)—prospectors Mathew Hilton and William Kemp. More than two years later, the Kootenay constable arrested and jailed two Kootenay Indians because they had Hilton's saddle. Outraged, the Kootenay band's Chief Isadore stormed into town, broke open the jail and freed his men, saying they had merely found the saddle and the men dead. A land developer, James Baker, expropriated favorite pasture lands of the Indians at St. Joseph's Prairie (Cranbrook). The Indians argued strenuously with Baker.

In came the Mounties to Golden. They engaged the *Duchess* to carry the officers' baggage, oats and supplies, instructing Armstrong to rendezvous each night with the mounted troops. After striking a snag, the overloaded craft sank in fourteen feet of water. The Mounties then hired the *Cline*, a miserable scow powered by the engine off a Manitoba steam plow and just as slow. It took three months to move the 60 tons of supplies stranded in Golden and intermediate points.

With swift Canadian justice the Mounties found the Indians could not be guilty, and they mediated the land dispute, mostly in Baker's favor. After patrolling the valley and "showing the flag," they left in August 1888, via Crow's Nest Pass. The community was so impressed with Commander Sam Steele and D Division that it renamed the community "Fort Steele."

Fort Steele remained a major commercial center until 1898, when an ungrateful Joseph Baker persuaded the CPR to build the B. C. Southern through his property (today's Cranbrook), instead of through Fort Steele, by donating part of his land to the railroad. Fort Steele's population sharply declined.

But Fort Steele lives again, restored as a living historic town in 1961. Now its rotting buildings are repaired and painted. Employees walk the streets in period costumes. Clydesdale teams clump through the dirt streets pulling wagonloads of delighted tourists. A steam train chuffs around a circular track.

Frank Armstrong (of the ill-fated *Duchess*) proved to be the lord of the rivers. Although he had competitors at times, Armstrong monopolized the steamer trade on both the Columbia and Kootenay until 1898 and continued on the Columbia until the railroad forced him out. One of his last boats sank in the river, just south of Columbia Lake, and is still distinctly visible.

Traveling from Golden to Jennings, Montana, was an adventure. From Golden to Columbia Lake (depending on high or low water), steamboats ran on the Columbia River ... maybe. Low water near the lake was a problem. In 1891 Frank Armstrong, his brother, J. F. Armstrong, and Thomas B. H. Cochrane organized the Upper Columbia Navigation and Tramway Company to construct a short tram from Golden town site to the Columbia River docks, and a longer one with a passenger and freight car from Adela or Mud Lake, south of Windermere, to the Kootenay River, where waiting steamboats churned downstream to Jennings.

The Columbia Lake, birthplace of the Columbia River.

In 1889, English big game hunter, mountaineer and entrepreneur William A. Baillie-Grohman conceived the idea of building a canal between the two rivers. He proposed to divert water from the Kootenay to allay flooding of fertile plains near the international border, to solve periodic low water problems in the upper Columbia River, and to provide a direct steamer route between the two rivers. The distant provincial government in Victoria gave him a permit for this rather ill-thought-out scheme, which could have raised havoc with salmon runs, river shores and towns from British Columbia to Oregon.

Fortunately, there was an outcry from Canadian Pacific Railway officials, who feared inundation of newly built rail lines. As a condition, therefore, the provincial permit required Baillie-Grohman to build a lock. He came to Golden with materials to open a sawmill and a supply store for the canal project. At Golden station, he had to unload his own freight within twenty-four hours and leave it in the open, since the station consisted only of a small office building. Baillie-Grohman grumbled that the lack of competition made the railroad company high-handed.

He completed his canal in 1889: 6,700 feet long, 45 feet wide and a small and flimsy log lock 100 feet long and 30 feet wide. The lock was to be opened only to allow the passage of a steamboat or to divert water from the Kootenay to the Columbia during flood periods. Without canal or locks, the Kootenay River did overflow into the Columbia River in the 1950s.)

Only one known boat went through the locks north to south, Armstrong's *Gwendoline*. In 1893, Captain Armstrong laid the steamer's hull and basic structure on the Kootenay River, then dragged her on skids and rollers over Canal Flats to Columbia Lake and towed her to Golden for completion. In 1894, the *Gwendoline* went south through the canal without serious incident. Not so with a 1902 attempt to take the larger *North Star* from south to north. Since the boat was too wide for the decaying locks, Armstrong sawed off its guard rails. The boat entered the locks but was too long; so Armstrong destroyed the rear lock and rebuilt a log and sandbag dam behind the craft. When all was ready, he dynamited out the northerly section and in a wild ride careened into Columbia Lake (destroying any hope of restoring the locks in the process).

With all this activity on the land barrier between the rivers, a small settlement had developed called first Grohman, then Canal Flats. The flats themselves enjoyed a brief gold rush. Today the handful of homes, a small logging operation and a few stores sleep peacefully in the summer sun, surrounded by fragrant sweet clover and pine. At the venerable, historic Columbia Inn, oldtimers swap stories of the days when the Atwoods, McCurchies, Coys and Tegarts fattened cattle in the valley to feed the miners.

The hopefuls who came on Armstrong's boats to prospect in the Upper Columbia Valley seldom made expenses. Among the better-known early mines were the Findlay Creek Mining Company, the Adela Mining Company and the Ptarmigan Mine near the Lake of the Hanging Glaciers in the Bugaboo Range. A gypsum mine still operates on Mount Swansea, east of Lake Windermere.

Three other mines did produce commercial quantities of ore: the Mineral King on Toby Creek, the Sheep Creek Mine and the famous Paradise Mine, originally spelled "Parradice." On August 29, 1897, the Paradise was staked as several claims. They were rich in silver contained in sand carbonates, the easiest form for processing—so easy in fact that, when a brush fire burned sacks of ore at a mine dump, the resulting lump was silver bullion. The original prospectors sold their claims to Randolph Bruce, a developer of many Upper Columbia Valley properties and later the Lieutenant Governor of British Columbia. Bruce built a good wagon road from the mine to Wilmer, where ore was loaded aboard Columbia River steamboats for Golden, thence to Trail for smeltering. In winter the ore came down by rawhiding; the ore was bound into a large steer hide hooked behind a docile horse. Hide flapping at his heels over the slippery snow, the horse pulled the material to the river.

Bruce was involved around 1911 in a land scheme, partly to attract investors who had quit South Africa during the Boer War. The Columbia Valley Irrigated Farm Lands Ltd. (CVI acquired a whopping 49,000 acres, extending north from Columbia Lake for thirty miles and advertised 10-to 40-acre parcels of land for fruit orchards. They built irrigation systems, wooden flumes, siphons and ditches, but not one ever contained water. This and two other similar schemes failed, disappointed immigrants left when World War I broke out, and CVI was left holding bankrupt lands.

A small portion of the CVI land included the site of David Thompson's Kootenae House. Basil Hamilton, accountant for CVI, Colonel Dennis of the

CPR, and Randolph Bruce—with the cooperation of Hudson's Bay Company—jointly bore costs of construction of a conception of Kootenae House. A splendid building of logs with a vaulted roof, it was completed July 4, 1922, and was used for twenty-six years as a community center. Residents enjoyed glittering social events and musicals in the building—although it had its drawbacks. Pioneer Ian Weir told me, "Every time the wind blew, the building drifted full of sand. Howard Cleland, a partner of Bruce, literally shoveled it out. There were bats living in that high ceiling, too. I was a saxophone player with a band there, and sometimes bat droppings became new quarter notes on the score."

No one would assume responsibility for upkeep of the David Thompson Memorial Fort, several historical associations refusing on the grounds that it was not authentic; so it was burned to the ground to make way for residential development.

The demise of CVI gave rise to a new industry: land was sold dirt-cheap to Christmas tree producers. Among buyers was the Kirk Forest Products Company, a Washington firm, which bought 35,000 acres of land near Cranbrook and Golden. During the Depression the demand for trees was a lifesaver, for a cutter could earn perhaps thirteen hundred dollars in the fall.

Walter Verge of Golden, who worked as a cutter, said the trees were cut as they grew at first. Later, crews pruned and shaped them. Independent horse operators brought trees into an assembly yard for sorting, bailing and shipment by train to distant points. In experiments plantation trees planted in rows did not thrive as well as those seeded by "mother trees" left scattered in a semi-cleared plot.

Land clearing had a secondary market—to provide ties for the railroad. Not only railroad ties but lumber for homes and stores was in demand as soon as settlement began. The enterprising Captain Armstrong operated one of the earliest sawmills in 1887 near Brisco, while McKenzie and McDonald opened another larger mill at Donald. Where proper roads did not exist, lumber companies often used portable mills hauled by horses along narrow tote roads clinging to the sides of mountains and along boiling rivers.

In 1902, Columbia River Lumber Company Ltd. of Golden was the largest holder of standing timber in British Columbia. Loggers stacked logs beside the Columbia during winter to be rolled into the river after spring thaw. The storage booms might be half as wide as the river and five miles long. The log drives were exciting and dangerous with men nimbly skipping over the rolling logs to "corral" them. Men lived in tents on shore, but the cookhouse on a raft moved along the river as needed. One became known as "the Ark."

Popular road cook Pete Faber came from a Luxembourg brewing family. He filled an oak hogshead with scrubbed potatoes, added black molasses and buried the closed barrel in horse manure for six months to produce excellent one hundred proof dark rum.

The enemy of the loggers was fire, set by lightning or by sparks spewing from locomotives. In 1912 a fire burned for three months near Cabin Creek. Valley residents could not see the sun, bears fled the fire to roam through the streets of towns and the air was full of cinders. Fierce fire storms blazed through forests so fast that only the branches were burned, the timber left intact. Loggers cut the "blackwood harvest," looking like coal miners each night.

In 1985, such a fire burned for six months on both sides of the upper valley, despite water bombing and the efforts of smokejumper crews. Smoke was so thick that Canal Flats was evacuated for a time. Again timber crews salvaged the singed tree trunks. An odd bonus appeared. In burned-over clearings, thousands of morel mushrooms popped up, where fire had sterilized the ground against parasites that otherwise destroy them. Locals earned good wages picking them for drying and export to Japan and Europe.

Still another giant fire destroyed the Columbia River Lumber Company in 1926, when it burned much of the firm's logging equipment. In 1931 a successor-Evans Lumber—began its British Columbia operations, using yellow cedar to produce battery separators. In 1969 Evans acquired Kicking Horse Forest Products Ltd., precious timber licenses, a veneer plant, sawmill and powerhouse, adding Selkirk Spruce Mills Ltd. of Donald. There, a major Evans plant operates today, employing eight hundred people.

The watershed of the Columbia produces a climate that, according to Brett Salmon, Evans' forestry manager at Golden, is "almost coastal, giving us the advantage in growing cedar as a crop. Much is second growth from fires of the 1880s, now 120 to 130 feet tall."

Fast growth is important because responsible loggers replant and "farm" every cut area, researching new ways to speed growth. Today's methods produce a tree three to four feet tall within five years, and in eighty years, harvestable at 125 to 130 feet tall.

Logging camps are a far cry from the tents of old. Men are housed two to a private room and have facilities ranging from laundry equipment to pool tables and television. Furthermore, with tough trucks and road systems, most loggers are able to sleep at home each night.

Chapter 4

The Railroads and the Tourists

With the coming of the Canadian Pacific Railway to Golden on the Columbia River in 1885, railroaders told their Eastern acquaintances about the beautiful Rockies, Selkirks and Purcells. First a trickle and then a flood of visitors came.

One of the first adventurers was William Baillie-Grohman, who came before 1883 to climb the peaks of the Purcells and Selkirks. In 1887 came two Englishmen, Lees and Clutterbuck, who wrote a whimsical book about their extraordinary experiences.

Tourists usually arrived at Golden. In about 1890 an English tourist, Edward Roper, unable to get rooms in the decent Queen's Hotel, stayed in a log shanty where small individual roomettes were walled and roofed with calico. He wrote cheerfully: "In many places the tacks with which the cloth was fastened had come out ... . We would lie in bed and converse with comfort, and there was an airiness about the place that was charming." (John Marsh, "Early Tourist Impression of Golden," in *Golden Memories*, [Golden and District Historical Society, 1982], 3.)

One might call Sir Sandford Fleming a tourist. Chief engineer while CPR was government-owned prior to 1881, Fleming was asked by the new private company, Canadian Pacific Railway, to assess the proposed railway route in 1883, including the formidable pass selected by Major A. B. Rogers. That summer Fleming, the Reverend Principal Grant and S. Hall Fleming, sitting at the summit of Rogers Pass in a field of flowers, organized the Canadian Alpine Club. The meeting was supervised by blue-white glaciers, the sentries of Mounts Macdonald and Tupper and the pyramid-shaped peak Cheops.

One of the earliest ramblers was the Reverend William Spotswood Green, an Englishman and experienced "Swiss mountaineer," who mounted an exploration in 1888 with the cooperation of the Royal Geographical Society. Green is considered the top pioneer climber and topographer to enter the Selkirks, and he named many points in use today. Emil Huber of the Swiss Alpine Club visited the Selkirks in 1890, also Harold W. Topham of the English Alpine Club. Huber was scornful of comparing them with the Alps, but Green suggested that in purity, sheer numbers of peaks and attractive glaciers, the Selkirks could "hold their own" with the Swiss and Italian Alps. Members of the prestigious Swiss Alpine Club, and the Appalachian Mountain Club of Boston, explored the Selkirks more thoroughly in the 1890s.

In 1888, CPR built a charming hotel, Glacier House, elevation 4,093 feet, in the trees at the base of Mt. Abbott, facing a lovely 1,200-foot waterfall. Like several other lodges, it was intended to house and feed passengers and crews, so that locomotives did not have to pull dining cars over steep passes. However, mountaineers soon made it their base. With a huge dining room but only a half-dozen bedrooms, Glacier House needed more space for overnighters and a sleeping car was parked on a nearby siding. Later there were ninety rooms and a sightseeing tower. A high fountain graced the lawn. For some years a tame bear, chained to a post by a collar, entertained visitors. D. W. Wilcox, author of a century-old book, said of his visit to Glacier House in 1893: "There is something pre-eminently comfortable and homelike about the Glacier House. ... One .. . scarcely realizes that civilization is so far distant ... writing his diary, or enjoying the pleasure of music or literature, while the rain is falling constantly. ... The manner in which the clouds come sweeping up the Illecillewaet valley at the base of Mount Cheops and turn toward the flank of Eagle peak or Mount Sir Donald is very impressive...." (A. O. Wheeler, *The Selkirk Range* [Ottawa: Government Printing Bureau, 1905], p. 298-99.)

Responding to the influx of tourists, the Canadian Pacific Railway constructed lodges and tourist hotels along the railway from Banff in Alberta to Victoria, British Columbia. The company hired Swiss mountain guides to work for them in the Rocky Mountains and Selkirk Range. A "Swiss mountain guide" was the epitome of skill and reliability.

The first two Swiss guides, Edouard Feuz and Christian Hasler of Interlaken, came West in 1899. In 1900 Hasler went to Mt. Stephen House in the Rockies, and Jacob Muller, Karl Schlunegger and Friedrich Michel joined Feuz at Glacier House. They made several ascents of Mount Sir Donald and other peaks. Their climbing parties often went out for weeks at a time, using pack trains for supply.

From 1899 to 1911, guides came in the summer and went home to Switzerland in the winter. (Climbing was impractical in heavy snow.) Near the banks of the Columbia River in 1911, the CPR built a Swiss village for the guides and their families, urging them to stay all year and assist with tourists. The elite group remained small; among them were Edouard Feuz, Sr. and Jr., and later Ernest, Gottfried and Walter Feuz; Chris Jorimann, Christian Hasler, Rudolph Aemmer, Charles Clark (an interpreter), F. Michel and Karl Schlunegger. Edward Feuz, Jr. died at Golden in 1981, after working as a guide for seventy-three years; he climbed difficult mountains until he was over ninety-five years old.

Glacier House closed in 1922 and was torn down in 1929. A new, modern Glacier House is a center for Rogers Pass travelers today. The descendants in spirit and in blood of the Swiss guides today work from Revelstoke, Golden and Invermere. Peter Schlunneger, Karl's grandson, works out of Golden. He guides mountaineers and also owns Alpine Rafting, the oldest company offering white water raft trips on the Kicking Horse River. Rafting is the latest "mountaineering" adventure of this area.

Quickening the Columbia's pulse as it flows northerly are the Spillamacheen, Kicking Horse, Blaeberry, Wood and the huge Canoe rivers. Beyond the Big Bend on the southerly flow are the Goldstream, Illicillawaet, Jordan and others. These tributaries frequently rush to the Columbia over impressive rapids. On a world-rated scale of 1 to 6 (a 6 gives one a 50/50 chance of survival!), many are rated 4.

Young mountaineers like Peter Schlunneger, and John Buffery and Ralph Koerber of Glacier Rafting, are guide rafters in summer, alpine enthusiasts in winter. Buffery talks of the rewards, such as his appreciation of the rapids, of wildlife and interpreting the experience for a blind rafter. He rhapsodizes about the purity of winter snow and the awful beauty of the Selkirks.

Hans Gmoser is the pioneer of heliskiing in the Selkirks and Monashee Mountains. His company, Canadian Mountain Holidays, operates trips from several locations. "Rabid" skiers often save for years just to have one exultant week of heliskiing, for it is not an inexpensive sport. Lodges are luxurious; some have European chefs, saunas and whirlpool baths at mile-high locations.

Phil Hein, who opened the David Thompson trail on the Wood River, is one of few native Canadians who is a licensed Senior Guide of the Canadian Association of Mountain Guides, a member of the International Union of Mountain Guides. Like the old Swiss Guides, Hein put in years of apprenticeship before taking an examination. He operates an alpine lodge at 6,700-feet elevation, north of the Wapta Ice Fields (northeast of Golden).

Newest of the wilderness ski sports is snowcat skiing, a bit tamer than heliskiing but still done along ungroomed slopes. For nonskiers the Invermere, Golden and Revelstoke areas have wilderness tour guides in four-wheel drive vehicles to show such sights as the Lake of the Hanging Glaciers in the Bugaboo Mountains, the Columbia River at sunset from Mount Swansea or old mine diggings. Don Yanko of Incredible Mountain Tours told me of a surprise one trip: "I shined my light on a mossy looking thing on a ledge, and it began to pulsate like an alien being. Spooky! I was about to take off, when I looked closer. It was a big hibernating glob of daddy longlegs, all huddled together."

Mountain adventures are part of the offerings at historic Fairmont Hot Springs Resort, one of the valley's oldest spas north of Columbia Lake. Succeeding John Galbraith and George Geary, Sam and Helen Brewer owned the property in 1890, when an English sightseer, Adela St. Maur, wrote about visiting the spa. She tramped over a steep trail and found two large basins, the first of which was 8 or

9 feet long, about 2 feet deep and 4 feet wide, and quiet. The second bubbled up boiling hot like champagne, while an adjacent mountain stream was icy cold.

Owner William Heap Holland improved the property in 1923 by building a flume from the springs to a pool 40 by 60 feet, a restaurant, tent camp and cabins to accommodate seventy guests. The place even had electricity generated by overflow from the pool. Over the years visitors waded the Columbia River, rode horseback, played tennis on gravel courts, camped, fished or soaked in the therapeutic waters.

Columbia valley entrepreneurs Lloyd Wilder and family acquired the springs in 1957, and the resort now sprawls over four thousand acres—a four-star lodge, golf courses, recreation center, indoor and outdoor pools, public lands and five-star time-share villas. Wilder family members form the executive corps, with Carol Seable the general manager.

To supplement cross-country skiing the resort developed downhill ski runs catering to beginners and families. During the planning stage, a pilot was flying Lloyd Wilder over the hill to reconnoiter, when a sudden downdraft forced the plane to the ground, killing the pilot and, quite literally, scalping Wilder. Half-conscious he stumbled down the mountainside and was tracked by rescuers from the trail of blood. He later joked that although doctors sewed his scalp, he picked pine needles out of it for years afterward..

The Wilders preserve almost half the historic Fairmont property for environmental concerns—the beginnings of the Columbia River, the Pacific Flyway, an elk herd that considers the golf course its private grazing ground, a cabin used by Baillie-Grohman, the Golden-Columbia Lake stage stop (now home of a Fairmont owner) and Captain Armstrong's last sternwheeler lying surprisingly well-preserved beneath the cold Columbia.

Between Fairmont and Columbia Lake are traces of the Spirit Trail of Kootenay Indians. The narrow, steep path through heavy forest was an ideal place for ambushes by traditional enemies, the Blackfeet or Piegans. At the beginning, end and hazardous midpoint of the trail, the Indians broke off a branch and laid it on an altar-like heap, an entreaty for safety or gratitude for a successful trip. Ancient pictographs were painted on the cliff face using vermilion (ground iron oxide mixed with bear grease and fish oil, sealed to the rock with chewed fish eggs and saliva), of braves with arrows in hand, animals, a papoose board and other items. Most of the pictographs have disappeared through natural erosion.

Something about the Upper Columbia Valley evokes a sense of mystery and spirit. In 1912, local resident Charles D. Ellis captured the feeling as he walked the historic headwaters trail: "Smoke from the funeral fires of many a mighty forest, hung like a pall across the valley. Distant trees, wrapped in the purple mist, lost themselves as the enfolding clouds grew thicker, reappearing at intervals like the wrath of their departed kindred; ... a fitter place to be peopled by fairies and elves never was ... ." (From Charles D. Ellis diary, Windermere Valley Historical Museum.)

Spiritual feeling touched many races as they entered or traveled this overwhelmingly beautiful birth valley of the Columbia River and its adjacent canyons. In times misty with age, at Radium Hot Springs, Indians soaked in the springs to ease their pains. Dale Zieroth told the story of Kootenay Indian Amelu, who came to the springs searching for his guardian spirit "nipika." He had gone without food for three days and had drunk sparsely in his pilgrimage, waiting for a vision. On the fourth day near the pool he heard the spirit of the trees singing in the wind: "He followed the song until he stood at the edge of the pool. The mist rose up in one great swirl ... he knew his guardian nipika was there. ...With one step, he was in the water, the hot mist wrapping around him like smoke ... and he felt the spirit go deep in his chest. ... He heard the nipika tell him that now he was a man and that he would be protected all his life." (Dale Zieroth, *nipika*, [pamphlet, Parks Canada, 1978], 7.)

The springs lie a scant two miles from the Columbia River in Sinclair Canyon, which is entered through a narrow cleft between cliffs towering 120 feet high; the sun's rays hardly penetrate to the canyon floor. In 1841 Sir George Simpson passed through this valley and called it a "horrid gorge, an angry stream, a dreary vale," and was glad to escape it. He apparently did not discover the springs. Later in 1841, leading a group of fractious settlers from Red River (Winnipeg), James Sinclair detoured to search for the springs—having heard of them from his guide Mackipictoon. Disgruntled and weary, Sinclair eased into the pool and found himself relaxing and dreaming dreams that soared beyond logical bounds and reached into the past.

Modern man tends to dismiss such mysteries, but a marvellous cure was responsible for raising money to develop the springs. Financier Roland Stuart purchased the springs and 160 acres of land from the crown for $160 on May 27, 1890. He planned to develop the springs as a spa and to sell bottled water. However, he needed a road to bring tourists—tourists that were beginning to swarm into Banff on the CPR or to come north from the United States to Golden. He created Radium Natural Springs Syndicate Ltd. in 1913 and published a prospectus for development.

The scheme came to the attention of a wealthy man associated with the Perrier waters company, St. John Harmsworth, who was paralyzed from the hips down following an accident. Eager for a financial backer, Stuart made sure Harmsworth got to Radium. The crippled man was lowered into the springs in a hammock, and each day for four months he soaked in the springs. Whether his "nipika" or spirit came or whatever, Harmsworth was able to move his feet for the first time since the accident. He financed Stuart.

Despite the financing, Stuart did little except build a concrete pool and a bathhouse, until the Banff-Windermere Road backers took matters out of his hands. Among them was developer Robert Randolph Bruce of Invermere. The group looked to the government for finishing the western slope of road. The government agreed, on condition that the province of British Columbia give them five miles of land on each side of the road as a national park. On April 21, 1920, the Kootenay Dominion Park was declared. Then the government pressured Stuart and others to sell private holdings along the proposed road. In 1922 the Park expropriated Stuart's property for $24 ,692 (plus a later sum of $15,000), and the springs became park property.

In 1923, the Banff-Windermere Road was completed, a one-lane gravel road in places, but a road. Travelers came to the springs and the Columbia Valley. In 1929 five hundred cars a month traveled the road. Fine lodges were built, still serving visitors today, including Radium Lodge, Radium Hot Springs Resort (not at the springs itself) and the more modest Blakley Bungalows. The springs were encased below a concrete pool, which could be chlorinated, and a handsome Aquacourt with food and change facilities constructed.

Chapter 5

The Big Bend and Revelstoke

West of the Selkirks, Revelstoke was settled by CPR workers in the mid-1880s. Before any white settlement, the site was popular with Shuswap Indians, who caught fish near the dangerous whirlpool called the Big Eddy, formed by the rush of the Jordan River into the curving Columbia River.

Continuing to enter the valley at Boat Encampment over the route David Thompson pioneered, fur traders, missionaries and a few settlers had a hazardous introduction to the West. Among the famous traveling this way were Sir George Simpson of Hudson's Bay Company and frontier artist Paul Kane, whose inscription on a tree "Paul Kane 1847" was found by a twentieth century traveler. The wood has been cut out and is in the Provincial Archives, Victoria.

Boat Encampment at the Big Bend of the Columbia possessed a lonely, harsh beauty that made gnats of humans. Some of North America's heaviest snowfalls occur there. In the nineteenth century the exquisite Kinbasket Lake, a relatively quiet widening of the Columbia, usually froze over. Eminent author Stewart Holbrook suggested that, if one saw Kinbasket, he needn't bother with the alpine lakes of Switzerland. In places one could see the glittering Columbia Ice Fields.

If a traveler were going downriver, however, tranquility ended at Boat Encampment. As the Columbia turned southward, its roar was heard miles away. Intermittent, violent rapids awaited the hapless canoeist—all the way to Revelstoke's site.

It is a tribute to the skills of Hudson's Bay brigades that they could use this stretch as a thoroughfare. Not far below the Big Bend, Les Dalles des Morts or Death Rapids was a chain of killer whirlpools. Ross Cox told of his passage upstream in April 1817, where between Les Dalles and Boat Encampment, the river was so swollen with spring melt that—even by lining canoes and portaging supplies—it took an entire day to make it three miles upstream.

In 1838 the infamous Dalles claimed twelve lives of an expedition that included almost forty men, women and children. With them were Father Francis N. Blanchet and Father Modeste Demers. Hudson's Bay Company officials had sanctioned the sending of priests to establish missions on the Cowlitz and Willamette rivers, and the only way to get there was in Hudson's Bay Company canoes bound for Fort Vancouver. The party arrived at Boat Encampment on October 13. This day, a Sunday, Father Blanchet offered the Holy Sacrifice of Mass, the first time in Oregon (Blanchet's designation). It was a good thing he did.

After looking at Les Dalles des Morts, the leaders decided to run the hundred miles of river to House of the Lakes near Arrowhead, in relays. The two boats set out with about one-third of the party, including Blanchet and Demers, and arrived safely. One boat returned to transport those left behind. Unwilling to wait for another round trip, the passengers all crowded into the boat. At the next rapids (thereafter called Priest Rapids) the overloaded boat wallowed and took on water. Crying to passengers to sit still, the pilot headed toward shore. Before he touched the bank, English botanist Robert Wallace grabbed his wife Maria (unacknowledged daughter of Sir George Simpson), stood on the gunwale and jumped over, capsizing the boat. Not only they but ten others drowned from this impetuous departure.

In 1865 Walter Moberly almost drowned in the Little Dalles just north of today's Revelstoke, as he returned downriver after discovering Eagle Pass for the railroad route by watching the flight of two eagles. He was taking bearings when the canoe's bowman shouted, "Bad water—all will be killed!" As they swept into the Little Dalles, Moberly leaped to the paddles. The two men managed to escape being sucked into the whirlpools, but Moberly said, "Sometimes one end of the canoe became the bow, and at other times the opposite end."

Significant gold was discovered in 1865 near the Big Bend, along Goldstream, Carnes, French, Downie creeks and other tributaries. Prospectors thronged in from Wild Horse Creek, from eastern Canada and the United States. The early rushes were no more successful than those of Wild Horse, but men swarmed down the Columbia, which claimed more lives as unsuspecting miners swept around the Big Bend in makeshift boats.

More came from the south. Captain Leonard White brought a supply boat, the *Forty-Nine*, upriver from Washington to the foot of Death Rapids in 1866— quite a feat. He continued to serve the prospectors for the brief time it took for enthusiasm to run out. After three trips, paying passengers northbound were few, free passengers southbound, many.

Poor prospectors sometimes lived on flour alone and developed scurvy. They spent grimly cold winters, isolated in a typical cabin of chinked logs heated by a sheetrock stove. An egg case nailed to the wall made a shelf. Other furnishings were a small bench with a wash basin and soap, a crude bed and a miner's candlestick stuck in the wall. Most of the prospectors went on to new Eldorados, leaving the mosquitoes to feed on a handful of stubborn or better-funded miners who persisted into the twentieth century.

With the arrival of the railroad around 1885, surveyor Arthur Stanhope Farwell laid out the settlement of Farwell at Big Eddy. Only twenty-eight miles of railroad west of Farwell remained unfinished, and prospectors could reach Golden and Revelstoke easily. This led to renewed prospecting along the Big Bend. The Columbia River was still the north-south avenue.

Harbinger of late twentieth century catamarans, the *Despatch* was launched in 1888, running from Revelstoke to Sproat's Landing (Castlegar). The futuristic craft had two 54-foot pontoons with the paddlewheels between. Although designed for two engines, her owners could afford only one; so she was slow and difficult to manage in a blow. The design permitted minimal freight. Partners in the venture were J. F. Hume, 'W. Cowan and Captain Robert Sanderson.

Watching the freight enterprise from the wings were men known on British Columbia lakes: J. A. Mara, a steamboat operator from the Shuswap Lakes waterways; Captain J. Irving of Fraser River experience; and Frank S. Barnard, whose father had organized the Barnard Express to Barkerville's gold fields. The three bought in, naming their new company the Columbia and Kootenay Steam Navigation Company (CKSN), capitalized for $100,000, a solidly managed firm and eventual thorn in the corporate flesh of the CPR.

CKSN launched the *Lytton*, on July 2, 1890, and bought Captain Frank Armstrong's *Marion*, transported from Golden to Revelstoke by rail and re-launched at Revelstoke.

In 1897, the Lytton came from Arrow Lakes to Revelstoke, but she had to have her stack shortened to pass under the CPR bridge. With fairly powerful engines she managed to travel through the vicious Little Dalles to carry heavy mining machinery to La Porte, two miles south of Les Dalles des Morts. It is said that she took six hours to ascend the Little Dalles but only six minutes and fifty-one seconds to descend. Five years later Revelstoke residents combined to build a powerful vessel, the *Revelstoke*, that could manage the rapids. Instead of braving the Little Dalles every trip, it started upriver above them and went to La Porte. She was almost wrecked on February 18, 1903, in Arrow Lakes when a massive wave caused by a thundering rock slide slammed into her.

Packers jumped into the supply business, too. George LaForme trekked north from Revelstoke with as many as thirty-five animals. He was wiped out on a return trip from French Creek in November, 1896, when rain crusted the snow and horses broke through and cut their legs. There was no forage, and no help to be had. LaForme wound up shooting all the horses.

Andrew Rupert Westerberg was a legendary mailman to the Big Bend for thirty-five years, mostly trudging the hundred-mile route. Another colorful local man was "Ole the Bear," a miner who had won a hand-to-hand fight with a grizzly. He had a tame, trained black bear that would obey his commands. One day he left home, telling the bear to stay. A mile or so away he noticed that a bear was following him. Thinking it was his disobedient pet, he yelled at it, threw a rope around the startled animal's neck and dragged it home—a very unwilling captive. Only when he approached his home did he discover his tame bear was still there.

Farwell's townsite thrived, but very few decent women helped to civilize the place. A visitor, Colonel Edward Mallandaine, said of Farwell: "The town consisted of one street on either side of which were wooden and log shacks; chief among them was the Columbia Hotel ... the life was exciting, especially on paydays. There were brawls continually and gambling night and day with men of all nationalities throwing away their hard-earned pay at faro, stud poker and other games of chance. What the gamblers and saloon men did not get the women of the town did." (From *Revelstoke Review,* June 29,1940.) To avoid being cheated by card sharps, players threw the decks out the window between card games, to the point that the street was "paved" with playing cards.

The Canadian Pacific Railway refused to pay Farwell's prices for land to build a roundhouse, marshaling yard and station, and built it on land uphill from Farwell. In 1899 the new town of Revelstoke was incorporated around the railway center, named for a lord who had bailed out the CPR during a financial crisis. It absorbed Farwell to become both a rail and river port. Local sports founded a racetrack along Big Eddy, patronized by riverboat passengers. The Turf Club building is the clubhouse today of Revelstoke Golf Club; faint outlines of the racetrack are visible.

Four smelters were established to process the miners' ore—at Revelstoke, Nelson, Golden and Trail. In 1889 at Revelstoke, the Kootenay Smelting & Trading Syndicate constructed a smelter, boarding house, store, brickyard and railroad spur on the east side of the Columbia River. The smelter itself probably was a rectangular water-jacketed furnace perhaps 6 feet long and 3 feet wide. On July 23, 1891, it produced the first lead bullion drawn from any Canadian smelter. But that was its entire claim to fame. The Columbia River began to undercut the smelter's land, and because land titles were a subject of contention between British Columbia and the Dominion of Canada, neither would assist in allaying the erosion. The entire installation fell into the river in 1898.

The Revelstoke smelter was inefficient, anyway. About 1920, a war veteran purchased the smelter's ore dump for $5, hauled some of it to the Trail smelter and made his fortune.

The CPR consolidated its offices in 1899 by moving the Donald operations to Revelstoke, dismantling and moving most of the Donald buildings. The tiny wooden church was scheduled to be transported by railroad flatcar, when Lake Windermere stagecoach operator, Rufus Kimpton, and others spirited it away on a riverboat and reassembled it at Lake Windermere. Kimpton and his wife Celina had become fond of this first Anglican church in the Rockies. They and their friends weathered the outraged protests and threats of Revelstoke residents, and there in Windermere the church remains today. The "stolen church" was rededicated for Christian use in 1905.

The "stolen church" at Windermere.

Pleased with the profits from tourism that resulted from bringing Swiss Guides into the region, the CPR was happy to see the establishment of national parks in the region. Glacier National Park was established in 1886 and Mount Revelstoke National Park in 1914.

With the emphasis on tourism and snow sports, competitive ski jumping began at Revelstoke in 1915, with Norwegian-born Nels Nelsen jumping 240 feet in the 1925 Mount Revelstoke tournament—a record until 1932. Bob Lymburne also broke a world record at Revelstoke, and much later Johnny McInnes, hometown boy, was a many time Canadian ski jump champion. The Tournament of Jumps was held annually from 1950 to 1972; among the local champions was Larry Nelles, later coach of the Canadian National Ski Team and a resort rancher.

The lore of the railway workmen who operated over Rogers Pass has been touted in numerous books—the avalanches, loneliness of station attendants, the storms. Problems included the invasion of caterpillars in 1923, making the rails so slippery that train service stopped. Colossal snowfalls of nine feet a week were not uncommon. Often the crews had to stay in the mountains for days, clearing tracks with snowplows. On March 4, 1910, sixty-two men died in an avalanche while clearing a slide from the tracks at the 4,300-foot level. The railway finally built the five-mile long descending Connaught Tunnel *inside* Mount McDonald.

Railroad operations changed. In 1940, Revelstoke Division of CPR stretched from Field to Kamloops. The eighteen-stall roundhouse and outdoor freight car repair operations bustled. Between 1950 and 1960, the trains were being converted to diesel, reducing the need for a roundhouse (although it was used for repairs until 1990). Making Revelstoke the busiest terminal in Canada were the 108-car coal trains from Natal (near Alberta) to Roberts Bank, a seaport near Vancouver. An average of six trains each twenty-four hours rolled through Revelstoke. The car repair division moved to Golden in 1989.

Until 1962 the only way to cross the Selkirks from Golden to Revelstoke was by train. Retired CPR employee Al McAskill told me, "Almost everything was transported by rail—food, fuel, heavy machinery. There also was a special train from Revelstoke toward Golden each Sunday night called the Hobo. It took men from town to their various camps (railroad, logging, forest) and stopped anywhere." As autos became more practical, drivers ventured cross-country. In response to the need for this link of the Trans-Canada Highwoy, work began on the Big Bend Highway adjacent to the Columbia River in 1929. The scenery was inspiring—one worker remembers the sun setting "into" the Columbia during midsummer—but conditions were not comfortable for workers.

Construction began around May 1 each year and ended with the first heavy snowfalls (October or November). Workers lived in camps of about fifty men in buildings with wooden floors and walls and canvas roofs. Clouds of mosquitoes, devil's club as high as a man's head, insistent skunks in and under the cabins and cookhouses and bears added to the challenges for men and horses.

Boats took supplies up Kinbasket Lake where waves 4 to 5 feet high drove them to shelter at times. Teams pulled Fresno scrapers and plows to break up the earth. So far from any town, workers spent their Sundays off fishing or playing cards. About once a month they got to town, usually Golden.

One can imagine the lively times in the taverns and Helen's Sporting House, when lonely men—hungry for diversion—arrived for a couple of days or, in November, for the winter. Prudent workers bought next year's supplies first before they spent the rest of their money in riotous living. Golden was variously described as "one of the toughest towns anyone could imagine," and "a surprisingly pleasant and orderly community." No doubt it was both; if you were with Scarface Stewart who drank a mickey (about 13 ounces) of overproof rum without stopping and died there on his barstool, you saw one side. If you were a sawmill worker, taking home your pay to a wife and seven kids, sitting on a porch enjoying the scenery of an evening, you saw another.

Crews built a steel bridge to cross the Columbia River at Boat Encampment, and travel was possible by 1937. Rough, graveled, with few facilities, the highway was a stepchild of a road, but it served its purpose, though sometimes flooded by the Columbia or closed by snow. Deep snow made the landscape so featureless that a logging company near Boat Encampment had to send a helicopter out to locate its buried D-8 caterpillar tractor. A man was employed solely to shovel snow off Big Bend Highway bridges in winter, tramping from one cramped shelter to another.

Its travails are not forgotten. Gordon Bell, past owner of Three Valley Gap Resort in Eagle Pass, traveled the highway in the 1960s, hauling building materials from Alberta. Once the road north of Golden was marked "closed" due to flooding, but Bell said, "I just took off the fan belt and drove through water as deep as two and one-half feet for about two miles, following the edge-of-road stakes."

Bell treasured the local history and gathered original historic buildings and replicas on his resort property. Among the truly precious structures are the original St. Stephen's Church from Donald, built in 1886, rededicated in 1967 (in big demand for weddings); C. B. Hume's general store from Revelstoke built in 1892; the entire Hotel Bellevue from Mara Lake, Sicamous, British Columbia; and Halfway House, a roadhouse from the Big Bend Highway.

The old highway is under water now from Donald to Mica Creek. Death Rapids, the Little Dalles and others between Boat Encampment (which is under 600 feet of water) and Revelstoke have vanished beneath the lakes formed by Mica Dam and Revelstoke Dam. Spurred by the need to control destructive flooding and, in the process, to create more power, Canada and the United States signed the Columbia River Treaty on September 16, 1964. Among its terms, Canada would build three dams to provide 15.5 million acre-feet of water storage. Since British Columbia then did not need the power, the province sold its share of power for the next thirty years to an amalgam of American utilities, the Columbia Storage Power Company.

The original three dams were: Duncan on the Kootenay River completed July 31, 1967; Hugh Keenleyside Dam above Castlegar operational October 10, 1968; and Mica Dam finished March 29, 1973. Revelstoke Dam came along in 1985. Keenleyside impounds runoff from the Arrow Lakes and includes locks for transport of logs to the Castlegar mills. Mica is the more dramatic, looming 800 feet above bedrock in the narrow canyon upriver from Death Rapids.

About two thousand workers lived in three-story bunkhouses below the damsite, scattering after the dam's completion. Only a handful remain to staff the dam, some of them living ninety miles away at Revelstoke.

Marg and Jim Sproat stayed, often isolated in winter storms; yet the couple loved living next to nature. Marg worked at the Interpretive Center, Jim as maintenance foreman. Grizzlies, cougars, caribou and pine martens were among their companions. One day in 1977, Marg wondered why her husband was making so much racket on the porch. She opened the door to come face to face with a huge grizzly that had come over the porch rail and gotten stuck between the rails somehow. She slammed the door and waited for the furious bear to get loose and leave. He went off but returned the next day to do the same thing. Common black bears would open doors and appear in the powerhouse; now the doors are always locked.

Still operating in 1992 between Mica and Revelstoke at Downie Creek was a historic roadhouse. It was purchased in 1946 by Margaret Ruth Wallis and her son Edward. Loggers, road builders, and shaken-up motorists rested there at the tearoom and cabins. Mom Wallis' homemade soups, breads and huckleberry pies were legendary, and during construction of Mica Dam, the place was always packed. When Wallis cooked, the sweet smells lured bears to the kitchen. If the door was not closed tightly, a bear would walk in any time. If it was closed, one came in, anyway, after ripping the screen door off. Last time I was there, the roadhouse was a timber employee residence and cafeteria, and at the moment I cannot find anyone to verify its current status.

Mrs. Wallis' grandson, Don Munk, took over the resort in 1986. It offered a step back in time, and Don also demonstrated the art of gold panning to guests.

Curious phenomena accompany the variable river levels since construction of the dams. At Mica the larger lake surface has moderated temperatures somewhat. Revelstoke sustains smothering dust storms. The Columbia River carries immense quantities of silt, depositing it in the riverbed. Now, when Keenleyside Dam "draws down" to allow for spring runoff, the Columbia River channel returns to normal width, uncovering a broad band of powdery silt. It blows easily, causing dust storms so dense one cannot see the surrounding mountains, "like the Sahara," say locals. A potential solution would be a low weir dam to retain enough water to cover the river bottom.

Only thirty miles south of Revelstoke lie the Upper and Lower Arrow Lakes, one hundred thirty-four miles long, really broad portions of the Columbia River. Early Arrow Lakes travelers such as Ross Cox expressed appreciation of their beauty, Cox writing in 1817 that he enjoyed a fine view of the snow-covered Rocky Mountains.

A century or so later the Arrow Lakes Board of Trade described them passionately in a promotional pamphlet: "The sunset glow suffuses the far flung arch of the sky with scarlet and gold, ... the deepening shadows set the sombre masses of the mighty hills into sharp relief against an iridescent sky ... here is a setting, a panorama of scenic beauty and mountain majesty."

Written in the flowery language of the time, the tribute is yet an accurate sketch of the beauties of these remote and appealing lakes, named because Hudson's Bay travelers saw mysterious groups of arrows in a hole in the cliffs of Lower Arrow Lake, their meaning unknown.

The Columbia River and its sister river, the Kootenay, bracketed the gold mining operations, large and small, that sprang up after railroads came. From 1886 on, CPR anchored the north end of the district and the Northern Pacific roughly formed a southern boundary in Montana. The Great Northern and others came along later; indeed, one needed a program to make sense of the cast of characters in the tic-tac-toe pattern of railroads and connecting steamers. The pace of laying rail accelerated as Canadians feared the entire largesse of the upper Columbia would bleed down into American coffers.

Truly promising gold mines opened all over southeastern British Columbia, among them the North Star and Sullivan at Kimberley, the Paradise in Invermere, and legions of others in the central Selkirks.

Sprawling between the two rivers, a bevy of towns sprang up like mushrooms after a fire and boasted "a thousand people" within weeks, but most of them were soon abandoned. These are lovely hills, often carpeted with blue daisies and dotted with serene lakes, but few miners really saw the beauty. The wise built supply stores; the eager dug in the mines. Camborne was a booming town. Cody had two thousand residents and a concentrator mill for the Noble King Mine. New Denver on Slocan Lake and Nakusp on Upper Arrow Lake became important shipping points. Silverton clustered around the Mammoth Mine Mill, the largest at Slocan Lake. Kaslo was an important center at one end of Kootenay Lake, Nelson at the other; both remain so. In 1893, rails were laid between Sandon and Nakusp to connect with riverboats for shipment of ore to smelters.

A sad chapter of North American history was played out in the ghost towns of the Selkirks-Rosebery, Lemon Creek, Popoff Farm, Sandon, New Denver. When war with Japan came in 1941, the Canadian government transported to that beautiful but hard wilderness thousands of Japanese from coastal towns. Of the 21,439 Japanese removed, more than half lived in abandoned mining towns—old homes converted to apartments, a saloon dance hall housing three families.

At the Popoff farm in Slocan Valley, hundreds of Japanese spent 1942 in tents, waiting for shacks 16 feet by 16 feet to be completed. The Japanese worked at construction, on road crews, did stoop labor, or sewed on piecework, clerked and did office work, usually at low wages. For the first year there were no schools for the 1,811 school children. The resilient Japanese earned the friendship of local residents, and soon compassionate villagers helped as they could. In October 1942, to prove their loyalty to Canada, the Japanese organized a Victory Bond Drive. When the war ended, the Japanese went home, often to find their properties were gone.

Sandon had been repaired, but in 1955 an old flume plugged up during runoff and overflowed to wash out most of the town. Treminco Resources Ltd. today operates the Sandon mine, and a museum remembers the poignant past of those towns in the "Valley of the Ghosts."

Keenleyside Dam flooded out many lakeside peach orchards along Arrow Lakes, plus the buildings at Halcyon Hot Springs (not the springs), shoreside wrecked sternwheelers, the old railroad barge docks at Arrowhead, Renata, Forest Glen, Fosthall, Deer Park, Graham's Landing and the saloons and card rooms of Brooklyn town. There a determined preacher, the Reverend John Munroe of the Presbyterian Church of Trail, played one hour of popular music in a saloon whenever the patrons would agree to listen to an hour's sermon afterwards.

Nakusp, Burton, Fauquier, Needles, Edgewood, Galena Bay—these small towns still enjoy the broadened reaches of Arrow Lakes. Thirty miles below Revelstoke, the Shelter Bay-Galena ferry, part of the highway system, provides a free thirty-minute "scenic cruise." Captain Roy Peterson says there is a 70-foot variation in the lake's level. Storms still blow up suddenly, and the ferry stops running when waves get five feet high. On rare occasions the lake freezes. One winter the captain saw two deer stranded on a small ice floe. He edged the ferry up to the floe, the deer calmly walked aboard the car deck and jumped off near the opposite shore like veteran ferry travelers.

Chapter 6

Mining and Tourism

For several decades the most practical and comfortable access to the towns between the lakes was by water. Both the Kootenay and Columbia rivers teemed with sternwheelers, the soft sigh of their passage hardly disturbing the waters.

One of the finest sternwheelers on the Columbia was launched at Nakusp on July I, 1895. The town's namesake *Nakusp* was 171 feet long, with luxurious appointments, although she could carry 300 tons of freight. From balconies on the "Texas" deck one looked down to white linened tables with bouquets. Artistic chandeliers swung from the white and gold ceiling, 17 feet high in the dining room.

Near Christmas, 1895, the ship was trapped by ice in Lower Arrow Lake. Owners sent the smaller *Arrow* to break up the ice in the narrows and open a path for the *Nakusp,* but the *Arrow* capsized in a killer gale and drowned its captain and engineer. In 1897, the *Nakusp* fell victim to fire at Arrowhead. Despite weather problems, such sternwheelers operated regular routes from Arrowhead (fed by a rail spur from Revelstoke in later years) to Castlegar, Trail and Northport.

Trail was founded by Eugene Sayre Topping when he preempted 343 acres of land on Trail Creek and the Columbia River. He was a deputy mining recorder in Nelson, a modest man on a workman's salary. One day he was confronted by two excited miners who had five claims to stake and were allowed only two each. They offered Topping the fifth if he would pay all five recording fees. Thus Topping acquired a share in the soon fabulously rich LeRoi Mine at Red Mountain above Trail.

In 1890 to 1891 Topping brought samples of ore from his LeRoi Mine to Butte for analysis, then sold his interest to ecstatic purchasers for $30,000. The mine later sold for $3 million, but after all, he had paid only $12.50.

Enter Fritz August Heinze in 1894 on the steamer *Lytton* from Northport, an experienced smelter man and speculator from Butte. He purchased 40 acres at the present site of Cominco and built a smelter in six months. Heinze's company was incorporated in New Jersey as British Columbia Smelting and Refining Company Limited and the furnace fired up in February 1896.

Workers flocking to steady employment found conditions little better than the mines. J. R. Widmer said about Trail, population three hundred: "There were no sanitary conveniences. Water was delivered from house to house by water wagon. Smoky gas lamps lit the eight or ten hotels and the log and rough board cottages that huddled at the foot of smelter hill. Some of the hotels had double-deck bunks filled with loose straw for mattresses." (From article in *Orbit*, Cominco Magazine, September 1988, 8.) A later employee, Frank Verzuh, told me that the bed bugs became so bad in the hotels that he and three other men scrounged lumber and built their own rough cabin.

Heinze was juggling lawsuits in Butte from past dealings, development of the smelter and construction of the narrow gauge Columbia & Western Railway from Trail to Rossland—all the while staving off intense competition. The Northport smelter was ready to open in 1898, and American D. C. Corbin had thrust a rail line from Spokane to The Dalles below Northport in 1890 (then the foot of riverboat traffic), plus a spur to Red Mountain (Rossland) by December 1896.

Both speculators, Corbin and Heinze, sold their holdings to the titans in 1898. Heinze sold his smelter and railway holdings to Canadian Pacific Railway. Corbin sold the Spokane Falls and Northern to the Great Northern. Corbin had bitterly opposed the Great Northern, and some say he was unaware that his line would wind up in their hands during third party sale negotiations.

The CPR was forced to buy the smelter with the rail interests and although not keen about being in that business, they determined to do a good job, putting a capable engineer, Walter H. Aldridge, in charge.

Too late, he discovered that the CPR had paid only for railway and smelter, not for certain rolling stock and supplies to operate the smelter. A grinning Heinze suggested that he and Aldridge play poker for the $300,000 additional purchase price, but the more conservative Aldridge asked for arbitration. Upon resolution of the matter, the outfit was known as Canadian Smelting Works until 1906, when the Consolidated Mining and Smelting Company of Canada, Limited, was formed (Cominco), a subsidiary of Canadian Pacific Railway.

Meanwhile, workers clamored for better conditions at the LeRoi Mines of Rossland, impetus for the whole matter. In 1895, Rossland miners organized Local 38 of the Western Federation of Miners, the first in Western Canada, and built the still-standing Miners Hall. In 1898, they obtained an eight-hour workday credited to the efforts of Jim Martin, Rossland legislator. The miners were on strike for nine months in 1901, a bitter time but with no violence. Miners eventually were represented by United Steelworkers of America.

Among the workers at Rossland were about two hundred Chinese, employed as cooks, houseboys or proprietors of small stores. Laundrymen delivered clothes carried in one big sheet, the corners tied together. From verdant gardens, the

Chinese "vegetable man" delivered produce door to door from two enormous baskets slung over his shoulders. He marked the recipient's accounts on the door frame of the house, consternation reigning if a paint job covered the reckoning. Relationships were quite amicable between Europeans and Chinese. White guests were invited to the opening of a Chinese Masonic Lodge with a membership of one hundred men. Guests described the event: "In the lodge room were altars at either end of the room bearing lighted candles . . . joss sticks smouldered. Chickens well browned and inviting, candles of the Chinese varieties, cakes ... and sam suey galore graced the refreshment stand but the Celestial Masons did not bother with refreshments until noon. ... The concluding feature was a procession about the lodge room, each making obeisance to the master and other officers." (From Alice Martin manuscript, Rossland, British Columbia, Museum.)

When a Chinese person died, he or she was laid to rest with a twenty-five cent piece in his or her mouth to pay the way into the other world. The departed one was buried for three years, then disinterred and the bones returned to China for burial. In later years Canadians attempted to return numerous sets of bones to their Chinese homeland, in accordance with old custom, but the Communist government refused to accept them.

An inventor flared briefly into fame in 1902. Lou Gagnon built and flew the first helicopter ever to get off the ground in North America, a contraption that skeptical Rosslanders called the "Flying Steamshovel." Since it crashed after takeoff, a humiliated Gagnon left town.

Today Rossland is a prime ski destination. It is also the hometown of Olympics and World Cup ski champion Nancy Greene. A prophet, perhaps, was Olaus Jeldness, a Norwegian miner. On a dare from cohorts in 1896, he raced on 9-foot carved wooden skis from the summit of Red Mountain to the streets of town. Urging him on were the cheers of crowds well-oiled from the five local breweries and forty saloons. The feat led to Rossland's first annual winter carnival, still held each year in February.

The transportation war continued. Alarmed by the encroachment into Canada of the Great Northern, which touched the Kootenay in Montana, the Canadian Pacific Railway bought out the entire Columbia and Kootenay Steam Navigation Company. Thus, it could squeeze out competitors by changing ports of call while it built more spur lines in Canada. By World War I the Canadian Pacific Railway won the battle, only to renew rivalry with the Great Northern farther west.

The sternwheelers continued to serve. However tranquil the Arrow Lakes and Kootenay Lake might be usually, winds and ice took their toll. On Kootenay Lake on November 29, 1898, nine people lost their lives. Art Downs described the incident:

> The *City of Ainsworth* left Nelson for Bonners Ferry but got caught in a gale. Eight cords of firewood on her bow made her sluggish

41

and she began to ship water Her paddlewheel virtually stopped and she swung broadside to the waves ... each roll worse than the preceding one. Then she heeled over so far that water poured into her smokestack.

When she began to wallow, First Officer Perrier launched a small lifeboat but it swamped. Four of the five aboard vanished into the snow-lashed waves. Then Captain Lean and some crew members launched the other lifeboat ... it capsized. Five more people vanished into the storm. (Art Downs , *Paddlewheels on the Frontier* [Sidney, British Columbia: Gray's Publishing Ltd., 1972] 126-28.)

Despite further rescue efforts, the final toll was two passengers and seven crewmen.

Newer sternwheelers of the 1900s included staterooms with private washbasins, raised dining areas for better passenger visibility, stained and leaded glass windows and other amenities. They were powered by more efficient engines and designed for the rough waters of the Columbia rapids. Many of the vessels were built at Nakusp. The four-decker *Bonnington* went into service April 24, 1911, on the Arrow Lakes. Furnishings were of golden oak and Australian mahogany and, in the ladies' salon, there were plush carpets and soft armchairs. With a steel hull and relatively powerful engines, she was designed to manage shallow water. Her chief problem was her great height; the large amount of freeboard made her tricky to dock in a wind; however, passengers enjoyed her luxurious accommodations until she ceased operations in 1931 . Construction of the *Bonnington* was part of a master plan by the Canadian Pacific Railway to extend its tourist lodges to the Arrow/Kootenay scenic areas. The company built a luxury hotel on Kootenay Lake, accessed by a short train ride from Robson (Castlegar). The *Bonnington* brought passengers from Revelstoke, and a sister ship was available for passage or pleasure cruises on Kootenay Lake.

Tourists did come to the Arrow Lakes, especially to the hot springs resorts. On Upper Arrow Lake two locations opened to serve tourists, miners and loggers with aching muscles. In 1901, the Hotel St. Leon on Halfway Creek was open, lavishly decorated by owner Mike Grady with proceeds from sale of the Standard Mine, Slocan Lake. It was open sporadically, but few tourists came because the pipes carrying water from the springs were too small, and the water grew cold before reaching the hotel. Old travelers remember Grady as a lake character, a man with a flowing white beard who always met arriving steamers.

Riverboat Captain Robert Sanderson started the Halcyon Hot Springs Hotel in 1894, merely a dressing room of cedar bark nailed to poles and a sod-roofed log structure over the springs. Eventually the springs were purchased by Governor C. H. Mackintosh, who built Swiss-style guest cottages, seeded a lawn and built a wharf for steamer service.

In March, 1924, Halcyon was sold to retired Brigadier General F. E. Burnham, a World War I hero and Head Surgeon at Sarajevo, Serbia. He established the hotel as a White Cross sanatorium with healthy food and strict rules—no drinking and lights out at nine (although this was partly because of a low-powered generator). His friend Jack Harris remembers him as somewhat eccentric but a dedicated philanthropist and doctor who predicted smoking would cause cancer.

Burnham felt the waters were a gift from God and should be available to everyone who needed them. Burnham's rates remained very low and if one could not pay, he could cut firewood for the aging steam plant. Later he changed to fuel oil, and his parsimonious ways became his death sentence. He refused to hire a repairman to fix a leaky oil stove, catching the drips in a pail instead. One morning in 1955, the hotel exploded in flame, becoming Burnham's funeral pyre.

Not so grand, the Nakusp Hot Springs continuously operated and remains open as a public springs and pool, with camping facilities and overnight chalets. Historic Ainsworth Hot Springs on Kootenay Lake still is an operating spa.

Of the sternwheelers on the lakes, two survived into the 1950s to serve isolated miners and loggers, farmers and retirees. The *Minto* on Arrow Lakes and the *Moyie* on Kootenay Lake were fabricated at Toronto to be reassembled for duty in the Klondike gold rush; when plans changed, they were rerouted to the Kootenays. The *Moyie* was reassembled at Nelson. From a thousand labeled parts the *Minto* was reconstructed into a vessel 162 feet long and launched at Nakusp on November 19, 1898, three weeks after the *Moyie*.

The *Minto* was destined to become a legend on the broad Columbia River lakes. As the twentieth century wore on, the vessel became the only link to the outside world for isolated settlers—the occasional prospector, loggers in remote camps, the brave orchardists growing peaches on meager flatlands along the lakes. The ship carried mail and freight ranging from a spool of thread for a housewife to mining machinery, tractors or horses.

In 1949, a traveler reported the *Minto* had fifty-six berths and a crew of twenty—the berths sharply in demand. Passengers otherwise had to sit up and snooze in chairs for the twenty-six hour trip between Arrowhead and Robson. To see mule deer, caribou, elk or bears cavorting along the shores was a common experience—all the animals accustomed to the throbbing whoosh-whoosh of the *Minto's* paddlewheel. To hail her anywhere, one just waved two white flags or built two small fires; for an emergency it was three of either. The ship ran day and night except for the narrows between lakes, which the captain traversed only in daylight, determined not to add his beloved ship to the hulks rotting there on shallow, shifting gravel bars.

Locals said Captain Otto Estabrooks of that period could "take the Minto across a tureen of consomme without disturbing the vermicelli," according to Richard Neuberger writing in 1949 in the *Saturday Evening Post*.

43

Paddlewheel from an original riverboat, the Moyie, being restored at Kaslo

The ship's colorful 134-mile voyages seemed doomed to end before World War II, with only four thousand passengers a year; however, young men who trained for war at camps in the Selkirks returned after the peace to visit or settle the region again. Capacity crowds came once more to the *Minto's* decks.

Finally, weary from three decades of continuous use, and outrun by cars and railroads, this last sternwheeler quit. On her farewell voyage, April 24, 1954, under Captain Robert Manning, the teary farewells of locals and dignitaries could have floated the vessel. There were flags and songs, a wreath from Burton citizens on the ship's bow, a bagpipe lament and a welcoming crowd when she pulled in to Nakusp, the place of her "birth."

Outraged at the idea of scrapping the historic *Minto,* elderly John Nelson of Upper Arrow Lake purchased the vessel and planned to restore her as a museum, but he was too old and his project too ambitious. After he died in 1967, the stripped *Minto* was towed out into the lake and burned as part of the Dominion Day celebration in 1968.

Her memory lives on, though, in her sister ship, the *Moyie,* which was reconstructed as a museum at Kaslo on Kootenay Lake. The former luxury of her interior was restored: a ladies' salon with piano and upholstered chairs where tea and crumpets were served; a forthright men's saloon that had gambling tables, a bar and spittoons. Wood carvings over the cabin doors that provided openwork for ventilation are repolished. As work proceeded, a veritable treasure house of "garbage" was uncovered—candy wrappers, beer labels, newspapers of a century ago, where they were stuffed into apertures in the walls by passengers.

The foundation sponsoring restoration searched with modern sonar, diving gear, and cameras for the *City of Ainsworth* that sank in 1898. So far the only item located has been an intact jar of pickles thought to be from the vessel.

Tugs once pulled huge log booms along the Columbia River/Arrow Lakes. The trees were felled by independent loggers who used continuous track tractors or high lead logging to move them, instead of horse teams. A high lead system involved a logging jammer, a central small A-frame device that wound logs into the center from about a 500-feet radius. Hauled to the shore, the logs were scaled or measured before being rolled into the lake, where they were corraled in bag booms—big round enclosures—to await tugs. The tow sometimes was a quarter-mile-long procession down lake, a week's trip, to the locks of Hugh Keenleyside Dam. There booms were cut loose, lowered to river level and picked up by another tug for transport to Westar's lumber mill.

In 1960, Celanese Corporation of America opened the first pulp mill in interior British Columbia at Castlegar, to make bleached kraft pulp from waste material—chips and small softwood logs. Shipped all over the world, the end product is fine finished, coated papers.

At first Celanese bought and consolidated many small mills upriver and managed Celgar Pulp, Celgar Lumber and Celgar Woodlands Divisions. In 1986, the firm sold the timber operations to Westar Timber Limited and retained the pulp mill.

Westar used independent truckers and loggers to harvest blocks of trees from crown lands, after which they replanted the cleared areas within five years. James Cavaliero of Westar told me that the private companies bought or grew their own seedlings to reforest the areas.

The marine division of Westar managed the river craft, including tugs and boom boats (small, almost circular "tubs"—powerful craft that surge in among logs to sort and bundle them into rafts). One boom boat is fortified as an ice breaker for infrequent use.

Not surprisingly, a pulp mill like Celgar wrestles with emissions of unpleasant odors and materials into the river. Today the company asserts that its recycling plant returns water to the river cleaner than it entered, but totally eliminating odors is an ongoing and costly project.

Area telephone books show many Russian names. By 1912, about five thousand Russian religious dissenters called Doukhobors had settled in British Columbia, perhaps half around Castlegar and the central Selkirks. Their lifestyle involved no physical churches except community homes where the people met for prayer (religion was within the heart, not the Orthodox Church), vegetarianism, rejection of killing anything or anyone, abstinence from alcohol, tobacco and—

in rare cases—minimizing sexual intercourse. They recognized only God as their authority.

This independent attitude led to frictions with governments. In Russia it was objection to conscription; in Saskatchewan, their first Canadian home, it was refusal to make an Oath of Allegiance required by the Homestead Act before properties could be deeded. Doctrinal differences developed. While still in Saskatchewan, the Doukhobors became divided into three groups, of which vestiges linger: (l) Independents, who live on individual homesites; (2) Community, who live in communal villages; and (3) Freedomites or Svobodniki, the dogmatic arm that seeks return to absolutely nonmaterialistic living.

By 1924, under leader Peter V. Verigin, the sect had acquired 21,648 acres of land. In Castlegar it lay mostly south of the confluence of the Columbia and Kootenay rivers. The Doukhobors set up villages with thirty-five to fifty people per home, each family having a separate room, but sharing meals and property. Industrious and creative, the people cleared and farmed land, planted orchards and eventually had saw mills, oil presses, flour mills and a jam factory—the latter highly praised. The Castlegar Golf Course is the site of old blacksmith shops, barns, kitchens and a pit for distilling oil from birchbark for water proofing shoes, all gone before the course was built.

Old ways changed. Children were forced by the Canadian government to attend schools, a ruling that caused arson of schools laid chiefly at the door of the Freedomites. Doukhobor extremists also were blamed for the purported assassination of Peter V. Verigin on a Canadian Pacific Railway train between Brilliant and Grand Forks in 1924. Several miles west of Castlegar a massive explosion blew up the railway coach in which Verigin was riding, killing him, a female friend, and nine other passengers. The consensus is that the helpful Doukhobor man who carried Verigin's suitcase aboard had planted a bomb in it. Others say, since miners often illegally carried dynamite on trains, that unstable explosives caused the blast. In recent years a CPR employee said that the explosion was typical of a gas light malfunction. We will never know for sure.

In 1943, extremists burned down the Doukhobor jam factory above the Columbia River at Brilliant, as well as leader Ivan Verigin's home. The main body of Doukhobors shuns turmoil and tried to disassociate themselves from the violence. The Freedomites also were blamed, fairly or not, for using fire and nude parades as protests between 1958 and 1962, when—for nearly the first time—the protests involved burning Canadian governmental properties. Before that, it seemed that the protesters burned out their own.

Peaceful ways prevail today. Most Doukhobors now live in individual homes but retain their gentle ways and faith, including the belief that love is of paramount importance. The Doukhobors have developed wonderful choral groups that perform worldwide. The scores are unusual, possibly deriving from

Gregorian polyphony, the original, ancient style of Greek-Orthodox singing, a style so ancient that other Russians may have forgotten it.

A non-Doukhobor Russian, Alexander Zuckerberg, a high-born refugee from the Bolshevik Revolution, came to teach Russian to the Doukhobor and Castlegar children. He discovered a small forested island in the Columbia River, a few yards from shore, and inquired about its purchase. The provincial government was amazed, saying there was no such island, but Zuckerberg finally convinced them that it existed. There he built a Russian-style country home, paths, gardens irrigated from the Columbia through a waterwheel, and sculptures—including one commemorating his wife when she died in 1960. It is a park now, compliments of Zuckerberg and funded by the Rotary Club, a haven of peace reached over a suspension foot bridge.

World War I brought an urgent need for zinc used in munitions. Cominco researcher Ralph Diamond discovered new extraction methods that resulted in profitable expansion at Trail, a boon to the community, very dependent on the smelter. In World War II, Cominco developed "heavy water" used in the atomic bomb, a project so secret researchers did not know the reason for the project until very shortly before the bomb was dropped on Hiroshima.

Cominco got consistently fine marks from local citizens as a good corporate citizen, but its early-day emissions of sulphur dioxide led to complaints from downwind Washington farmers of damage to foliage. Research resulted in new ways of capturing 94 percent of the sulfuric emissions to use in fertilizers. Instead of polluting the atmosphere, the fertilizers marketed as "Elephant Brand" speeded the growth of crops in the Prairies. Today lead for auto batteries constitutes 70 percent of Cominco's output; zinc for galvanizing steel against rust is next.

Necessarily, emissions continue to be sharply reduced. "We definitely get the heavy metals out of waste water returned to the river," says a spokesman. But the damage of decades ago, when industrialists did not recognize such hazards, is not entirely healed, even though the river is coming back swiftly. Trail "river rat" and avid fisherman Joe Biagoni claimed there are good stocks of rainbow trout and kokanee. Kokanee are landlocked salmon that have adapted to living their entire lives in fresh water and do reproduce. They tend to be smaller than the wild strain, but for two years there were dramatic increases in numbers and sizes after introduction of fresh water shrimp to the Arrow Lakes as fish food. Fishermen take huge sturgeon from the river, and there are increasing numbers of walleye pike.

In past days fishermen built cedar slab boathouses, mounting them on logs and anchoring them to shore. An elderly resident who owned one had an ongoing battle with a beaver that tried to dam up the opening to his boathouse. One week he found it half full of branches. A pair of otters called the boathouse home, a mixed blessing since they ate fish and excreted on the boat. However, the "river rats" delighted in such small problems, because it meant the river was recovering from pollution. Bear, wildcat and an extremely rare albino cougar have been seen coming to the river.

Below Castlegar the Columbia River runs into Washington State largely unchanged from the old days. Here is the Columbia of the impressive Waterloo Eddy below Castlegar that bounces off a rock promontory to form whirlpools as big as a house Biagoni has watched large logs upend there, disappear and emerge 300 feet downriver), of the rugged canyons at Murphy Creek, the killer rapids at Deadman's Eddy just below the border—where the remains of anyone who falls into the river and drowns are usually found.

Chapter 7

Travel and Trivia • The River in Canada

For a twelve-hundred-mile river, I am suggesting only those activities or places of unusual interest or my personal enjoyment. Ask tourism centers for visitors' guides or Internet addresses to gain comprehensive information about attractions in any area. Almost all settlements along the Canadian portion of the river celebrate Canada Days, July 1st, of importance similar to the Fourth of July in the United States.

Captain Robert Gray's ship was the *Columbia Rediviva*. Maritime artist Steve Mayo of Bellingham, Washington, was commissioned to do an official oil painting of the ship, from which posters were made. For prints contact Kirsten Gallery, Seattle WA or Steve Mayo, Bellingham WA.

General tourist information for British Columbia is accessible from the website: www.hellobc.ca Six different areas are listed.

High Country Properties is only one of several firms that handle vacation homes and condos in British Columbia and Alberta. www.highcountryproperties. com

Fort Steele Heritage Town. Connected to earliest Columbia River Valley history. Sixty restored buildings. Demonstrations of quilting, spinning, ice cream making (interactive). Mother's Day Tea and 1890s Fashion Show in May. Sam Steele Days in mid-June honor the frontier Mounted Police Commander and include a parade, Sweetheart Pageant and logger sports. Farming Day using horse-drawn equipment in August. Father's Day event. Open year-round www.fortsteele. com

Recommended reading. *Fort Steele* by Derryll White, available at gift shop or by mail order and in Columbia Valley bookstores.

CRANBROOK:

Cranbrook has two visitor centers. www.hellobc.ca   Ask about "Explore Historic Cranbrook," a self-guided tour of 1800s architecture and other or "Baker Hill" tour of residential and railroad lore of a later period. Sam Steele Days July. Rodeo at Wycliffe Exhibition Grounds mid-August.

Cranbrook Museum of Rail Travel. Slide shows, guided tours, old engines and cars of Canadian Pacific Railway, and rail lore. Dining in dining car. Crambrook Archives, Museum, and Landmark Foundation. Railway Downtown Cranbrook on Highway 3/95. http://www.destinationcranbrook.com and www.cranbrooktourism.ca

Kimberley, site of one of the world's largest lead and zinc mines , Sullivan Mine. The town has converted its downtown area to a charming Bavarian theme. Browse through shops or dine at sidewalk restaurants. Numerous festivals include: Magic of Christmas Artisan Market, Platzl Holiday Light-Up. Bavarian Iron Legs Competition similar to Ironman Race. Spring Splash. Round the Mountain Festival in June attracts runners and bikers, the major 40th annual JulyFest mid-July with a parade, Canadian Bocce Championships, music, etc. Art on the Edge in August, Kimberley Fall Fair the last weekend of September. www.Kimberley.ca or www.hellobc.ca

Fairmont Hoodoo Mt. Resort, adjacent to weird sandstone formations, near Dutch Creek (a Columbia River source), a simple country resort, housekeeping cabins. 130 campsites. 5398 Highway 93/95, Fairmont BC V0A 1H1.

Canal Flats is a settlement on what was/is a permanent gravel bar 1.2 miles wide that separates the Columbia River at its birth from the Kootenay River, born several miles northeast and headed S/SW as it skirts the easterly side of the bar. Aboriginal people said the two rivers came close enough to kiss but were married at Castlegar, where the Kootenay merges with the Columbia. Surveyor David Thompson called the sandbar "McGillivray's Portage" in 1808. The name "Canal Flats" resulted from the 1880s attempt to build a canal through the barrier, fortunately unsuccessful. (See text.) Canal Days Party on first weekend in June.

Tilley Memorial Park is at the southeast end of the Columbia Lake with a lovely swimming beach, wheelchair access and standard park amenities. It's thrilling to stand there and know it is the birthplace of the mighty Columbia River.

O'Henry's Saloon, formerly the historic Columbia Inn at Canal Flats. A place where old-timers hang out and newcomers listen. A few rooms, bath down the hall, modest but clean.. Canal Flats Days in June coincides with Canada Day.

Fairmont Hot Springs Resort straddles the newly born Columbia River. Splendid golfing on three courses in the area (imagine driving your ball over the river, tiny at this point). Recreation resort, first class rooms and food, skiing in winter including a family ski hill, natural hot mineral springs. Historic, see book text. Guests pampered in every way. Handsome time-share villas, too. On Highway 93/95, and accessible by air to Fairmont Airport. Winter Wonderland Carnival in

December and New Year's Gala at Fairmont Hot Springs. www.fairmonthotsprings. com 5225 Fairmont Resort Road, Fairmont BC V0B 1L1

Suggested reading. *The Legacy of Fairmont Hot Springs* by Janet Wilder, part of owner family. Book available locally or write to the resort.

Columbia Valley. Numerous campsites and RV locations. Contact www. hellobc.ca or www.columbiavalley.com .

INVERMERE AREA:

Tourist Info Centre, Main Street, Invermere, BC. www.cvchamber.ca 651 – 93/95 Highway, RR#3, Invermere BC, or postal Box 1019, Invermere BC V0A 1K0 Also www.hellobc.ca and www.columbiavalley.com Pond Hockey Championships in February. Nipika Toby Creek Nordic Skate Loppet in February. Wings Over the Rockies Bird Festival in May to celebrate the return of the birds to Columbia Valley area. Horsethief Hideout Backwoods Blues Festival in May, Heart of the Rockies Triathlon in mid-July.

Invermere on lovely Lake Windermere is a resort town with fishing, horse trips, pack trips, tours by off-road vehicles, boating, hiking, mountaineering. The main street of town has sidewalk cafes, small shops and gift shops. The well-known White Way provides 10 miles of groomed trails for cross-country skiing and skating www.hellobc.ca

KOOTENAE HOUSE NATIONAL HERITAGE SITE. The site of the first trading post in the area, David Thompson's "Kootenai House" is at the junction of Toby Creek and the Columbia River near Wilmer. Site has interpretive signage. See text for Thompson information.

Larry Halverson, retired from Kootenay National Park, wrote a bird guide to the upper Columbia Valley that was/is available at the Friends of Kootenay store in Radium Hot Springs, BC. He also writes a blog about natural history (2012) for the Friends of Kootenay National Park Society (www.friendsofkootenay.com)..

Windermere Valley Museum. Small museum with displays and considerable local lore in archives. www.windermerevalleymuseum.ca 222 – 6th Avenue, Windermere BC V0A 1K0

Invermere Inn, Best Western full service inn right downtown, great food and night club atmosphere, too, at Copper City Saloon. Popular with visitors and residents. Walking distance to shops and Lake Windermere beach. www. invermereinn.com 1310 Seventh Avenue, Invermere BC V0A 1K0

Strand's Old House Restaurant serves a sophisticated menu created by chefs imported sometimes from Europe. The restaurant is in a heritage home with leaded glass windows, occupied n the early 1920s by Dr. Elmer E. Coy, the only doctor from Golden to Cranbrook. Three generations of the pioneer Weir family lived there later. www.invermere.com 818 – 12th Street, Invermere BC V0A 1A0

Incredible Mountain Tours. Tours to scenic sites such as the Bugaboo Range, Lake of the Hanging Glaciers, the wildlife refuge, Paradise Ridge or

Mount Swansea to watch the sunset over the Columbia River. Rent a cabin at two different and remote locations. Complete ski program in winters for downhill, cross-country, snowcat and heliskiing. www.imtours.ca

Mount Swansea is a good spot from which to launch hang gliders.

At this writing **Babin Air** is one operator from Invermere Airport that provides scenic flights over the Canadian Rocky Mountain Trench that include views of glaciers. www.babinair.com

The **Invermere Soaring Centre** supports gliders. The Canadian Columbia Trench is considered one of the best mountain soaring sites in the world with a wonderful mix of thermals and dynamic soaring. The prime season is May to September. Twenty minute gentle glider rides with experienced pilots afford unforgettable scenic views above the Columbia Valley and Lake Windermere. www.soartherockies.com

St. Peter's Church in Windermere was "stolen" from the town of Donald, once a thriving little railroad workers' town, by Rufus Kimpton. The CPR had offered to transport stores, hotels, and personal effects to Revelstoke after it moved its headquarters there. Kimpton and J.C. Pitts dismantled the church and moved it to Windermere. Despite loud outcries from Revelstoke, the church stayed reassembled at Windermere and was reconsecrated on August 27, 1905. It's a popular place for wedding ceremonies.

Bavin Glassworks. Founder Jim Bavin attended the prestigious Pilchuck School in Darrington, Washington, internationally known for glass-blowing art. Bavin is an amateur archaeologist and has done many Kootenay Indian pictograph designs in glass. www.bavinglass.com

Village Arts, an artists cooperative, displays the handcrafts for sale of at least 55 local artists in downtown Invermere. http://villagearts.ca

Kootenay National Park staff suggests that visitors consider canoeing the Columbia River. It is quiet through much of the Columbia Valley, passes through huge scenic lakes, and offers views of wildlife and birds, especially at Wilmer National Wildlife Area five miles north of Invermere. Canoes may be rented fom Columbia River Kayak and Canoe in Invermere. The company also offers Voyageur canoe tours from Fairmont Hot Springs. Ask staff about pack trip outfitters in the area.

Panorama Mountain Village. About 20 miles from Invermere in the Purcell Mountains. A comprehensive summer and winter resort near the historic Paradise Mine, one that actually paid off. Resort accommodations including condos and apartments and amenities such as fireplaces, hot tubs, children's programs, seasonal sports – skiing, riding, golf, fishing, salmon barbecues. Murder Mystery Dinner Theatre in July and August, Panorama Grand Prix-Canada Cup Cycling Series in May, and more. www.panoramaresort.com

Mountain and Valley Shuttle. Supported by the Columbia Valley businesses, the shuttle operates in winter only to serve Invermere-on-the-Lake, Radium Hot Springs, and Panorama Mountain Village. www.invermere.net

Canada's only Bonspiel-on-the-Lake is in January. Hang Gliding and Paragliding Splash Landing Contest in May at Invermere.

In winter the **Bugab0oo Mountains** in the Purcell Range offer prime heliskiing daily. This sport requires a least a good to expert skier, although runs have guides familiar with the local terrains and weather conditions. Expensive but thrilling for dedicated skiers or snowboarders. Usually available from Invermere, Golden, and Revelstoke airports. Some lodges offer cross-country ski trips, as well. Summer helihiking trips are offered by a few operators. Ask infocentres for names of providers and check them out thoroughly.

Among the heliski companies is **Canadian Mountain Holidays (CMH).** Father of heliskiing Hans Gmoser worked with this company and is accepted by most as the first or inventor of the sport. CMH offers trips to several mountain ranges of the Columbia Valley area and beyond. www.canadianmountainholidays. com

RADIUM HOT SPRINGS:

Radium Hot Springs Chamber of Commerce. www.radiumhotsprings. com Wildlife, big horn sheep. Starlight Challenge (ski, snowboard) in February. Trail Run at Nipika Resort in June. Radium Hot Springs Festival held in late May annually includes a dance, beer garden, parade, and golf tournament. www. radiumhotsprings.com Classic Car Show and Shine Festival in mid-September exhibits as many as 800 cars and trucks that culminates with a car parade from Radium to Invermere. A few days following this event is a major trail run from Radium into the Kootenay National Park to support the Bighorn Sheep Project.

Columbia River Wetlands adjacent to town. Largest continuous wetlands in North America.

Radium Hot Springs Aquacourt is the original Sinclair Springs or Radium Hot Springs (see text). The parking lot is just east of the springs across from a massive red rock formation. Nominal fee for using the springs. Modest food services and gift shop. In the adjacent town are many motels and restaurants, often with a Bavarian or Swiss appearance.

 Radium Resort (formerly called Radium Hot Springs Resort) is a golfing resort in the foothills a mile south of the town. It is one of the older but full service resorts of the area. Tennis, indoor pool, squash, patio dining, lounge, golf and views. Meeting facilities up to 500 people. Site of BC Men's Amateur Golf Championships. www.radiumresort.com Mail: Box 310, Radium Hot Springs BC V0A 1M0

Towering Rocky Mountains east of Golden and psuedo-covered wagons of Beaverfoot Lodge.

Prestige Lodge at the junction of Highways 93/95 offers panoramic views of the Columbia Valley. Has meeting facilities, deluxe rooms, pool and easy access to Aquacourt. http://prestigehotelsandresorts.com

GOLDEN AREA:

Kicking Horse Chamber of Commerce. www.goldenchamber.bc.ca Mail: Box 1320, Golden, BC V0A 1H0 Municipal campgrouind with variable programs for public, including evening interpretive programs, review of history at the District Museum, or walks to the Columbia River Valley Wetlands. Kicking Horse Country Fall Faire, September. Dogtooth Dash mountaineering race in March. Wrangle the Chute ski-based affair in March and other snow-based bashes.

Golden Field Office of Columbia Forest District. Information on Forest Service Recreation Sites, fishing and hunting regulations, and general information. Set up appointment or seek information through the Main office in Revelstoke. 1761 Big Eddy Road or PO Box 9158, RPO Office, Revelstoke BC V0E 3K0 http://www.for.gov.bc.ca/dco/#first

Golden District Museum has displays and archival material. Open every day in summer. 1302 11th Avenue South, Golden BC V0A 1H0

Raft trips on the Kootenay River. Several companies offer tours north of Canal Flats (which forms a barrier between the Kootenay and Columbia rivers) and on the Kicking Horse River beyond Golden. The latter has swift and wicked rapids such as: "Hopi's Hold," "Flying Hot," "Penny's Plunge," "Witch's Rock," "Last Waltz," and "Table Saw." Rated up to #4. Among the operators are Alpine

Rafting Company and Glacier Raft Company Ltd., Kootenay River Runners, and others. Close to Invermere is Toby Creek Adventures and other. Most of the operators serve Invermere, Golden, Radium Hot Springs, Fairmont Hot Springs Resort, Panorama, and other visitor sites. Suggest contacting tourism information outlets. Operators do tame river trips, as well.

Amiskwi Lodge north of Golden, accessed by Alpine Helicopter at Golden Airport. Backcountry lodge in remote Blaeberry River alpine area at 6900' altitude. Comfortable beds and cooking facilities, catered or bring-your-own food. Hiking, helicopter skiing. All season service. See text for Blaeberry River historical significance. Scenic flights to Yoho and other glacial areas including Columbia Ice Fields from Golden. www.amiskwi.com www.alpinehelicopter.com (at Golden but serves other northern airports).

Please note that flight, raft, and other service names might change over time, so check Internet or tourism information sources.

Northern Lights Wildlife Wolf Centre focuses on educating the public about wolves. An estimated 10,000 to 15,000 visitors a year mingle with a few tame wolves, some more comfortable with humans than others. Interpretive center/refuge is near Blaeberry River about 10 miles from Golden www.northernlightswildlife.com 1645 Short Road, Golden BC V0E 1H1

Flying W Trail Rides operating out of Kicking Horse Mountain Resort includes rides along the Blaeberry River made memorable by explorer David Thompson. See text. Also offers ATV trail rides. www.flyingwtrailrides.com

Beaverfoot Lodge off Highway #1 is historically famous in that the Pallliser Expedition passed through its grounds. The isolated country log lodge, with the turnoff onto a dirt road about 13 miles east of Golden, has basic second-floor rooms and top-notch wholesome food. A dude ranch atmosphere with lots of horseback riding, river fishing, hiking, wildlife. Unusual circle of 20 pseudo covered wagons in a secluded valley for visitor lodgings, a complex that includes a cookhouse and modern bathrooms. A wilderness experience for guests. Cross-country skiing in winter. Very scenic at the edge of Yoho National Park. www.beaverfootlodge.com Box 388, Golden BC V0A Canada 1H0

GLACIER NATIONAL PARK is an hour's drive west of Golden. It includes **Rogers Pass Historic Site.** The mountainous area between Golden and Revelstoke was a barrier to transportation but teemed with international class skiers and outdoors people who came from several countries. (See text about Swiss Guides.) Today's park protects a major area of the Columbia Mountains Natural Region in the interior wet belt of British Columbia. Among its assets are stands of huge old-growth cedars. Wildlife abounds, including caribou and grizzly bears. Rogers Pass is honored because of its location for building the first coast-to-coast railroad in Canada and, even later, finally Highway #1in 1962. Glacier Park Lodge at the summit of Rogers Pass has a limited number of rooms, basic services, hiking trails, sweeping views. www.pc.gc.ca/glacier Mail: Glacier National Park, PO Box 350, Revelstoke BC Canada V0E 2S0.

Kinbasket Lake Resort is one of few structures on the huge lake. The Columbia River runs through this 150-mile-long lake, joined at the site of the resort by Beaver River. Remote and wild but accessible by road for cars to RVs. Six rustic cabins have amenities and decks facing the lake. www.kinbasketlakeresort.com

Columbia Ice Fields loom over Kinbasket Lake but are not accessible from there, except by challenging foot trails. Accessed more often from the east side of the range.

Mica Heli-guides is a back country lodge across Kinbasket Lake from Mica Dam above the hairpin bend of the Columbia, served at this writing by Arrow Helicopters . Accommodates 16 people in 12 bedrooms with amenities. www.micaheli.com www.arrowhelicopters.com (Revelstoke).

National and provincial parks abound along both sides of the Columbia River.

Kootenay National Park is known "from cactus to glacier," because it represents the southwest region of the Canadian Rockies with extremely diverse topography from the Continental Divide to the Rocky Mountain Trench where cactus grows. For information: www.pc.gc.ca/kootenay Mail: Kootenay National Park. Box 220, Radium Hot Springs BC Canada V0A 1M0

Yoho National Park. Although it is about an hour's drive from Golden, it should not be missed. Yoho is a Cree word expressing awe and wonder. Sheer rock faces and broad glaciers. Center of the Yoho area is at the town of Field on Highway 1. In 1909 the Burgess Shale was discovered. Scientists are uncovering the best examples in the world of pre-Cambrian marine life and fossils, 530 million years old. It was named a World Heritage Site in 1981. www.pc.gc.ca/yoho Mail: Yoho National Park, PO Box 99, Field BC Canada V0A 1G0.

It is near **Mica Dam** that the river turns abruptly from northwesterly to southerly. See text and map, for it was here that David Thompson realized this river was the same as the one flowing south from the international border more than 200 miles away. The Columbia's long northwesterly path had long deceived explorers as to the river's birthplace. A gravel road on the south side of the lake takes you to the plaque commemorating David Thompson's discovery of the Columbia River. The actual site, the junction of the Columbia, Wood, and Canoe rivers is under Kinbasket Lake today.

The river from the Big Bend to Revelstoke had some of the most dangerous rapids to navigate before Mica and Revelstoke dams were created. History records several incidents ending in loss of life for those trying to pass this stretch by canoe or boat. The area also had vast snowfalls.[See text] Significant numbers of grizzly bears inhabit the forests there. Author was fortunate enough to see in her rear view mirror a mother and cub crossing the road a hundred feet behind the car.

Canoeing, boating, fishing and camping along the river described above is delightful at this writing, after taming of the river through dams. Boat launching ramps at Five Mile Provincial Park, Martha Lake Provincial Park, and other. Several campgrounds and RV sites are available, including one at the historic Downie's Resort, 43 miles north of Revelstoke. Before dams and the Rogers Pass highway, a primitive road followed the Columbia River from Golden around the Big Bend and south to Revelstoke. Sometimes portions were under water during flood stages. Downie's Resort, then little more than a few cabins and a country restaurant, was a welcome sight to intrepid automobile visitors. *Reminder: This is prime grizzly bear country. Respect them.*

REVELSTOKE AREA:

Revelstoke Chamber of Commerce. www.revelstokechamber.com or www. hellobc.com/Revelstoke The Rogers Pass section of Trans-Canada Highway #1 from Golden to Revelstoke was completed in 1962. Until then, it was accessible from the east only by rail. Today it is a significant Southern Interior city with charm and industry. Father's Day at Skytrek in Revelstoke celebrates in an adventurous way – zipline through forest or slide through on a skateboard, pass over swinging logs or a suspension bridge. Other festivals include a Vintage Car Club Show in early June, Timber Days early July and Stoked to get Spanked Cross-Country Mountain Bike Race in later July. An important link of the CPR, Revelstoke celebrates four days of Railways Days in August. Snowflake Wine Festival in later November. Ask about snowmobiling and hiking map. Mountain bike rides down Boulder Mountain, extensive trails for mountain bikers.

On its southward flow from the Big Bend Revelstoke is the first town the Columbia River bisects after passing through the large Revelstoke Dam built in 1985.

Revelstoke Dam Visitor Centre north of the city. Recently renovated Centre includes 14 new interactive displays, First Nations gallery, and theatre. Elevator to summit of the 175-metre-high dam. Scenic views. Interpretive information and self-guided tours of the dam.

http://www.bchydro.com www.hellobc.com

Revelstoke Walking Tour. Brochure available at the Visitor Centre at 204 Campbell Street to the many historic sites of this small city, steeped in alpine, railroad, and road building lore. [See text.]

Revelstoke Historical Museum and Archives at 315 First Street West.

Revelstoke Railway Museum across the tracks. Comprehensive story and artifacts about the building of the Canadian Pacific Railway **(CPR)** across Canada and especially across Rogers Pass from Golden to Revelstoke.

Revelstoke Nickelodeon Museum in a historic building downtown that has been a pool hall, disco, dance hall, dental surgery centre, bowling alley, and now an official Heritage Site. Owners of McKinnon Block Building restored its tin ceiling, the largest tin ceiling in Canada, it is claimed. Automated music devices, juke boxes, player pianos, barrel organ, music boxes. One-hour tours. http://www. revelstokenickelodeon.com

Apex Raft Company. www.revenstokechamber.com

Mount Revelstoke National Park. Adjacent to Revelstoke town. Downhill, heli-skiing, and cross-country available each winter on Mount Mackenzie. Meadows in the Sky scenic drive. Giant Cedars hiking trail, Skunk Cabbage hiking trail in jungle-like wetland. Other hiking trails, sweeping fields of wildflowers in spring, all the facilities of a typical national park. www.pc.gc.ca/revelstoke Mail: Mount Revelstoke National Park, PO Box 350, Revelstoke BC Canada V0E 2SO

Revelstoke Mountain Resort on and around Mount Mackenzie Ski Area. A major resort construction project began in 2005 that is estimated to be completed by 2020 with all amenities of a major ski destination. Smaller visitor facilities will be or have been absorbed. Two high speed gondolas (Revelation) serve the ski facility plus two chair lifts, two detachable quads, and a beginner lift. In 2007, Selkirk Tangiers Helicopter Skiing Ltd. purchased an existent smaller heli-ski operation. Revelstoke has the highest lift-served vertical in North America and hosts the Canadian Championships of the Free Skiing World Tour annually. A Spirit Festival of music and multiculturalism occurs in February.

Mustang Cat Powder offers snow-cat skiing or snowboarding in the deep powder of Monashee Mountains near Revelstoke, simply called cat-skiing or cat-boarding. Certified guides. Mount Copeland near Mustang Powder has held the record for 80 feet of snow in one season. The company has acquired a vintage mansion for a Bed and Breakfast ski facility near Revelstoke Mountain Resort, as well. www.mustangpowder.com K3 Catski and Revelstoke Mountain Resort also have snow-cat operations.

`**Scenic flights** over glaciers, the Columbia River, and wildlife viewing from Revelstoke Airport at this writing (2013) from Silvertip Aviation in a twin-engine plane (Access by current phone or mail) or by helicopter from Arrow Helicopters (www.arrowhelicopters.com) and Selkirk Moutains Helicopters (www.smheli.com). Glacier Helicopter at Three Valley Gap .

Williamson's Lake Campground. RV hookups, tent sites, mini golf course on a lake with swimming beach. www.williamsonlakecampground.com

Revelstoke Golf Club above the Big Eddy section of the Columbia River on the site of the 1904 Revelstoke Turf Club . 18 holes, lounge, restaurant, open to the public. www.revelstokegolfclub.com

Three Valley Lake Chateau. Scenic location in Eagle Pass 12 miles west of Revelstoke. Lake, beach, heritage ghost town. Surveyor/explorer Walter Moberly discovered the much needed pass for the CPR by watching eagles soar on the pass's updrafts. Descendants of original builder Gordon Bell still are involved with the Chateau[see text]. Twenty-five displaced historic buildings were moved to Three Valley site, including St. Stephen's Church popular for weddings. On site, also, are the Antique Automobile Museum and a Railroad Museum. Helicopter tours leave directly from Three Valley. Frequent booking of live entertainment for groups. www.3valley.com hello@3valley.com

Arrow Lakes ans Kootenay Lake areas:

Arrow Lakes, the Upper and Lower, are part of the Columbia River beginning south of Revelstoke. Two ferries across the 162-mile lakes are the only ways to cross the vast waterway: Shelter Bay-Galena Bay Ferry 32 miles south of Revelstoke and Fauquier-Needles Ferry 34 miles south of the town of Nakusp (this feeds Highway 6 toward the Okanagan Valley of Canada).

To understand the juxtaposition of the Arrow Lakes portion of the Columbia and Kootenay Lake (an expanded section of the Kootenay River), please refer to a BC map and read in this text about the area between the two large lake systems. The Kootenay River flows past Canal Flats opposite the fledgling Columbia River and, after much meandering by both rivers, the Kootenay empties into the Columbia near the United States border at Castlegar.

Visitors are advised to obtain travel guides of the land between the lakes, such as "Go Kootenays" or other. In the text the period of mining and settlement is discussed.

Nakusp on Upper Arrow Lake is a village with most amenities. Beach open to the public. Outstanding fishing is normal, and several small marinas or sports store have rental boats. Creative Hands Craft Fair in November. Arrow Park south of Nakusp has a cable ferry that provides access to the western shore of the lake and its country roads. www.nakusparrowlakes.com

Two of the Nakusp hotels represent differing views of décor. The **Leland Hotel** with lake views claims to be the oldest continuously-operating hotel in British Columbia, since 1892. When steamers docked in pioneer days, passengers would race to the hotel to compete for the few available rooms. Within the last 20 years the owners have worked at restoring the hotel, especially old grillworks and woodwork, stove-heated water heaters and such, but 21st century passengers have varying opinions of antique restoration. Lakeside view dining (Write or telephone.)

Another century-old hotel and spa, the **Halcyon Springs Hotel** has chosen to go more to the modern. It has a heated mineral (Lithia) pool from the natural springs that is popular, affording lake views from the patios surrounding the pool. Housing is in individual cabins. www.halcyon-hotsprings.com

Nakusp Hot Springs, eight miles e o the village itself has a modern pool with change facilities, overnight Cedar Chalets, and at least 30 campsites beside the Kuskanax River. www.nakusphotspringschalets.com

Interesting **books concentrating on paddlewheelers** (such as those operating on the Arrow Lakes and Columbia in past times) include: *Paddlewheels on the Frontier* by Art Downs (Sidney BC, Gray's Publishing, 1972) and *Sternwheelers and Steam Tugs* by Robert D. Turner (Victoria, Sono Nis Press, 1984.)

In the area between Arrow and Kootenay lakes is the **Slocan Valley**, once an active gold mining area and still of mining attention. It is a charming and historically interesting area to explore, an area related to this, a saga of the Columbia River. Among the settlements on Slocan Lake are **New Denver** and **Silverton**. Silverton has a mining museum of small and very large artifacts that are kept outside. New Denver has the Silvery Slocan Museum, open in summer. New Denver is the site of the **Nikkei Internment Memorial Centre,** dedicated to the 22,000 Japanese-Canadians who were removed from their homes in Canada during World War II and settled in camps in the Slocan Valley. A small village, Hills, between New Denver and Nakusp is the host for the large Hills Garlic Festival held annually.

The website: www.slocanvalley.com shows "Journey Through the Valley," a series of illustrated vignettes to describe the little towns of the valley and key events.

Ten miles east of New Denver is the halfway ghost town of **Sandon,** site of the Silvana Mine of the Treminco group, which was closed in 1993. A mining museum and old buildings at Sandon recognize the active production of the Silvana only 20 years ago.

Idaho Peak at 7,480 feet (2,280 meters) is the acknowledged peak for a prime scenic view. It is on a rather steep, graveled road, 4 WD recommended. Noted for its spectacular array of alpine flowers in spring. *Remember: this is bear country!*

Kaslo, about 60 miles from Arrow Lakes on Kootenay Lake, survived the mining period to settle into a charming village with an art and summer stock facility housed in the Langham Cultural Centre, an 1883 hotel building. Featival of the Arts for two weeks in mid-August. *S.S. Moyie*, a 1900s paddlewheel passenger boat, was renovated here and became a museum to commemorate the fleet of such large boats that served residents and visitors on the Arrow Lakes and Kootenay Lake as late as the 1950s. A village of myriad festivals, the most recently conceived in 2010 as Sufferfest, a bike and run event. www.visitkaslo.com

The land between the lakes from Nakusp and Kaslo to Nelson is a vacationer's paradise for fishing, boating, swimming, hiking, winter sports, The Lardeau River that runs into the Kootenay has produced huge rainbow trout as big as 25 pounds. On the Columbia side the Lower Arrow Lake does not have "through" roads. From Kaslo southward one can drive along the west side of Kootenay Lake toward Castlegar, crossing the Kootenay to explore Nelson. A ferry also operates for crossing the lake from Kaslo to Nelson.

Ainsworth Hot Springs Resort south of Kaslo has first-class rooms and dining. The springs emerge in an eerily lighted, horseshoe-shaped cave. www.hotnaturally.com

Nelson is a sizable town that has maintained as many as 350 turn-of-the-century Victorian buildings from its days as a prominent mining and boating supply centre. Ask for a brochure entitled "Architectural Heritage Tours." Said to be the most impressive hotel between Winnipeg and Vancouver, the Hume Hotel built in 1898 with great fanfare became rundown by 1980. It was renovated and restored to its 1898 splendor and operated 25 more years as the Heritage Inn. Locals donated antique furnishings and monitored the works with keen interest. In 2005, a new owner restored the hotel's name to Hume Hotel. The attractive, tree-lined streets belie Nelson's former reputation as a rough frontier-style town. In the 21st century Nelson is known as the #1 small arts town in Canada. A continuous Artwalk occurs for the three months of summer between July and October with more than 70 nationally-known artists' works shown in 17 of the city's restaurants and shops. Performing arts events are booked regularly into the heritage Capitol Theatre, as well. Nelson, Castlegar, and Trail share their history, to an extent, since the vast water system of the Kootenay discharges into the Columbia River at Castlegar, and at Trail the Keenleyside Dam arose to assist flood control on this impressive water heritage, amplified by the melt from adjacent mountain ranges, as well as producing electric power. Nelson hosts numerous festivals all year, many of them shared by Castlegar and Trail. Attracting international students is one focus of the unusual Selkirk College with campuses in all three towns. www. nelsonkootenaylake.com and www.hellobc.ca

Castlegar is a small city at the confluence of the Kootenay and the Columbia River. The two mighty rivers are only 11 miles apart at Canal Flats BC, near the birthplace of the Columbia to the west. The river promptly heads northwesterly. The Kootenay rises several miles northeast of Canal Flats, and is headed south as it passes the Flats. After running different courses for hundreds of miles each and in opposite directions, the Kootenay joins the Columbia at Castlegar. The town became populated with many Doukhobors, people of Russian ethnic heritage, religious protestors who moved to Canada in the 1800s with an unusual cultural background. Kootenay Festival in late July. www.castlegar,com

Zuckerberg Heritage Park is on a little island in the Columbia River accessed by a suspension bridge 474 feet long and with a span of 300 feet. Follow signs to parking. Walking paths, picnic grounds, sculptures. A Salish pit house was discovered on the island that dates back probably 20,000 years. Alexander Zuckerberg built a lovely Russian Orthodox chapel house for his wife and himself that is open at suitable times for viewing. www.gokootenays.com

Doukhobor Discovery Centre is a reconstruction of a typical Doubhobor village with tools, buildings, and exhibits. Near the junction of Hwys. #3 and #3A. (See text).

Brilliant Cultural Centre is named for an original Doukhobor settlement at the site. It serves both religious needs of the Doukhobor Union of Spiritual Communities of Christ (USCC) and as a secular multi-purpose community centre and venue for visiting cultural groups. It especially welcomes events that deal with multiculturalism and world peace. www.usccdoukhobors.org

Kootenay Gallery of Art, History and Science hosts traveling art and cultural exhibits, including those from the Royal British Columbia Museum, Canadian Craft Museum, Communications Canada, and other. It is a handsome building near the Doukhobor Discovery Centre. Exhibitions have included diverse showings such as Canada's fur trade, quilts, ancient Chinese ceramics, www. castlegar.ca

Verigin's Tomb above the Kootenay River contains the remains of Peter V. Verigin (Peter the Lordly), important to the Doukhobors, also the son, Peter P. Verigin (also called Christiakov, Peter the Purger, Peter the Cleanser), their wives, and Anne P. Markova (daughter of Peter P. Verigin and mother of John J. Verigin, Doukhobor leader). Take Broadwater Road toward the town of Robson.

Hugh Keenleyside Dam is 6.5 miles upriver from the town of Castlegar. Because it is at the foot of the Arrow Lakes, it originally was called High Arrow Dam. Hugh Keenleyside was the chairman of the British Columbia Power Commission and 1962-69 co-chairman of the British Columbia Power and Hydro Authority. The dam was completed in 1968, one of three dams constructed not just for power but to control the levels of the Columbia River during potential flood periods. During one such past flood, the city of Portland, Oregon, far south in the United States was inundated. www.bchydro.com

Canadian Pacific Railway (CPR) Museum is housed in a original 1907 train station, one where the station agent lived upstairs. Local rail complex artifacts from the period when lead and zinc were shipped from Revelstoke to wind up at the Trail smelter farther south. www.stationmuseum.ca

Pass Creek Regional Park across the river from Castlegar is a 30-unit campground with a swimming pond and other visitor amenities. www.rdck.bc.ca

Syringa Creek Provincial Park is another big campground of 61 sites adjacent to Lower Arrow Lake itself. Fine for RVs. http://www.westkootenayparks. com or www.discovercamping.com for info or reservations.

TRAIL **and Trail Area** is the most southerly large city on the Canadian Columbia River before the river enters the United States. Between the Monashee and Selkirk mountain ranges, it is a haven for recreation, some of it in wilderness lands. Trail is the fourth largest city in British Columbia. See the Columbia River running swift and free at this point below the Canadian dams at Trail's waterfront **Gyro Park**, two miles long. The Columbia River always ran swiftly before dams and, on the longer undammed stretches still can develop impressive whirlpools, once a navigational hazard. www.trailchamber.bc.ca

Consolidated Mining & Smelting Company of Canada Ltd. founded in 1906, just five years after the incorporation of the city of Trail, changed its name to Cominco in 1966, Teck Cominco in 2008 after a merger of the two, and Teck Resources Ltd. in 2009. . With the discovery of large quantities of lead and zinc in the nearby Red Mountain before 1900, mines began operating and the above smelter prospered in Trail. During World War II the smelter cooperated with Hanford in creating elements needed for creating sophisticated arms. The mining operations in the area have been accused of polluting parts of the Columbia River, but at this writing the industry receives good marks for attempting to reverse past mistakes. www.teck.com

Colander Restaurant in downtown Trail gives a taste of boarding house days when throngs of single smelter and mine workers ate family-style at Kootenay Hotel. Angelina Infanti once operated that boarding house and, in 1990, worked for Colander. Today an Italian menu still retaining a huge spaghetti feed is available to customers who eat at common tables as the workers did. www.colander. readmymenu.com

Sports Hall of Memories. Trail has a long history of intense sports activity, winning championships at hockey, in particular. The adjacent Cominco Memorial Centre, a sports and recreational center is home to the Trail Smoke Eaters Hockey Club. The Sports hall has display cases of memorabilia, trophies, newspaper clippings, photos, and such. www.trailhistory.com

Rossland, home of the LeRoi Mine that produced fabulous amounts of gold around 1900. The mine no longer operates but underground tours take the visitor 800 feet into Red Mountain to showcase hard rock mining techniques. Rossland's site is within an ancient volcanic crater at 3,410 feet altitude, making it one of Canada's highest cities. It re-invented itself after mining days as a ski resort. Famed Canadian ski competitor Nancy Greene grew up there. Today the Red Mountain Ski Area has several lifts and alpine skiing, plus a Winter Carnival in February that includes a torchlight parade, ice sculpture, tobogganing and a lively time. The second weekend of September during Golden City Days Rossland celebrates its historic mining past with entertainment such as can-can dancers and kite flying! Considered a prime outdoor vacation city Rossland adds to the year-round events with the Rubberhead Festival in mid-September, a no-holds-barred mountain bike competition. http://www.rossland.com

Although technically not in the Columbia River basin, a remarkable 17,000-acre, wild wetland near Kootenay Lake between Trail and Creston is managed Crown land as Creston Valley Wildlife Management Area. Here and there are towers where one can watch for wildlife without disturbing these natives. www. crestonwildlife.ca

U.S. Border to Priest Rapids

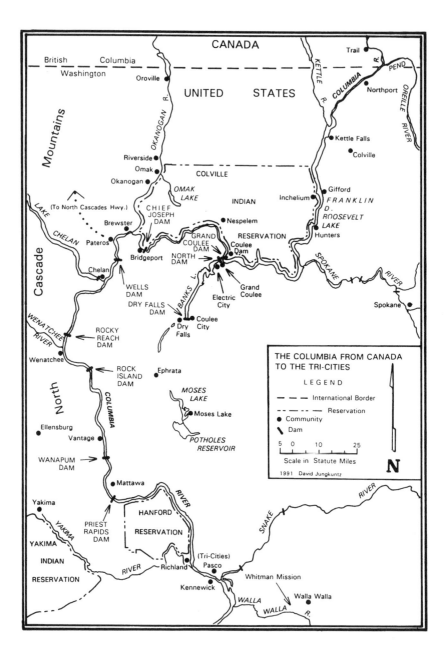

THE COLUMBIA FROM CANADA
TO THE TRI-CITIES

LEGEND

— — — International Border

— · — · Reservation

● Community

◣ Dam

5   0   10   25

Scale in Statute Miles

1991   David Jungkuntz

Chapter 8

South of the Border

L ittle has changed today along this free-flowing turbulent stretch of water from Castlegar to the upper reaches of Lake Roosevelt near Northport, except that powerful boats whisk water skiers along the deadly whirlpools. One skier said with an evil grin, "You can look right down into the dark center hole, and it makes it more fun."

Twenty miles south of the border, the hamlet of Little Dalles was settled about 1865 to serve as the southerly terminus for river boat traffic. No sensible riverboat captain regularly challenged The Dalles below town, a washing machine of a rapids. However, when the *Forty-Nine* was launched near The Dalles in 1865 to serve Big Bend prospectors, its captain, Leonard White, did challenge The Dalles rapids to rocket downstream and dock in front of old Fort Colvile to pick up Christina McDonald for this premier voyage. (Her father Angus saluted the sternwheeler with a volley from a little brass cannon.) Little traffic ensued after White's few trips until the Canadian Pacific Railway came to Revelstoke and interest was rekindled in the Columbia River area.

To tap the growing north/south traffic, D. C. Corbin swiftly extended his Spokane Falls & Northern Railroad to Little Dalles by 1890, where he connected with riverboats of the Columbia and Kootenay Steam Navigation Company. Responding, also, to the profitable mines at Rossland (Red Mountain) in British Columbia, Corbin hastened to extend his railroad ten miles north in 1892, where the resulting new settlement, Northport, eclipsed The Dalles. From there the logical course toward Red Mountain was across the Columbia and up Sheep Creek Canyon.

Angry Indian police were guarding the far shore against encroaching would-be settlers. The Congressional Act of July 1, 1892, restored the north part of the Colville Reservation to the public domain but provided for initial allotments of 51,653 acres to 660 Indian people, before non-Indians could apply. It took a senate bill to grant permission for the railroad to cross the land.

While Corbin's railroad proceeded, a stage line ran between Northport and Rossland, and the steamer *Lytton,* Columbia and Kootenay Steam Navigation Company's early sternwheeler, operated between Northport and Trail.

Meanwhile, entrepreneurs were constructing the Northport Smelter, opened for business in 1898, especially hoping to process ore from Rossland's LeRoi Mine and beat out the Trail Smelter. While Corbin's railway supplied ore, the Northport Smelter prospered, employing about two hundred men initially, six hundred at its zenith. The sound of saw and hammer was constant as two thousand people struggled for housing. By 1904, the Trail smelter had won out, and there was insufficient ore to feed the furnaces.

As suddenly as it began, Northport became a virtual ghost town, flickering to life briefly in 1915, when the smelter processed lead. The only significant mining was for gold; transient Chinese worked the Columbia River bars, and the outlines of their unique "washings" or gravelly flumes are still visible. A sawmill, logging companies, farms and orchards kept Northport alive for a few hundred residents. All that remains of the old smelter is its smokestack on the sawmill grounds.

During prohibition days such border communities were accustomed to strangers in autos or pack trains passing through the back roads. A most innovative bootlegger sent cargos down the Columbia from Canada in sealed hollow logs especially marked so a waiting American accomplice could identify them and pull them in.

At China Bend one evening, two men requested the ferry operator to take them across as fast as possible. It was too windy to be safe, the operator said. The fidgeting passengers offered the operator big money if he would risk it. When the wind died down a little, the operator made the trip, receiving $25, big money, indeed.

Cable ferries linked small communities on either side of the river. Such transport across the Columbia could be adventurous. Cables could break, stranding passengers in midstream until someone came by row boat to rescue them. A high wind or extra-strong current could cause the ferry to revolve completely and make braids out of the cable. Where cable ferries were not available, settlers (even young children) rowed across the river to socialize, with little thought as to what could happen should they be swept downriver into the rapids or over Kettle Falls.

On one occasion a cable ferry did break loose entirely and hurtle down river. Twenty-seven miles below lay Kettle Falls, a 20-foot drop. That evening at Marcus, just above the falls, Carl Brauner was fixing dinner when he heard pounding hoofbeats. A wild-looking man threw himself off his lathered horse, crying to Brauner, "Quick, get your boat! The Bossburg ferry is coming down the river with passengers aboard." Brauner raced to his boat and rowed strongly to the middle of the broad river, managing to remove the screaming passengers before the ferry boat fell to destruction over Kettle Falls.

Brauner's home at Marcus was within sight of the decaying buildings of Fort Colvile. Until its official abandonment in 1871 (although various McDonalds lived on there), Fort Colvile was one of the most influential trading posts in the Hudson's Bay Company system.

Sir George Simpson, Hudson's Bay Company governor, ordered the construction of the fort in 1824, upon the earlier recommendation of Alexander Kennedy that Fort Spokane should be replaced. David Thompson of the North West Company and Finan McDonald had built Spokane House as a distribution center ten miles northwest of today's Spokane in 1810 to 1811. The location was delightful for living, located in a pleasant valley, but was out of the way for fur brigades, since it was not on the Columbia River. Spokane House personnel moved to adjacent Fort Spokane (Hudson's Bay Company) after merger of the two companies in 1821 , and abandoned Spokane House. Now the fort, too, was to be phased out.

Thus, in 1825, Fort Colvile began to rise about a mile above Kettle Falls in a broad valley protected from wintry winds by low mountains. Construction was entrusted to John Work, a tough, capable man living up to his name. He and his crew completed enough buildings that Spokane personnel could move.

The complex closedown of Fort Spokane took place in March, 1826. Two strings of packhorses, one of sixty-two animals, the other of eighty, augmented by several boats, transferred everything. Employees unscrewed the iron hinges from doors. The formerly lively post became a shambles overnight, and friendly Spokan Indians viewed the move with consternation.

Construction continued over the next few years. The trading post itself was a wooden fort enclosed with high pickets. At one corner there was a blockhouse or bastion with a four-sided roof and three portholes for rifles and another for the cannon, a small, ineffectual piece never fired in anger. The factor's home was a relatively substantial place with a large living room warmed by an odd adobe fireplace so narrow that one could insert logs only vertically. There were offices, storage areas for furs, storage granaries, a blacksmith shop, a carpenter's shop, two houses for visitors, an Indian hall to shelter native dignitaries who came to call, trappers' barracks and other structures. Outside the stockade were extensive farming areas, barns, servants' housing, bakehouses and a boathouse.

Responding to Simpson's orders that forts should be frugal and grow their own food, post personnel planted fields of potatoes, vegetables and grain between the river and the chalky-white limestone bluffs. The Catholic fathers at St. Paul Mission operated a school, available to all, especially Indian children; and in 1863 Mary Meyers opened a school on the Colville River for white and mixed-blood children.

In his memoirs, Ranald, the son of Archibald McDonald (Chief Trader 1834 to 1842, Chief Factor 1842 to 1844), remembered the gracious parties in the commodious dining room of the fort, when the supply boat or the semiannual express came from Fort Vancouver or York Factory. Guests were pampered from a richly stocked cellar of liquors and a groaning pantry of meats and vegetables. Those invited might include hunters, Indian chiefs, Hudson's Bay Company inspectors, trappers, all seated in order of importance, his father at the head of table, women and children at the foot. From newspapers and letters received in the express, Archibald often read aloud to those hungry for any information about the world beyond the Columbia River.

Below the fort the river quickened to enter a canyon leading through rock-strewn rapids to two great falls. The main torrent swirled boulders around with such force that they wore depressions like kettles in the rocks, hence its name Kettle Falls or, in French, *Les Chaudières.*

Kettle Falls was the most revered Indian fishing site on the upper Columbia River. A rich variety of tribes, cousins from ancient days, lived all across the boundary country—Spokan, Lake, Nespelem, Okanogan, Sanpoil and others. In late June, these tribes and distant visitors gathered on the west bank, the fishing preceded by the First Salmon Dance. Presiding over the assemblage was a salmon chief, whose sacred duty was to apportion equitably all salmon caught. A number of salmon were allowed to pass above the falls to spawn upstream. Then the salmon chief directed a fisherman to catch one fish, boil it and let him taste it. If all was well, the salmon chief approved the start of fishing.

The Indians used spears or uniquely shaped baskets of willow, about 4 feet deep, 5 to 6 feet wide, 20 feet long. Salmon attempting to leap up through the falls usually fell back several times before attaining the top. Fishermen thrust the baskets beneath the falling salmon, and when the catch filled the basket or became too heavy to handle, they dumped it out on shore. Waiting hands butchered and salted down the fish in containers or hung them on drying racks.

A spear fisherman stood precariously on a platform hanging out over the river, spear poised. Spears and gaffs had an ingenious "fail safe" character so that, if the fish were too weighty, the spearhead would detach and play out along a strong cord. Otherwise, the fisherman might be yanked into the river, a foaming caldron.

Witnessing Indian fishing in 1860, Lieutenant Charles Wilson of the Royal Engineers said that two men stripped and jumped into the water beneath the falls, where they knocked the caught salmon senseless and passed them to handlers on shore. The men stood right in the falling water, half-drowning.

Salmon-gathering time was not all work. Dancing, stick or bone games, and horse racing filled idle moments. In later years when settlers had formed the towns of Kettle Falls and Colville, Indians (and sometimes settlers) raced through the streets of town. A popular event was the salmon relay. A contestant grabbed a big live salmon up to 30 pounds from a trough, ran 100 yards with the struggling and slippery fish, then back to the trough. Often salmon and contestant wound up rolling around together in the dust.

When construction began on Grand Coulee Dam in 1933, the Kettle Falls salmon runs began to fade. In 1940 the Indians held a poignant "mourning ceremony" to mark the loss of the traditional fishing ground, since fish cannot go upstream beyond the dam. At the Colville Tribal Museum, Grand Coulee, one may see replicas or original baskets and spears, and fishing scenes painted from memory. An Indian historian and tribal volunteers answer questions.

Heavily intermarried, the Indians and settlers have a remarkably amicable history—especially since the initial behavior of the intruding Americans was sometimes unsavory. In pioneer days Indians and settlers starved together when times were tough, and worked together at logging and ranching—in fact, often the "Indians" were the "cowboys."

Among the earliest settlers of Kettle Falls was Carl Brauner, rescuer of the cable ferry passengers. He came from Austria in the 1920s to work on the Columbia River, building a tough rowboat to catch drift logs—logs that escaped from booms far upriver or trees that fell into the river naturally. During high water the logs might have come all the way from the Pend Oreille River in Idaho or from the Columbia's Big Bend country. He boomed them and sold them to a mill on the Kettle River.

So turbulent was the Columbia River that logs would "jump out" of standard booms. Brauner screwed a metal eye into each log and threaded chains or ropes through to hold them in. One spring, as Brauner attempted to tow a log boom into the mouth of the Kettle River, the engine on his 26-foot boat quit about a half-mile above the falls. Stubbornly refusing to lose the boom and boat over the falls, Brauner jumped into the icy spring water to replace a key in the propeller.

This intrepid pioneer also ran the Marcus cable ferry for a decade. He was known to climb over the river on the cable, hand-over-hand, to replace the pulley when it fell off.

The site of Fort Colvile is now a broad circular bay. The centripetal action of the river has deposited up to seventy feet of silt there along a bank. During a recent low water period, the river cut into the silt banks and drew it back into the mainstream. Bill Brauner, Carl's son, who runs the family logging operation and was on the city water board, said, "The water was thick as soup going over the falls for almost a month. The town of Kettle Falls fought to sort out the sand and silt from the drinking water, and save the pumps from being damaged by the sand."

Periodically water levels in Lake Roosevelt retreat so that Kettle Falls is uncovered, its roar heard again with nostalgia by nearby residents. In 1976, exceptionally low water uncovered the site of Fort Colvile and old fishing camp areas, yielding a rich harvest of artifacts.

When Lake Roosevelt backed up behind Grand Coulee Dam, the original town of Kettle Falls had to be moved to higher ground. Near the town's original site today is an extensive campground and a new marina and boat rental facility (including a few houseboats).

Nearby, Boise Cascade's plywood mill employs about four hundred people (1992) in the region, a successor to several smaller mills. The logs come in by truck, not river boom; the river is used only for occasional log storage. The plywood process uses, not large logs, but those 7 to 20 inches in diameter. They are peeled down to veneers of 1/8 to 3/16 inch for exterior sheeting.

Adjacent to Boise Cascade is the Washington Water Power Generating Station which is environmentally exciting. When the state's residents became concerned about environmental factors, wigwam incinerators burning tons of sawdust generated by sawmills were pinpointed as polluters. In 1983 Washington Water Power, the private utility for northeast Washington, installed a plant to generate power from sawdust, the first in the United States. Trucks haul waste wood and chips to the plant for burning in a closed system (the resultant ash is captured), creating steam to run turbines for power generation—an output currently that can serve twenty-three thousand residential customers per day. Like the Trail smelter, which alleviated pollution by turning sulphurous emissions into useful fertilizer, the new generating plant turns potentially wasted or damaging by-products into "good" channels.

In 1921, two adventurers made trips down the 1,214-mile length of the Columbia River. Lewis R. Freeman was accompanied by a photographer to make a movie of the trip and got away first. M. J. Lorraine, age sixty-seven, did it in a rowboat just for fun weeks later, reading Freeman's feature in *Sunset Magazine* when he passed through Northport. Both men wrote books that reflected great respect for the seemingly endless series of rapids between Kettle Falls and Pasco at the time. It is interesting to touch on their travels before relating the saga of two major dams that would seriously change the channel of the Columbia River-Bonneville Dam on the lower Columbia, Grand Coulee on the upper, the latter to drown Kettle Falls.

Freeman traveled as far south as Hunter's, seventy-five miles below the border, with riverboat pioneer Captain Frank Armstrong as his guide. The men spent their last night together in a farmer's barn, where belled cows kept them awake and licked their faces.

As Armstrong's replacement locals suggested (always with a devious grin) river pilot, Ike Emerson. After much difficulty, Freeman did locate Emerson and found him to be quite a character but seemingly capable. Emerson suggested that Freeman and the photographer should throw their boat atop his lumber raft to go through Hell Gate Rapids (below Hunter's). The raft was 100 feet long, 30 feet wide and stacked several feet high with cordwood for downriver markets. Through the stacks one could see the river, flowing darkly beneath. Onlookers told morbid stories of those who had failed to manage Hell Gate. As if to emphasize the dangers awaiting them, Emerson's youthful helper fell into the river first thing, disappearing under the raft, only to come up safely at the rear and clamber aboard.

En route downriver toward Hell Gate, Freeman reported that "the sun painted the sky and the weird pinnacles and bluffs of the bleak shore with colourings brighter and more varied than any I had believed to exist outside of the canyons of the Colorado and the Yellowstone. Saffron melting to fawn and dun was there, and vivid streaks that were almost scarlet. ... A fluted cliff-face ... flushed a pink so delicate that one seemed to be looking at it through a rosy mist." (Lewis Freemoil, *Down the Columbia* [New York: Dodd, Mead and Company, 1921], 249.)

The dramatic 1,000-foot face of Whitestone signaled the approach to Hell Gate—"a pair of black rock jaws, froth-flecked and savage ... closing together in an attempt to bite the river in two." A long black reef, jutting out from the left bank, choked the river into a narrowing channel against a rocky wall, the water shooting between the two obstructions to split against a rock island 100 yards farther down. Thereafter, it negotiated a Z turn.

Emerson had built an oversized sweep to steer the raft, its handle a 4-inch in diameter wooden piece about 20 feet long. A motor launch steadied the head of the raft. Freeman's impression of the whole wicked rapid was blurred activity ... the water of the black-walled chasm ricocheting off the basaltic walls, a foam geyser of water tumbling over the stern, which swung broadside and straightened out with mighty efforts on the sweep. And then they were through.

Elderly Lorraine, an unruffled pragmatist somewhat smug about his ability to handle any kind of water, also wound up at Hunter's in late September. About a mile below, he was hit suddenly with a wall of wind that sent sand flying and whipped up the river into whitecaps. Dust from the Big Bend farms obscured the sky (a condition the author experienced there in 1990). Retreating to shore, Lorraine spent a fitful night. In the morning he found that his boat had broken loose with all his possessions aboard, even his camera and typewriter. After searching all day along the shores, he found the boat six miles down river, her mooring line luckily caught on an obstruction. Nothing was lost.

When Lorraine reached the infamous Hell Gate, he approached it stern-first in his heavily built rowboat and slid quickly through the opening. He deliberately steered his craft toward the perpendicular wall Freeman mentioned, skillfully turning when 100 feet away, running across the rushing water bow first. Again he turned the rowboat stern-first and came out of the rapids without shipping a drop of water.

After further such adventures, Freeman finished the long journey at Portland. Lorraine went all the way to Astoria; his last view from his battered boat was the white crest of Mount St. Helens hanging above the river like a cloud.

Chapter 9

Primeval Times and Indians

A hundred miles below Kettle Falls, the mighty Columbia River's destructive force was turned into electrical power generation with the completion of Grand Coulee Dam between 1941 and 1951. It was here that the original Columbia River once changed channels.

Witnessing the power of an ordinary river is an awe-inspiring experience—the grinding and churning of massive floes as big as a house, when river ice breaks up in spring—the deafening thunder of falls—the unstoppable power in flood stage, over its banks, relentlessly tearing apart houses and stores, ripping away big chunks of earth and toppling trees. Think, then, of the power of the primeval Columbia River of central Washington, many times the size of today's river. (Modern place names are used for orientation.)

The early Columbia River drained glaciers through present channels. As the river came south past Kettle Falls, it was shunted westward by the massive Columbia Plateau or scablands, to skirt its edges. The North Cascades caused it to veer southward again, a channel described in Chapter 1 , *Discovery*.

These scablands were formed by lava upwelling like a fountain in southeastern Washington. The lava extended from slightly below Colville into Oregon, from beyond the ldaho border to send fingers oozing through the North Cascades Mountains all the way to the sea. Over and over the black basaltic material overflowed, spreading over the Columbia Plateau more than a mile thick. Then in the Pleistocene Epoch vast fields of glacial ice, no doubt blue-white and beautiful like the glaciers of the Cascades today, pressed forward to cover British Columbia and Washington in an irregular pattern. Ancient Lake Columbia filled the trench now occupied by Lake Roosevelt. A long finger of glacial ice, perhaps 5,000 feet thick, moved down the Okanogan River Valley across today's Bridgeport and overran the plateau as far south as Coulee City, blocking the course of the ancient Columbia River. Forced aside it turned south, wearing itself new paths.

A new era began, the earth warmed, and glaciers began to retreat unevenly. To the northeast the enormous Lake Missoula had developed behind an ice dam.

It eroded the dam and sent a torrent too massive to comprehend catapulting oceanward. The evidence is there in central Washington.

Crashing down the Spokane River channel, the waters came with unimaginable force into the Columbia above Grand Coulee. Blocked by the ice barrier at Bridgeport, the rampaging waters turned into the alternate southward channel of the Columbia, taking advantage of a natural fault to rip out weakened chunks of basalt and carve the coulees indenting central Washington State. First came the excavation of Grand Coulee, extending twenty-one miles south of today's dam, its virtually sheer walls more than 800 feet high in places, exposing the strata to be easily read by geologists.

The flood spread out briefly, then plunged seaward again over a falls three and a half miles wide, dropping more than four hundred feet. (Niagara Falls is one mile wide and drops 165 feet.) It must have washed away rhinoceros, woolly mammoth, mastodon, the great lion, short-faced bear, sabre-toothed tiger and more in its unchecked rush, for fossils of some have been found along the channels. The basin it scooped out holds a pathetic remnant of water as several small, extremely deep lakes. There at Dry Falls, standing at cliffside, one can imagine the torrent, the awfulness of that flood.

The water continued down a narrowing fault, carving out the coulees and lakes we know today—Sun Lakes, Soap Lake, Moses Coulee, Moses Lake, Potholes Reservoir. The flood became a temporary lake from the Cascades to Lewiston, Idaho, covering Pasco's site with 800 feet of water. Eventually it wore away the Wallula barrier and, in a cataclysmic rush, turned westward, widening the Columbia Gorge through the Cascade Range, and emptied into the ocean. The site of Portland was under 400 feet of water.

Most scientists believe that disastrous floods recurred from a freeze-and-melt, melt-and-freeze cycle on Lake Missoula. At any rate, when ice near Bridgeport melted, leaving behind large boulders scattered randomly on the dry plateau, the Columbia River resumed its present channel.

Grand Coulee, then all but dry except during rainy seasons, had a stark and frightening grandeur of its own, described best by Alexander Ross in 1855:

> The sight in many places is truly magnificent: while in one place the solemn gloom forbids the wanderer to advance, in another the prospect is lively and inviting, the ground being thickly studded with ranges of columns, pillars, battlements, turrets, and steps above steps, in every variety of shade and colour. ... Thunder and lightning are known to be more frequent here than in other parts; and a rumbling in the earth is sometimes heard. According to Indian tradition, it is the abode of evil spirits. ... It is the wonder of Oregon. (Alexander Ross, *Fur Hunters of the Far West* [Norman: University of Oklahoma Press, 1956], 31-32.)

Today the Grand Coulee's battlements are reflected in the deep blue water of Banks Lake, the vistas akin to those of Lake Powell in Arizona/Utah on the Colorado River. The massive rock formation, Steamboat Rock, formerly sailing through a dry wash, is more fittingly almost surrounded by water.

Around the perimeters of the hot, dry Columbia Plateau, aboriginal people thrived, arriving eight to thirteen thousand years ago on some sites. Northwest Indians said of themselves only that they came "from the north." In Columbia River country the tribes belonged to two distinct linguistic families—Salishan, the more northerly and coastal, and Sahaptin from south central Washington on. Two decades after Gray startled the Indians of the Lower Columbia, David Thompson and Finan McDonald came in from the north to establish Spokane House to trade with the Spokans and Coeur d'Alenes, as mentioned earlier. Relationships with the Spokans were amiable; they were a largely peaceful people living in a richly endowed land.

Several Indian tribes or bands lived periodically along the Columbia River, moving with the seasons to customary fishing sites, hunting camps, root-gathering places and permanent winter camps. Few called any one specific place "my land." Indigenous to northern Washington were Salish-speaking Okanogan, Sanpoil, Nespelem and Lake. Despite often shabby treatment by white people, more by the transients than the governmental figures, these Indian people were staunch friends and still today point out that they never warred on Americans. The painful process of accepting an encroaching culture unquestionably was eased a little by earlier contacts with Hudson's Bay Company and North West Company fur traders.

David Thompson of the North West Company tells of meeting the Indians on his first Columbia voyage. About 70 miles below Kettle Falls he met the Sanpoils, commenting on their foods, including camas and a small onion, plus moss bread (considered by the Indians as the last resort before starvation) and their hunting practices. To catch deer, thirty or forty persons gradually encircled a herd until a signal came to start shooting them.

Near Box Canyon he encountered Nespelem Indians, who were taller and fairer. He noted that the women daubed their faces with red ochre and the men painted a stripe down the parting in their hair. At the mouth of the Methow River he met the Methows, cautiously friendly.

At the Wenatchee River and south to Priest Rapids, Thompson met Indians who apparently had not seen a white man before. They examined Thompson with wonder, even feeling his leg to see if he was real. Beyond that point, Thompson entered the Sahaptin-speaking country, and his interpreters were replaced.

The Salish Indians exhibited few or no warlike weapons, and usually were friendly. In 1841, in Canadian Okanagan Indian country, when an Okanagan killed a Hudson's Bay Company trader whom he wrongly blamed for his father's death, Okanagan Chief Nicola thundered out against the perpetrator: "The winter is cold. On all the hills around the deer are plenty; and yet I hear your children crying for food. Why is this? You ask for powder and ball. ... The powder and ball he gave you that you might get food ... you turned against him. ... I cannot look at myself in the glass, I cannot look at you. ... Wherefore did you kill him?" (Quoted by Sister Maria Ilma Raufer, O.P., in *Black Robes and Indians* [Milwaukee: The Bruce Publishing Company, 1966], 21.)

Chief Nicola's father, Chief Pelka-mulox, once said to the white traders: "You are my white children, and I do not want to lose you. I want you to live in my territory. I have a big country, big enough for all of us and for our children and our children's children. ... As long as the waters run and until yonder hill is no more, you and I stay here, your children and my children. " (*Ibid.,* 3)

The upper Columbia tribes were mariners, not horsemen; they built and paddled canoes where few would go, through the Columbia River's rapids and up treacherous shallows in their commerce and fishing. Not until late in the nineteenth century did horses become important.

Their equally friendly cousins, the Spokans, were inordinately fond of horses. One of the chief horse trading fairs was near the Little Spokane River. The sellers lined up, holding their horses; the buyers started piling up goods until a seller handed over the lead rope. Like the Nez Perce, famed for their racing steeds, the Spokans might stage races as long as five miles over hill and dale.

The Spokans were happy to supply traders with skins, since the payment in guns and metal gave them a chance against traditional enemies, the Blackfeet and Nez Perce. They entered wholeheartedly into the social life of the trading post, learning European-style dancing, and the women adopted the foreigner's clothes. Many traders and trappers, including John Mcloughlin and Peter Skene Ogden, married native women. One poor soldier almost lost his head over marrying an Indian bride, only to have her husband come home—understandably furious, but later willing to relinquish her for suitable presents.

Moving like leavening agents throughout the meetings between cultures were the missionaries, Catholic Fathers deSmet, Demers, Grassi, Joset, Ravalli, who established St. Paul's Mission at Kettle Falls and St. Regis near Colville, and the Protestants Cushing Eells and Elkanah Walker among the Spokans. Often they visited their converts by canoe, a dangerous journey at times. In the spring of 1842, when Father Pierre de Smet came to visit the Okanogan Indians, he walked along the Columbia River and watched helplessly as the canoe he had just left was drawn into a whirlpool. Five people were drowned.

The Indian's faith was tested severely in 1853 and 1854 during a dreadful smallpox epidemic. Because most of the white settlers were vaccinated, they did not get the disease, and prostrate Indians (many of whom had declined vaccination) believed the infection was some deliberate ploy of the Americans to reduce their numbers. New Christian converts returned to the dreamer-prophets, Skolaskin of the Sanpoils (his grave is in Keller Cemetery, and his old log church is at Nespelem) and Smohalla of the Wanapums, and their mystical religions. Most of them clung to old ways of dealing with disease—the sweat house and a plunge into cold water, disastrous as treatment of smallpox sufferers. Still the steady hands of wise chiefs kept the peace.

Confusion among the Indians as to beliefs of Catholics and Protestants led to some friction. When surveyors for the railroad and for the Mullan wagon road from the headwaters of the Missouri to the Columbia came with tape measures, the Spokans realized that the white people intended to take some of their lands. They wondered if they had been wise by being friendly. Word came of the Whitman massacre in southern Washington; the Spokans hoped their white friends would not blame them as accomplices.

Then gold seekers in northeast Washington and Idaho capped the uncomfortable changes, bringing liquor that inflamed these previously sober Indians. Many prospectors did not honor Indian lands or ways. Finally, despite the steadfast friendliness of leaders like Spokan Garry, a devout Christian, the Spokans' regard ruptured over the matter of going onto a reservation—not even a convenient reservation on their homelands, but the threat of being moved west of the Columbia.

This was too much. Meeting Colonel E. J. Steptoe in May 1858, while he marched north from Fort Walla Walla to placate the Indians, the Spokans and allied bands soundly beat him in a well-executed attack. Three months later, the Spokans, aligned with bitter Nez Perce, Coeur d'Alenes and others, were decisively defeated by Colonel George Wright in bloody battles at Four Lakes and Spokane Plains. Afterward, the American force shot hundreds of Indian horses. Relenting somewhat later, the authorities did establish a reservation along the north bank of the Spokane River, part of the Spokans' original homeland, although a small group of Spokans chose to go to the Colville Reservation west of the Columbia River.

At least one military man, General W. S. Harney, formerly an avid Indian opponent, spoke mercifully about the necessity of protecting the remaining Indians from the unscrupulous white miners and settlers, not vice versa.

Schools eventually came to the reservation, the most beloved teacher sent there being Helen Clark, a Quebecois, who taught at Wellpinit between 1894 and 1899. She was protector and friend to her charges and once said indignantly, "Every white man seems to think that it is his legitimate privilege to ... trick an Indian in any kind of a trade or business transaction, and as a rule they have very little confidence in the white man's honesty. I tell them I am ashamed of my people." (Quoted by Ruby and Brown in "The Spokane Indians" from *Lincoln County Times,* March 20, 1896 ,7 .)

Meanwhile, to trade with the Indians living farther west, the North West/ Hudson's Bay Company Fort Okanogan served the area between 1814 and 1848. The fort was superbly situated on a promontory overlooking the confluence of the Okanogan River and the Columbia near today's Brewster. There the fur brigades transferred from Columbia River canoes to pack trains to supply posts at Kamloops and Alexandria (near Prince George). With the establishment of the forty-ninth parallel as an international border in 1846, Hudson's Bay Company moved its headquarters to Fort Langley north of Bellingham, Washington, on the Fraser River, and abandoned the Okanogan post (and others).

Okanogan Indians were friends of Fort Okanogan personnel. Clerk Ross Cox told of an eerie prediction by a Chief Ye-whell-come-tetsa that wolves would come after the post's horses. Discounting the premonition, Cox went about his business, but the very next night wolves killed five horses. Grimly, Cox and a hunting party went after the wolves and among those shot was a monster white wolf estimated at over 125 pounds. Cox gave the skin to the chief, a special treasure, because the insignia of an Okanogan Indian chief was a white wolf-skin, fantastically painted with figures, the head and tail decorated with bears' claws and animal teeth, suspended from a pole near his lodge. In 1858 and later, miners traveled past Fort Okanogan's derelict remains on their way to the fabulous gold fields of Barkerville (Canada), 300 miles north of the border. More sagacious adventurers drove big herds of cattle north to feed them.

The sheer numbers of a large party moving north in 1858 were alarming. The party under David Mcloughlin (son of John) moved north from Walla Walla, bound for Barkerville. South of the border at a defile thereafter called Mcloughlin Canyon, the party walked into an ambush by Indians encouraged by Chiefs Moses and Sarsapkin. Six men fell in the first volley. Taking cover, the miners held their own until nightfall, escaping across the Okanogan River. A day or two later, they were attacked again, but Chief Tonasket came to stop the fighting.

Then, all Indian-settler relationships became strained in the Columbia country. Government representatives attempted to conclude treaties with hostile Indians and to fashion reservations for many. The bands called "Colville" today did not sign any treaties but eventually accepted a reservation that extended from the Columbia River on the south and east to the international border on the north and to the Okanogan River on the west. Later agreements would pare the reservation.

As Indians moved, willingly or not, to reservations, governmental authorities were often confused about their tribal backgrounds. Disparate people were assigned to the Colville Federated Tribes, often likened to "Colville United Nations." Tribes had differing customs, religions, governments and languages. Two groups especially were foreign to the others—the Moses Indians and the Nez Perce band of Chief Joseph.

Moses' people came from near Wenatchee, around Rock Island Rapids, and were intermarried with Entiat and Yakima bands. They considered lands in Douglas and Grant counties as their own, south of today's Colville Reservation. They also had signed no treaty or reservation agreement. In June 1877, Chief Moses agreed to move to a reservation if he could help to select it. Certain lands were proposed in May 1879, at a most colorful gathering at the Wenatchee and Columbia rivers that included Territorial Governor Elisha P. Ferry; General O. O.

Howard, the military leader; local trader and settler Sam Miller and "Dutch John" Galler; Chief Moses, Chief Innomoseecha of the Chelan band; Chief Harmelt of the Wenatchi (original spelling); and hundreds of Indians and troops. The gathering was described by Lieutenant C. E. S. Wood:

> Hour after hour the Indians arrived, singly, by families, bands, and almost by tribes, trooping in with herds and loaded pack animals. ... The tepees of buffalo-skin were put up, the smoke of many campfires arose, and the hillsides became dotted with grazing ponies. All the life was barbaric. ... The shy women in buckskin shirts and leggins (riding astride), their saddles hung with bags, strange utensils, and sometimes the papoose swinging in his swaddling cradle at the pommel; wild-eyed, elfin-haired, little bronze children, perched naked on top of some bales of household goods. ... In the train came the grave, anxious looking men in fur mantles or loose buckskin shirts, or with yellowish copper-colored, naked bodies, and only the breech-clout and fringed leggins, their hair loose or braided, and their faces painted black, red, yellow, white. ... The ponies ... sometimes gay with interwoven feathers, and sometimes ears, tail and mane all cut close to the body. ... Then the camp ... its color, its gorgeous setting in the evergreen and snow-clad hills; the eternal snow peaks high in the air against the blue sky. ... (Lt.C. E. S. Wood, "An Indian Horse Race," *Century Magazine* 33 [November 1886-April 1887], p. 448.)

The Indians listened but made no decision, preferring to stay where they presently lived until forced to move. Besides, they had brought their horses to the council—the best to be found—for wildly competitive horse races on the broad council plain.

Later in 1879, Moses approved a reservation centered on the west side of the Columbia River, but by then, miners were flocking into the upper Methow River Valley where gold in paying quantities was found. Many Wenatchi, Chelan and Wapato bands stayed where they were. Chief Moses collected rentals from squatters on his new reservation for awhile. In 1884, he sold the reservation back to the government, and his band was assigned to the Colville Reservation.

During Indian negotiations with the government, Moses was represented as a chief of the Okanogans, absolutely incorrect and resented by the latter. A Colville Tribes historian suggests that the government needed a "chief" with whom to deal, not several leaders, and seized upon the personable Chief Moses.

The Moses and Wenatchi bands, at least, were Salish-speaking and were akin to the locals. After the famous flight of Chief Joseph and a band of Nez Perce from the U.S. cavalry, the defeated group was sent to Oklahoma. Most miserable there, Chief Joseph's band agreed to live on the Colville Reservation, to which Chief Moses invited his old friend, Chief Joseph, in December 1885.

The other tribes indigenous to the Colville lands were outraged; they said it was the Nez Perce who, long ago, raided their lands and killed many of them along the Columbia River. Furthermore, the Nez Perce are not of Salish but of Sahaptin language. The proud old Chief Joseph lived his life out among hostile "friends" on the reservation. Nonetheless, a memorial to him stands near Nespelem, Colville Federated Tribe headquarters. To the south, the Columbia dam quelling Box Canyon's rapids is Chief Joseph Dam.

Today the Colville Federated Tribes with college-educated leaders and sophisticated management techniques operates a timber mill, extensive logging operations, a very successful rental service of large houseboats on Lake Roosevelt, and other enterprises. Former tribal differences have lessened. A usually easy relationship prevails with the white settlers and business people around and within the reservation; after all, large numbers of the indigenous peoples were intermarried with Europeans (Hudson's Bay men) and with later American settlers.

On festival days, though, the spectacular finery comes out of mothballs, the feathers are brushed and the leggings are donned. The drums set up their hypnotic beat, and half-remembered chants begin. Old stories come alive of days before the Americans came to make "Americans" of them, the country's aboriginal people. It is well that they do remember and revere their tribal arts.

During the 1890s and early 1900s horses helped stuggling boats traverse through rough stretches of river currents. From an original oil painting by Frederick L. Hubbard entitled "Extra Horsepower." Used by permission

Chapter 10

Uncertain Times

In eastern Washington, the earth itself was changing. Between 1872 and 1906, earthquakes were puzzlingly frequent. It all started out with a real shaker on December 14, 1872, that brought down an entire bluff north of Entiat, blocking the Columbia River for several hours until pent-up water broke through. One can imagine an Indian's astonishment, coming to the river for water that day, only to find it completely dry! The formation left behind—Ribbon Cliff or "Cock Shoot," "Broken Mountain" as the Indians called it—is clearly visible today.

Stinking sulphur water spewed over food supplies of nearby Chelan Indians, and yawning cracks opened and closed in the earth. For a time a tremendous geyser shot up at Chelan Falls adjacent to the river, subsiding into springs. Nineteen miles up Lake Chelan a water eruption sent 6-foot waves toward shore, washing a small boat onto the rocks. Throughout the following year there were frequent aftershocks. Smohalla, the dreamer prophet, had predicted that the Great Spirit would show his displeasure by shaking the earth. Terrified Wenatchi Indians fled to the Wenatchi trading post run by Sam Miller, asking him to read from the magic black book, the Bible, while others turned to Smohalla. Again in 1887, there were three days of severe earthquakes, recorded by settler James C. Bonar, "I can hear [the cannonading] and feel the jar of the earthquake nearly every hour."

Robert Byrd, in his annotations in *Lake Chelan* in the 1890s, speculates that earthquakes may have lowered the lake bed. He tells of a Spokane visitor to Stehekin in 1891 who mentioned seeing extensive Indian petroglyphs on smooth rocks at the head of Lake Chelan, figures of war parties and large animals. They were so high on the cliffs that they must have been painted from a canoe at a time when the lake was higher.

In 1906, above the present Keller Ferry site on the Columbia River, a cliff gave way under an Indian on horseback, carrying them across the river unharmed, but damming the Columbia for a time.

The Indian unrest described in the previous chapter led to establishment of forts on the Columbia, along what is now Lake Roosevelt-Fort Colville (not the

Hudson's Bay Company fort) fourteen miles southeast of Kettle Falls, and Fort Spokane on a pleasant bluff above the confluence of the Spokane and Columbia rivers.

To protect the crews surveying the international border, Fort Colville was established in June 1859, under orders of General W. S. Harney, commander of the Department of the Columbia. Major Pinkney Lugenbeel came with a battalion of the Ninth Infantry to do the job. Lugenbeel found that the Spokans were peaceful and wanted only to obtain farming tools, medical supplies and missionaries. When his troops (regulars) were ordered into the Civil War, they were replaced with more rowdy volunteers, Companies C and D, Second Infantry, California Volunteers. They were unruly and frequently drunk.

Unscrupulous traders set up distilleries and shops at nearby Pinkney City, a sordid civilian village growing up near the fort, illegally selling liquor to the troops and to the Indians. Prostitution thrived there, with diseases shared by Indians and soldiers alike. The squalid situation was not aided by Indian Agent W. P. Winans, unpopular with the Indians and accused of dealing in liquor himself.

One terminus of the new military road from Walla Walla, Fort Colville served as a distribution point for government supplies to Indians and, most notably, as a site for conferences between Chief Moses and government representatives during the treaty period. In 1878, troops were sent to a temporary encampment on Foster Creek and the Columbia, then on to Camp Chelan.

Fort Colville was awkwardly located for dealing with the Spokan Indians on their new reservation. To replace it, Camp Spokane was established in 1880 at the

Visible Indian art on rocks.

junction of the Columbia and Spokane rivers, close to the Spokan Indian lands. By 1883, when General William T. Sherman visited Fort Colville, it was largely decommissioned.

Fort Spokane proved to be a substantial and long-lasting installation, every inch the military post with West Point lieutenants, disciplined troops and extensive drills. By 1890, there were fifty sturdy buildings, including officers' quarters, barracks, recreation hall and hospital.

Nevertheless, duty there was dull, and the vastness of the area was intimidating—especially to soldiers from the East. There were desertions each spring. To enliven the deadly routine, for there were no wars, sergeants periodically led their troops on long field trips to work off excessive frustrations. The first wilderness survival programs were staged out of forts Colville and Spokane, where recruits would be "abandoned" in the wilderness to live off the land for a period of time.

On the cultural side, visiting dramatic troupes performed, grandly formal dances were held, and lecture series on tactics and other military matters were given for officers. There was a well-stocked library.

Of historic importance was the ministering by fort personnel to Chief Joseph and his band of Nez Perce immediately after they were assigned to the Colville Reservation. They encamped across from the fort, bitter, disillusioned, ragged and hungry, estranged from the other Nez Perce at Lapwai, surrounded by resentful local Indian bands. The Colville Indian Agent was suspected of embezzling supplies. Lieutenant Colonel Joshua Fletcher, commander of the post, angrily denounced the situation and attempted to get his superiors to act against the agent, which they finally did. Supplies to feed these wretched people were slow in coming, and Fort Spokane officers fed the Nez Perce from their own stores. Eventually the band moved over to Nespelem.

When the Spanish-American War broke out in 1898, the troops from Fort Spokane were sent into action, and the government abandoned the military post by 1899. In 1902, facilities were remodeled for use as a boarding school for Indian children. At first only about a hundred students enrolled, but more came upon the encouragement of the Spokan chief, who had asked for a school near his reservation. A health service was established, ministering to Indians until 1929. To occupy some of the vacant buildings, the Colville Indian Agency moved its offices to Fort Spokane. In 1914, the agency moved to Nespelem, and the school closed.

Four buildings survive today, including the old administration building facing the parade grounds. The grounds are open to the public as a national park.

Indians and settlers alike began to log the forests to supply sawmills such as the Lantzy Mill above Fort Spokane. They brought the trees to the Columbia by horse team for booming to the mill. After the Lantzy Mill converted the logs to rough lumber, they sent it to the railhead at Bridgeport by chaining lumber on rafts propelled only by the Columbia current. Near Whitestone, a cliff that resembles a grapefruit bisected with a knife, the Lincoln Lumber Company Mill opened, later managed by Crown Zellerbach. Operations ceased there in the 1980s, leaving only stark foundations on the shore of Lake Roosevelt.

The mariners who muscled the lumber rafts and log booms to Bridgeport installed oversized sweeps to help them steer through the rapids and around the curves. In Box Canyon above Bridgeport there were deep subcurrents. Booms would break up, the huge logs spinning around and going completely under water to emerge far downstream. One mill owner built a fin boom (an angular guide) to bring drifting logs into his sawmill. He worked with a logger upstream who stockpiled logs until the spring runoff floated them, but the mighty Columbia propelled the logs right over, around and under the fin boom. Despite several configurations, the idea never worked. Later, powerful tugs were added to pull booms downriver to the sawmills. In 1992 only one tug remained on Lake Roosevelt to serve varying needs.

On the windswept Columbia Plateau, a wilderness desert, nutritious bunch grass grew thigh-high from Davenport to Wenatchee, Mansfield to Pasco. Prospectors in the North Cascades foothills and along the border were hungry; in response, the area became cattle country, a frontier "Wild West." Cattle were driven northward, crossing the Columbia by swimming or ferry near Bridgeport and herded on to Conconully, Ruby or Republic.

This popular ferry was run by "Wild Goose" Bill Condon (Samuel Wilbur Condit), who got his name by mistakenly shooting tame geese. He established a reliable ferry in 1884 across the Columbia in Nespelem Canyon about twenty miles below today's Grand Coulee Dam (a location recommended by Lieutenant Thomas W. Symons during his reconnoitering trip on the Upper Columbia River in 1881). By 1889, Condon Ferry had a hotel, store and saloon, and was an official stage stop and post office.

Condon was quite a ladies' man, and this was his eventual undoing. In a classic love triangle, middle-aged Condon befriended and fell in love with a younger woman, who fell in love with a younger man. One day, when Condon was absent, she moved over to her lover's cabin. When Condon returned home, he calmly made out his will, then marched over to the cabin to take his sweetheart back. In the resulting melee, he and the lover shot each other dead before the woman's eyes.

After Condon's death, relatives and friends continued to operate the ferry until 1929. In "Gold Historian," John Weber told of seeing the old ferry cable during the Columbia River flood of 1948. Investigating loud rhythmic booming sounds, he saw that the center portion of the sagging cable was below water. The strong current swept the cable downstream where, "tight as a bowstring, it would clear the water and arc back upstream 40 to 50 feet, striking the water with the noise of thunder." Debris subsequently snapped the cable.

One by one the old ferries met similar fates. The only ferries remaining in 1992 were the Keller Ferry and a ferry from Inchelium to Gifford, both on Lake

Roosevelt. The latter, the *Columbia Princess,* was brought from Everett, Washington, in 1981, up the Columbia and Snake rivers to a point where it was taken on a tractor trailer to Lincoln on the Columbia. It was the widest load ever moved on the state highways.

Some of the best ranchlands were right in Grand Coulee, where small springs bubbled up to water the stock. Near Steamboat Rock was Devil's Lake, so named because any drowned bodies never rose to the surface. In this picturesque region one of the largest spreads in Washington thrived, the Steamboat Rock Stock Company, later called Lincoln Stock Farm. At least five hundred head of whiteface cattle grazed on native grasses supplemented by alfalfa hay grown on irrigated land. Often important guests came to stay, and Chinese cooks served superb dinners to guests in formal attire. The Stock Farm's trees, flowers and handsome buildings are now under the waters of Banks Lake.

Far from being totally barren, the Coulee was home to carpets of flowers; under the willow trees grew wild columbine, roses, iris, violets and wild mint. Service berry (when dried, a staple food of the Indians) grew profusely. There were blue lupine and gold balsam root. The Coulee area is on the Pacific Flyway, serving trumpeter swans, night hawks, ducks and geese. This area is enhanced today by marshes on the shores of Banks Lake.

Isolated as they were, children of the ranchers grew up on horseback, and their animals were friends. One family raised an abandoned sandhill crane. Because of his aggressiveness, he was boss of the farmyard and was dubbed "Nero." When the family went off to Wilbur for supplies, Nero—with a wing spread of 7 feet and looming as tall as the wagon bed—insisted on going, too, walking beside the horses or flapping his wings to catch up. Teams meeting this apparition often bolted in wide-eyed terror.

One of the most successful horse ranches was operated by Cull White north of the Columbia River on the Colville Reservation. He purchased horses and broke them to sell to the U.S. Army. Another was Peter Dan Moses, carrying on the family tradition, as his uncle Tse-Chila-wix of Ephrata was said to be the greatest horse rancher in Western Indian history, selling three thousand horses to incoming settlers. Such prolific herds of fine horses and cattle were bound to attract thieves and rustlers, the most infamous along the Columbia being the Fiddle Creek Gang and Texas Jack.

Times were tough enough without the pilfering; blizzards howled across the uninterrupted plains, killing horses, cattle and people. (In 1916, the snow was 6 feet deep near Waterville.) Water holes froze, so cattle went thirsty. And the cattle were wild as deer. Pioneer Emry Vance told of rounding up twenty-five head of wild steers on reservation and trying to get them onto "Wild Goose" Bill's ferry. Three men had managed to get the spooky cattle near the ferry, when the operator started to hammer on a board, then dropped some lumber. The cattle scattered wildly into the brush with the cowboys in hot pursuit. When the herd was reassembled and approached the ferry again, the operator called out to the cowboys. The sudden noise sent the herd, nostrils dilated with excitement, back into the brush.

As ranchers scratched the scablands to grow hay, farmers watched with interest the verdant crops that emerged. In the south part of the plains, farmers tried growing wheat early, but it was not until around 1890 that dirt farmers drifted into the plains between Chelan and Grand Coulee near Mansfield, where huge boulders lay tossed about by a giant's hand, the terminal moraine of the ancient glacier. Grain crops fairly leaped out of the ground, but that was a siren song for farmers; out of the sky came grasshoppers and hailstorms. Winds lifted the fine glacial silt into the air in dust storms that were like the night. Along the Columbia near the Methow River, a pioneer boy dug cricket ditches filled with water to protect crops, emptying shovel-loads of crickets from the ditches each night.

Lulled by the usually moderate climate, settlers were unprepared for renegade winter storms whistling down from the frigid north, freezing the fall wheat in the ground and the animals above it. Yet there were enough good years that dry land farming proved prosperous; soon this great Columbia Plateau waved with wheat. The next problem was how to get wheat to market. The Columbia River became the highway.

Until adequate railways were built, farmers hauled their sacks of grain to the river where sternwheelers docked to transport them to railroads. The river between Grand Coulee and Wanapum growled along between bluffs 1,000 to 2,000 feet high; passes to the water's edge were few and agonizingly steep. Soon someone dreamed up the idea of building chutes from the canyon rim down to water level. These chutes were similar to large stovepipes, but the wheat hurtling down the pipes created such friction that it arrived scorched at the boat. Engineers tried baffling to slow it down, and eventually the methods worked well. One wheat tramway came down the bluff south of Waterville to Orondo's docks, serving farmers well into the twentieth century.

A virtual parade of grain boats joined the complex fleet of passenger-freight steamers plying the Columbia. Among the grain ports above Rock Island were Chelan Falls, Virginia City (about half a mile south of Brewster), Central Ferry, Orondo, Troy and Wenatchee.

Basically, navigation was not practical between Pasco and Wenatchee because of the Priest, Cabinet, and Rock Island rapids. Boats plied the river from a port above Rock Island Rapids to Brewster and Bridgeport, even though the connecting trail from the railroad at Ellensburg was so steep that teamsters attached logs to their wagons on the downhill grade to slow the descent. Boats tended to carry mining and general supplies upriver, and ore, grain or animals downstream.

Joining the two sternwheelers late in the century were smaller boats, some that regularly went to Okanogan (and even farther in high water), including the *North Star, City of Wenatchee* and *Echo*. How the steamers made it through rapids was accurately, if ecstatically described by passenger Dora Tibbits Casey (at the Methow Rapids):

> The scene, too, beggared description. Just the first streaks of dawn coming over a desolate-looking plateau to the east. ... To the west the frowning mountains, and ahead, jagged rocks, almost filling the river bed, some towering several times higher than the smoke stack of the boat . . . whirlpools only surpassed by those below Niagara Falls. ... [Passage upstream] was possible by carrying a cable attached to the winch on the deck up to the guide rings ... anchored in large boulders. ... With the donkey engine turning the winch and slowly winding up the cable, the boat would not only be kept on her course, but her engines assisted in carrying the load up against the strong current. (Dora Tibbits Casey, "Reminiscences of a Ranch Woman." Unpublished manuscript, Binder l, December 30, 1930, at North Central Washington Museum, Wenatchee, Washington.)

Casey compared the scene to the eerie feeling one might have when an iceberg loomed in the fog.

Not far south of the Methow Rapids, Chelan Falls was the Columbia River port at the foot of a 375-foot waterfall, culmination of the three-mile Chelan River, shortest river in the state. It forms the overflow from lake Chelan.

The lake extends fifty-two miles into wilderness; even now there are no roads to its head; from Stevens Pass (Wenatchee to Everett) north almost 150 miles, only one road transects the mountains.

A steamer, *Belle of Chelan*, was placed on Lake Chelan in 1889, then as its successor is now, a tourist boat taking sightseers up the lake, over 1,500 feet deep in places. At the head of the lake surrounded by the crags of the North Cascades Mountains, the luxurious Field Hotel operated until the Chelan dam raised the water level and inundated it. Most passengers stayed at least one night there.

Land travel from Chelan to Wenatchee was impractical, but the settlement was only a small collection of farms and houses at that time. In 1885, the news of railroads building between Spokane and Seattle sparked land speculation. Seattle attorney Thomas Burke, L.C. Gilman, G. M. Haller and others bought 700 acres around Wenatchee in 1888, platting it into 100 feet by 30 feet lots priced at $100, land that cost them $10 per acre. Before many lots were sold, the Great Northern had acquired the railroad being built from Spokane, and the Wenatchee land company sold one-fourth of its lots to them, a shrewd move that merged their interests with the railroad's aims.

The railroad came to Wenatchee in October 1892, crossing the Columbia River on the sternwheeler *Thomas L. Nixon*. East and west links joined at Scenic on January 6, 1893, near the summit of Stevens Pass. Responding to the new rail connection, the southerly terminus of the sternwheeler fleet moved to a wharf at Wenatchee. When the Columbia froze over, boat crews dreamed up bizarre entertainment. One night a crew member won a quart of whiskey from a bet that he could run across the river and back stark naked.

With the commencement of rail service north, riverboat traffic declined. Three boats had been wrecked in rapids by 1906, and the final blow was delivered in July 1915, when the *North Star* (Columbia and Okanogan Steamboat Company) caught fire at her berth in Wenatchee, taking the *Columbia, Okonogan* and *Chelan* with her in the blaze.

At Wenatchee the railroad's arrival was the impetus for fruit growing to become a major industry. One pioneer grower brought a load of trees on muleback all the way from The Dalles to Wenatchee. At the Columbia River an onlooker watched in amazement as a queer procession swam across—mules tied together, appearing like a floating island of trees, and the owner swimming behind by hanging onto the last mule's tail. Orcharding had a long way to go.

Until convenient irrigation and transportation, though, settlers planted apples, peaches and cherries in backyard plots for their own use. The irrigation canal built by Jacob Shotwell in 1891 was the first in the Wenatchee area, utilizing water from the Wenatchee River that empties into the Columbia.

Shotwell and a partner, Arthur Gunn, organized the Wenatchee Water Power Company in 1896 to expand the irrigation service but ran out of funds. The Great Northern Railroad held their bonds and found itself owning the project. A new

View of Wenatchee sketched in 1904 from the east side of the Columbia River. Lithograph of a sketch drawn by Edward Lange, Great Northern Railway owner James J. Hill's personal artist. Used by permission of North Central Washington Museum, Wenatchee, Washington

group opened the Highline Canal, which still runs through the city of Wenatchee. Other systems followed to water lands in Wenatchee, Malaga and Manson.

The apple growers had "a bear by the tail," a fledgling industry that would place the lands along or near the Columbia River as the nation's prime area for fine apples, plus other fruits. The path to success was fraught with problems, however.

A tree took ten years (far less now) to bring forth fruit; depletion of nutrients in the soil was not understood clearly, quality fertilizers were unavailable and national marketing had to be learned. Pests were unwelcome settlers—aphids, which were unsuccessfully treated by dipping young branches in soapsuds, and codling moths, treated with arsenate of lead. Today, safer pest-control methods prevail.

The early picking and handling process was crude and was streamlined over the years—from metal pails to bags for less bruising, from hard boxes to "totes" (big plastic bins that could be handled by machine), from hand-sizing in arbitrary grades to machine grading.

No one grower could handle the marketing into national stores; cooperative marketing was developed, then better storage and refrigeration. Curiously, the first exports of apples went—not to the East Coast—but to Australia, Japan and England. Domestic demand grew later. In 1913, north-central Washington shipped 4,100 rail cars of fruit, in 1915 the area shipped 5,400 cars and more than three times that in 1923, but stores were unhappy with quality. Refrigerated rail cars had been diverted for military use during World War I, and without them, apples froze in winter or overheated from unreliable amateur heating systems.

Problems were ameliorated with the establishment of Wenatchee as a Great Northern Railroad division point and in 1923, with formation of the Western Fruit Express Company to schedule cars more efficiently.

As sweet-smelling fruit orchards spread over the benches of the Columbia River and its tributaries, the expense of irrigation and the need for a reliable source of water were constant concerns of growers. No practical way had yet been found to tap the vast water resources of the Columbia River, because it lay in a deep canyon, requiring installation of powerful pumps to raise water to the farmlands.

Rufus Woods, editor and publisher of the *Wenatchee Daily World* newspaper, electrified readers all the way to the national wire services in 1918 by airing a proposal by William Clapp, an Ephrata lawyer, for a dam to divert part of the Columbia River into the Grand Coulee and southward. Clapp's figures were incomplete; experts said that had his initial plan been implemented, the impounded water would have raised the Columbia 170 feet at the Arrow Lakes in British Columbia. The article was very influential, however, in stirring the imagination of local interests, politicians and government officials, who argued for the next fifteen years before a practical dam plan began to become a reality.

Chapter 11

Grand Coulee Dam

Today there are fourteen dams on the Columbia River from headwaters to ocean. Of these, Grand Coulee is the world's largest concrete structure. The bulky barrier stands 550 feet above bedrock, 350 feet above downstream water level. The total length of the dam is 1,223 feet. An incredible 11,975,521 cubic yards of concrete compose the structure, and more than 38 million yards of material was excavated to prepare the site. The total generating capacity of the dam is nearly 6.5 million kilowatts. In 1992 that was enough to serve the entire Northwest and occasionally sell power beyond. Transmission towers march away from the dam like children's stick figures, arms uplifted, their lines shimmering against the stark landscape. Besides generating power, the stored waters irrigate more than a half million acres of land in Washington's dry but lava-fertile plains.

The system includes 333 miles of main canals, 1,959 miles of lesser canals and 2,761 miles of drains and wasteways. Three huge reservoirs store the Columbia River's waters to be returned to the dam for power generation as needed, but mostly used to irrigate agricultural lands. These are Lake Roosevelt, Banks Lake and Potholes Reservoir—128,000 acres of lakes for the public to enjoy and on which wildlife thrives. Indeed, three times that acreage is managed to provide suitable habitat for fish and wildlife.

Beyond the statistics, which are necessary to fathom the immensity of the project, there are fascinating stories of political machinations and human adaptability. As early as 1903, the U.S. Reclamation Service considered proposals for a dam or for irrigation by tapping into the Pend Oreille or Spokane River and bringing water by gravity flow to a reservoir in central Washington. In 1918, Ephrata attorney William H. Clapp advanced a plan to use Grand Coulee as a natural storage basin. A dam would divert Columbia River water southward through Grand Coulee in the old Missoula flood channel. Both plans had backers and adversaries, equally feverish. However, the accounts in the *Wenatchee Daily World* and in the national news caught the attention of governmental groups. In 1919, the Washington State Legislature created the Columbia Basin Commission and appropriated $100,000 for a study of the two proposals. Panama Canal builder, Major General George W. Goethals, was hired to make a study of the situation and came out in favor of the gravity flow plan from the Pend Oreille.

Most Washingtonians credit James O'Sullivan, a contractor who came from Michigan to work out of Moses Lake in the 1920s, with dedicating his life to make the present Grand Coulee Dam a reality. He worked for minimal pay, talking to whomever would listen, neglecting his business to lobby for the dam—which he believed with the fervor of a messiah would make a garden of the barren scablands. Rufus Woods, through the pages of the *World*, focused attention on the proposed project.

Clearly the expense would require the project to be funded federally, and in 1926, Washington Senators Wesley L. Jones and Clarence C. Dill tried to secure a $600,000 appropriation for a serious study. When opposition seemed overwhelming, Jones quietly placed the appropriation request into a rivers and harbors bill, where it passed undetected by the opposition. Major John S. Butler of the U.S. Army Corps of Engineers was directed to make the study, started in 1928 and completed in 1931, at a cost half of that appropriated. Butler favored Clapp, Woods and O'Sullivan's plan over the gravity plan.

Washington proponents continued their media and speaking campaigns. National newspapers and magazines scoffed. In a national magazine, a writer said insultingly, "All this dam would do is provide water for thirsty jackrabbits and for

Dry Falls State Park below Grand Coulee in Washington, The ledge is where a cataclysmic waterfall rushed ouer during a break in the ice dam during the Pleistocene Era.

light bulbs in Indian tepees." Adversaries referred to the town of Ephrata as "that Dam University." Opponents included private power companies, which preferred to initiate developments at Kettle Falls on the Columbia River.

Curiously in 1929 and 1930, a pitiless sun shone down on drought-ridden central Washington. Advocates of Grand Coulee Dam pointed out that the Columbia River and its tributaries were fed by Rocky Mountain glaciers usually unaffected by such weather vagaries.

The fine silt peculiar to the Columbia areas blew suffocatingly across the plains. In April 1931, 600 miles out at sea, passengers on a Honolulu-bound ocean liner, reported being enveloped in a huge cloud of this dust.

The Great Depression had set in—bad news but good news for the dam project. In 1933 President Franklin D. Roosevelt made Grand Coulee Dam a project of the Public Works Administration. The Bureau of Reclamation was to supervise the dam-building, headed by Frank A. Banks, construction engineer. He and a small cadre of engineers drove survey stakes on the Columbia River's banks on September 9, 1933. The State of Washington allotted $377,000 to do preliminary work on the site. Initial offices and residence complexes were at Almira, twenty-one miles south.

The news spread rapidly across the nation. WORK, PAYING JOBS were to be had in Washington. In came the unemployed, the destitute, the ragged, hungry men willing to work in a country devoid of jobs. Some came in, on and underneath rail cars with a sandwich and a canteen, or nothing at all to exult in obtaining jobs, eking out food supplies while awaiting their first paychecks. In 1932 there were six people living at Grand Goulee; by 1933 and 1934, there were seven thousand men and a handful of women.

There were no facilities for these people. Dormitories and homes came later. Overnight a shack and tent town covered the rocky, rattlesnake-infested ground that today is the pleasant town of Grand Coulee. Fortunate were the Colville Tribes workers who came, for they could go home at night.

With eager workers and capable engineers the work moved swiftly. The original contractor in 1933 for the first stage of the dam was the acronym MWAK, a merger of several firms, chief among them Silas Mason Construction Co., the Walsh Construction Co. and the Atkinson-Kier Co. In 1938, the second stage of the dam went to Consolidated Builders, Inc., another joint venture.

Before workers could excavate the river bed, they built cofferdams to divert the Columbia River from its channel. Geologists drilled six miles of test holes to check the bedrock, while surveyors assessed just how much of the uplying lands would be flooded. Ten entire towns had to be moved or razed. Parts of the dam project were carried out by the Works Progress Administration and Civilian Conservation Corps, both governmental programs to furnish jobs for the unemployed. Construction began on a railroad spur and a highway from Coulee City.

In 1935, unstable wet clay on the east bank slid like grease into the excavation and refused to be stemmed. Through an ingenious method of inserting pipes into the bank, then pumping freon gas in to freeze the wet earth, the area was stabilized until concrete pouring could be completed. The broad footings were installed, 450 feet thick.

After construction of a tramway to haul cement into place and the building of forms, the wafflelike sections of the dam began to take shape. Over twenty-thousand interlocking segments were poured, from 25 feet by 44 feet, to 50 feet by 50 feet. The lowest forms were anchored by diagonal rods imbedded into the rock. Concrete was dumped in layers, each successive layer vibrated out by air-powered machines. To cool the concrete to "setting" consistency, pipes were installed through which cold river water coursed. The pipes remain within the structure.

It was on this operation that a particularly horrifying accident ensued. Two men operating the vibrator machines were buried up to their armpits when the crane operator above dumped a load of concrete on them. As rescue efforts escalated, every time a man was moved, he sank deeper—much like quicksand. Finally the wall of the form had to be removed, the concrete spilling out, to release the men. Both lived but one was a complete invalid, the other badly injured and leaving the job.

On any construction job there are accidents, since the work is inherently dangerous; seventy-seven men died during building of Grand Coulee Dam, most from falls or dropped objects. Charles Chase Parsons was appointed Safety Inspector for the project in 1940, his job to monitor conditions, instruct employees and train a "Mercy Squad." The job included monitoring field crew problems of rattlesnake bites and tick fever; snakes were so bad on a reservoir site that work was delayed one summer until hibernation time.

Soon after the project started, homes were erected for the engineers on a ledge above the Columbia River, called "Engineers Town," and later renamed Coulee Dam. Across the river was Mason City, named for the construction company, now part of Coulee Dam. Elmer City, called Elmerton at first, grew up downriver. Grand Coulee in a stark valley a mile south was the shacktown home of most workers.

Notorious women appeared almost immediately at Grand Coulee, attracted by the prospect of several thousand single men. On a Saturday night, or any night, really, B Street was wide open. The red light houses operated openly, saloons were crowded. A Grand Coulee resident says, as children, he and his sister used to go to the First Aid Hall on Sunday mornings to size up the previous night's injuries—lines of men with black eyes, broken bones or needing other medical attention.

Another oldtimer said he was sent to a house to replace a broken window early one morning; when he rang the bell, a blowsy woman answered and declared plaintively, "My gosh, you guys even come at this hour!" The startled youth protested, blushing to his hairline.

"Good" women began to arrive and found their determination to live with their men a challenge. Lots in Grand Coulee were platted 25 feet by 70 feet and, since some shacks were built prior to surveying, there were odd-sized properties. Most husbands built one-or two-room homes plus an outhouse, and while running water was soon provided, at first it came from big tanks on a truck. Electricity was yet to come; kerosene or Aladdin (gas-powered mantle light) lamps were customary. The iceman came. The grocery store was in a tent. Near the damsite in 1933, the Trading Post of E. A. Betz and William Rosholt opened for business on a large wagon. Later it moved to Grand Coulee, billing itself as the "Biggest Little Store by a Damsite."

Fires swept through the packed community, crammed between bluffs; over and over, the tar paper and wood shacks exploded into flame in the dry desert air. During the late 1980s Grand Coulee workers intentionally burned about 150 vacant shacks still marring the local landscape.

Dust was the worst enemy. One woman said she checked on her sleeping baby and was horrified to find even his eyelashes heavy with dust. The silt of the Columbia River moved around with the slightest breeze, and no one ever really felt clean.

The only restaurant in town served a limited menu of pancakes for breakfast, stew for lunch and steak and greasy French fries for dinner. A Mexican man sold tamales from a pull cart. Dining out was not attractive.

Yet, "we were all in the same boat," said Edith Lael, a Grand Coulee resident, "and we didn't mind. We had a real community spirit." Bored housewives and children formed a library and Girl and Boy Scouts, gave card parties and formed horseback clubs—one of which, the Ridge Riders, thrives today. Money for the first schools came from donations, and when it was learned that the greatest sums contributed came from the ladies of B Street, some huffy parents wanted to keep their kids out of school.

Contractors built dormitories, mess halls, recreation rooms and a hospital as soon as possible. In 1992 one of the dormitories was the Four Winds, a bed and breakfast house, and the Bureau of Reclamation's engineering office is the Coulee Dam city hall.

While workers built the dam, other workers cleared the lands upriver. They lived at riverside camps or barges with barracks. Kettle Falls and Marcus were moved to higher locations. Peach, Fruitland, Lincoln and others were razed, never rebuilt. Workers dismantled or burned structures down to the foundations, leaving no loose lumber, and cut all trees and shrubs. Finally, a huge cable was dragged between two tractors or horses to scrape all vegetation possible from the land, leaving nothing to float to the surface and cause trouble. The Columbia River Valley looked as sere as when the prehistoric flood roared down to scrape everything clean.

In 1934, President Franklin D. Roosevelt came to see the growing big hole into which the government was pouring money, and again in 1937, to review progress. Then twenty thousand people lined the streets and cheered their leader. On May 11, 1950, Harry Truman came to dedicate the dam and unveil a plaque naming the reservoir "Lake Roosevelt."

The dam was nearing completion when the Japanese bombed Pearl Harbor in December 1941. War-footing security measures were taken at Grand Coulee. Two months before Pearl Harbor one 108,000 kilowatt generator had been placed in service; to meet the sharply escalating demand by manufacturers for power, two generators scheduled for still incomplete Shasta Dam in California were installed in Grand Coulee. This boost provided the power needed, also, for Richland's Hanford Project. After the war, Shasta got its generators back and Grand Coulee received larger new ones. By 1951 the dam was the largest hydroelectric facility in the western hemisphere.

Once World War II was over, attention was turned to irrigation. Involved were Banks Lake that fills the Grand Coulee virtually wall to wall; Potholes Reservoir south of Moses Lake formed by O'Sullivan Dam on Crab Creek; and Main, West, East Low and Potholes Canals. A complex system of pumps moves water from the Columbia River to Banks Lake, which feeds irrigation canals as required. A portion of runoff or waste water returns to the system for reuse. When Grand Coulee Dam has need of stored water for power generation, the system reciprocates by returning water for power generation.

When irrigation systems were in place, the federal government advertised farming lands it owned. Between 1948 and 1967, screened buyers drew lots to buy 1,157 farm acreages of varying sizes. Veterans were given preference. Today about a third of the lands are devoted to raising alfalfa hay, the balance in potatoes, corn, various seed crops and wheat. The agricultural production has spawned processing plants and feedlots.

As Franklin D. Roosevelt Lake (commonly referred to as Lake Roosevelt) covered the clean-scraped land, a biologist's study theorized that fish could never live in the lake because of insufficient food. Perhaps at first that was true. But as the years went by, nutrients washed back into the lake, the sun shone and grasses grew in shallows. Fish began to appear in the lake in ever greater numbers—trout, kokanee or landlocked salmon and walleyed pike.

In 1984 Thomas R. Jagielo noted in his master's thesis that there was considerable plankton in Lake Roosevelt and Banks Lake, favored by young rainbow trout. Bruce Smith, eastern director of the Washington State Fish and Wildlife Department, introduced to Lake Roosevelt residents a man who operated fish net hatcheries in western Washington. Smith wanted volunteers to try raising trout in Lake Roosevelt.

An eager volunteer was Win Self, a real estate developer of Seven Bays, a residential community, marina and restaurant (the latter operated by Colville

View of the Grand Coulee Dam in early morning from above the dam.

Federated Tribes) about forty miles above the dam. Bucking many who believed the project would not work, Self invested about $1,500 of his own money in nets and supplies; Fish & Wildlife furnished the small fry. The fish thrived in their net pen near the marina, fed and cared for by Self and volunteers. A few miles upstream at Hunter's, High School members of Future Farmers of America installed more net pens as a school project, feeding and caring for hatchlings, aided by public donations.

Today four students are enrolled at Eastern Washington University in Cheney to study fisheries management. Other net pens are installed at Kettle Falls and Banks Lake. Self alone has sixteen nets on the lake now, all as a labor of love. Fish & Wildlife and Colville Tribes supply fry. These grass roots efforts have caused four hundred thousand trout to be released in 1990 and, it is hoped, five hundred thousand in 1991. In addition, a pilot project for twelve thousand kokanee is underway. Self and the Hunter's kids believe that "everyone has to become involved and not expect the government to do everything, that it takes individual effort to get things done."

An Eastern Washington University scientist has tagged some fish and will keep records of where they are found. Significantly, the tags have shown up in the lower Columbia River, indicating that fry have gone through Grand Coulee's giant turbines without injury.

That was the fortuitous partnership forged in 1933, of government money for a vast dam project and of volunteers willing to help ameliorate problems.

Chapter 12

Pioneers and Archaeology

W ater from the Columbia River indeed made Washington State a bread basket for the nation. Grains and vegetables grow profusely in the odd patterns dictated by irrigation machinery—circular, rectangular or between ditches. Along the river itself, orchards thrive on the benches and in the valleys, protected by bluffs from the chill winter winds, the temperature further moderated by the large volume of river water. The volcanic soil and long growing season (135 to 175 days) complete the ideal conditions for apple culture, enabling Washington to market over half the nation's apples by 1990.

Commercial orchards appeared about 1850 near Oroville, and at the Ahtanum Mission and Fort Simcoe in Yakima Valley in the 1860s. Although there are a whopping eight thousand varieties of apples, Red Delicious, Gala and Fuji are currently the most popular. Orchardists graft buds from a parent tree onto rootstock to duplicate the parent, some rootstocks dating back two thousand years, according to the Washington Apple Commission.

Despite the moderate climate, frost is an ever-looming danger. Some growers use giant wind machines and occasionally heaters. Others turn on sprinklers; when water turns to ice on the trees, it protects the buds at the freezing point.

Until the development of controlled atmosphere storage methods, ripening apples were rushed into insulated warehouses, opened to cool down by night and closed tightly to resist daytime heat. Archie Van Doren, a "local boy," worked with Robert Smock in 1940 on the theory of controlled atmosphere storage for fruits as his project for a Ph.D. in horticulture from Cornell University.

An apple uses oxygen as it ripens; thus, if you limit the amount of oxygen, the ripening process slows or virtually ceases. Van Doren returned to Wenatchee in 1956 and persuaded an orchardist to install the necessary machinery—a gas-tight room kept at 30° to 32° F from which 97 to 98-1/2 percent of the oxygen is removed. The spring after storing apples in a controlled atmosphere facility, the orchardist sold apples at the New York Fruit Auction for $14 a box, instead of four or five dollars. The process is now in common use. It can be used for preserving bananas and floral products, as well.

Van Doren also developed a chemical thinner. When a tree blossoms, it develops a king bloom in the center and several side blooms. After the bloom opens and is pollinated, if sprayed with this substance, side blooms fall off, leaving the strong main blossom only. Handpicking of side blooms is extremely expensive as an alternative. In 1966, the Washington Apple Commission honored Van Doren for his contributions to the industry.

In 1929 Wenatchee orchardist Herman Ohme envisioned an oasis near his home on a sere bluff overlooking the Columbia Valley. He brought in alpine shrubs and evergreen trees to shade the barren land and planted lawns. Over the decades the family has built rock-lined paths and a pool "so the kids could learn to swim." In 1939, yielding to popular demand, Ohme Gardens was opened to the public. The nine-acre garden is ranked among the top gardens of America.

An extensive interlocking park and trail system marks the western shore of the Columbia River, built by Chelan County Public Utility District (PUD), portions leased to the City of Wenatchee and the State of Washington for management. There is a wilderness wetlands. The trail adjacent to a 100-acre protected marsh is closed during eagle nesting season.

From Ohme Gardens on a bluff above the river looking south over Wenatchee and the Columbia River

A great deal has been done to recognize heritage and restore riverfront use all the way from Chelan to beyond Wenatchee. Old-timer Kirby Billingsley of the *Wenatchee Daily World*, now incapacitated, was a champion of the idea "Selkirks to the Sea," for creating riverfront parks, trails and information sites along the entire length of the Columbia. While his concepts have not been totally implemented, there has been marked progress toward his goal. The Oregon Historical Society sponsored the Lewis and Clark Trail along the Columbia and the Columnia River Heritage Canoe Trail.

Not marring the scenery in any way, a gold mine exists inside the Wenatchee city limits. For decades prospectors came through Wenatchee, passing by the real lode. Today the Cannon Mine, Asamera Minerals, Inc., mines and processes gold *inside* a mountain so quietly that there are residents who do not realize it exists, the second largest underground gold mine in the United States.

A different kind of dig excited archaeologists in 1987. In an orchard above the Columbia at East Wenatchee, during the installation of an irrigation line, men turned up the largest fluted stone projectile points ever found (up to 9.25 inches long), mostly struck from agate. Stone tools and bone artifacts subsequently uncovered date back to the Ice Age, ten to twelve thousand years ago. The site is one of seven known Clovis sites in North America, the Clovis people entering the area about eleven thousand years ago, possibly over the Bering land bridge.

Additional excavations were made under the direction of Dr. Michael Gramly, Curator of Anthropology at the Buffalo Museum of Science, in cooperation with the North Central Washington Museum of Wenatchee, where the artifacts are housed. If human bones are uncovered, they would comprise the earliest-known humans of North America. However, representatives from the Colville Federated Tribes, Yakima Nation and others question the propriety of disturbing human remains of any age.

The deep, primeval-appearing river canyon from Brewster/Bridgeport almost to Richland is a remarkable heritage site. Clearly these areas were inhabited heavily back into prehistoric mists. In a Moses Coulee cave, a stone pipe was found in a wooden case carved with figures similar to those on petroglyphs, also a stone knife with a charred wooden handle bound by sinew. Near Orondo just north of Wenatchee is an early rock shelter of primitive people, well above the current river level. There is evidence of an ancient earthslide near Wenatchee, another near Malaga; both may have dammed the river for a time, like the more recent 1872 Entiat slide. The area once was heavily forested with many edible plants and inhabited by primitive animals; among artifacts found are molars and parts of tusks, the huge femur of woolly mammoth and evidence of a cameloid creature.

While building the Milwaukee Railroad from Othello to Beverly, near today's Wanapum Dam, workers found a natural ice cave in which they stored foodstuffs. In the Columbia River above Priest Rapids Dam, a sequence of drawings on a rocky island was thought to depict creation and was called Genesis Rock.

Before rising waters from a succession of smaller PUD dams (Wells, Rocky Reach, Rock Island, Wanapum, Priest Rapids) buried significant artifacts, engineers frequently removed sections of boulders sporting petroglyphs and pictographs to museums within the dams. Bushels of arrowheads were removed and preserved.

Providing ideal storage for artifacts, the Wells, Rocky Reach and Wanapum dams have extensive galleries within each structure. They contain rock exhibits, geologic explanations, artifacts and historic photos and displays reviewing pioneer life, the rich riverboat history and gold mining. These dams have fish ladders (with public viewing areas); a thriving fish hatchery at Wells Dam contributes fingerlings to the river system.

Downstream from Rock Island Dam, from which a huge Alcoa plant and other industries receive their electricity, the Columbia River flows for thirty miles through a magnificent gorge unattainable except by boat or a road at the resort of Crescent Bar. On the old river bed were sand layers, topped by lava that cooled rapidly into angular six-sided columns, above which is lighter, more gaseous material called vesicular lava. The cliffs eroded to create weird formations and towers not unlike those at Bryce Canyon, Utah. The erosion is speeded by waters that leak into the basalt, then freeze and expand to fracture it. Early river travelers marveled at a large petrified tree upright on a high ledge, still there in the gorge.

Looking at the harsh landscape, one is overcome with the odd feeling that he or she has taken a wrong turn in time and wound up in a past eon when the earth was in a formative stage.

On the river's west bank at Vantage, the Gingko Petrified Forest State Park and Interpretive Center is surrounded by major petrified wood sites. In ancient times the Columbia River here was more than 8 miles wide and 600 feet deep. At least two hundred species of wood have been identified as growing in or near the swamps sixteen million years ago, among them oak, maple, hickory, gingko and—in the higher elevations—the great sequoia tree.

As described earlier, lava oozed repeatedly over eastern Washington. Between two of such outpourings, a big lake formed where Vantage is now. Trees then growing along the ancient Columbia fell over and sank to the bottom of the lake. Again the lava came and overcame the lake, covering the logs. Intense chemical activity and lack of oxygen caused petrification; different minerals present created the varying colors of the petrified woods. In a later period the land rose, leaving the desertlike area we know today, draining into the Columbia, the tilting and fracturing bringing petrified materials closer to the surface.

During the Depression of the 1930s, Civilian Conservation Corps (CCC) workers excavated petrified logs in the park for public viewing. The main site is two miles from Vantage, where there are hiking trails on the brown, sage-covered hills that rise like bubbles above the desert. An old-timer claims the ability to find petrified wood by "witching," as some people find water by "water witching."

Scientists question this ability, but there is no denying he has found logs buried as deep as six lava flows beneath the surface.

In the Interpretive Center (closed except by appointment in winter), one may view a film and see wood exhibits. Debby Hall, interpreter, says that fifteen varieties of gingko trees grew nearby after the Ice Age, the only known place outside of China. Chinese used gingko seeds for medicine and religious rituals. Ten seeds were supposed to make one slightly intoxicated but were beneficial for kidney, liver and respiratory diseases, and some claim they reversed the onset of Alzheimer's disease.

The area is a virtual wind tunnel. Locals joke that "when the wind stops, everyone here falls down." The sudden onset of wind is no joke, however, for boaters and pilots in the area. The wind has even blown railway boxcars over.

During winter when the winds seemingly carve knife paths through one's skin, animals flock to the sparse river bottoms beneath the Gingko Interpretive Center. One year the State Patrol closed Interstate 90 for a time to protect a herd of 150 elk bent on crossing the freeway. Gingko's groundskeeper even saw an infrequent gray wolf in 1989. In 1985, during severe weather, elk, deer and smaller animals, including a rare albino fawn, came to seek shelter; with no food, they browsed on Vantage residents' trees and shrubs. Kind ranchers came with pickup loads of hay to rescue them from starvation. In recent years the Department of Wildlife has developed a grain and hay pellet for such emergencies.

The Columbia River's basaltic banks begin to diminish south of Vantage. Before Wanapum Dam and Priest Rapids Dam quieted the rapids, a small band of Wanapum Indians made their home around the southeast bend of the river, living primarily from the marvelous bounty of fish in the river. When explorers and settlers came to Washington (then Oregon Territory), Smohalla led the Wanapums, a highly religious and peaceful people, in the Dreamer religion. Its precepts were diametrically opposite to the ways of aggressive pioneers. Smohalla said:

> My young men shall never work. Men who work cannot dream and wisdom comes in dreams. ... You ask me to plow the ground. Shall I take a knife and tear my mother's bosom? You ask me to dig for stone. Shall I dig under her skin for her bones? Then when I die I cannot enter her body to be born again. You ask me to cut grass and make hay and sell it, and be rich like the white man, how dare I cut off my mother's hair? (taken from display at Wanapum Dam Visitor Center.)

The Wanapum priests inspired Alexander Ross to name the rapids of their home "Priest Rapids." (There were two Priest Rapids on the Columbia River, the other north of Revelstoke.) The Wanapums were a peaceful people, never warring with anyone. Sahaptin-speaking and related to the Yakimas, Nez Perce and Cayuse, they lived in tule mat houses woven from reeds that grew 6 feet high near today's

West Richland. They roamed to the Cascades to hunt sheep, elk and deer, and to Ephrata to gather roots. They made canoes and fished the river for suckers, eels, salmon—both with nets and wooden hoops—and gathered fresh-water mussels.

They neither sought nor were given any reservation or treaty, and in 1942 quietly surrendered certain lands around White Bluff on the Columbia River for the Hanford Project, receiving protection for their ancient burial grounds. Under the wise leadership of Puck-Hyah-Toot, who learned ancient ways from Smohalla, the small group managed to live in two worlds successfully. Because of frequent marriage outside the tribe, only twelve full-blooded Wanapums remained in 1992.

Early pioneers and cattlemen used a ford on the Columbia River near the Wanapums' lands. Most famous was Ben Snipes, who came to the area in 1854 to found a cattle kingdom that spread from The Dalles to the Yakima River. With the assistance of several Indians, friends more than mere employees, Snipes ran more than a hundred thousand cattle (and large herds of fine horses, cayuse mares bred to Hambletonian stallions) on the rolling Horse Heaven Hills and Yakima Valley.

Years later a magnificent palomino stallion dubbed the "Golden Ghost" (a descendant of Snipes' Hambletonian, no doubt) roamed the wild country with his band of mares, cleverly escaping horse hunters. When he finally was caught, his captor patiently but unsuccessfully tried to train him. Soon afterward the rancher died, and Clayton Speck of Sunnyside bought the stallion, trucked him to the wilderness and turned him loose to roam wild and free.

Snipes' initial stake was made by driving cattle herds to the hungry miners at Barkerville (Canada), crossing the Columbia River twice—once near Priest Rapids, once above today's Bridgeport. The crossings at Priest were aided by Wanapum Indians who formed an "alley" of canoes upstream and downstream to prevent cattle from bolting during the crossing. Unfortunately, Snipes lost his fortune during the Depression of 1893. His original crude cabin is in Sunnyside City Park, his grave in The Dalles.

Snipes was not alone, just the largest cattle rancher. Before wheat farms and Grand Coulee irrigation, the tangled bluffs and flats of the Columbia were more suited to ranching. A legendary cowboy was Ben Hutchinson, a giant 6 feet 6 inches tall, who raised horses east of Wanapum Dam. Neighbors said that as he approached on horseback, erect in a saddle with long tapaderos (leather decorations from the stirrups), it appeared that his legs touched the ground. When he became old and frail, he built a pulley on the barn roof to lift the heavy saddle onto his horse. He had chased the wild horses on the hills, mostly fugitives from ranches. Their trails through Crab Creek to watering holes on the Columbia River can still be detected.

The vast plains broke some men's minds. Rabbits ate every green thing. Occasionally the residents would get together and have a rabbit drive to thin their numbers. Neighbors were few, the wind blew dust to and fro, narrow trails often were blocked by drifting sand and tumbleweeds and the lonely yip-yip of coyotes sent prehensile shivers down one's spine.

An eccentric settler wallpapered his home with rattlesnake skins, decidedly smelly. A paid worker on the new Milwaukee Railroad had a conviction that he and God were building a railroad from Quincy to Smyrna. The man cleared brush as a right of way for some distance from his home, but got into trouble with the law when he tried to sell unlisted securities to raise capital. Worse off was a miner who saw a woman walking right through the wall into his house. She gave him specific directions as to the location of lost treasure on his farm. After unsuccessful digging, the man bought dynamite to blast. As he was tamping the first charge, the dynamite went off, sending the tamping stick upward through his jaw, coming out through his skull, the end of his aberrations forever.

With an eerie beauty of its own, dramatic near dusk and dawn and when a storm approaches, the land between Wenatchee and Richland has attracted sun-worshippers today. At least two extensive condominium resorts are active. Utilizing Columbia River irrigation water, growers have turned the easterly desert shores into vineyards and orchards. West of the river and beyond the large Yakima Firing Center (army) and the forbidding, deserted Rattlesnake Hills, the verdant Yakima River valley is rich with commercial produce gardens and fruit orchards, Yakima apples, in particular, known worldwide.

Sunset over the Columbia River.

Chapter 13

Travel and Trivia • U.S. Border to Priest Rapids

NORTHPORT.

At the north end of town are the remains of a major sawmill and a smelter that boasted a tall concrete smoke stack long after the smelter ceased operation. Historically, the little village once teemed with mining-related industry. The smoke stack disintegrated and now is represented only by a modest replica 16 feet high that overlooks the smelter site near Highway 25. The Northport Historical Society is gathering and preserving the town's history with some displays at its museum, 318 Columbia Street, in the old town hall. Ask locals about the "Chinese ditches," sandy remainders mostly on the west side of the river of the efforts of immigrant Chinese workers to extract gold from the Columbia. Launch boats from a small riverside city park. Upstream toward the border is the infamous Deadman's Eddy, still a dangerous whirlpool. www.northportwa.us

Snag Cove Campground. Along the road from Northport to Kettle Falls west of the river, Snag Cove is a popular site for fishing the huge expanse of the Columbia that widens into **Franklin D. Roosevelt Lake or just "Lake Roosevelt."**

Kettle Falls.

Kettle Falls originally was a turbulent falls in the Columbia River with a 40-foot drop interrupted by huge boulders across the river's width. It was a prime traditional fishing site used by several Washington Native American tribes. (See text.) When Lake Roosevelt downstream backed up to flood the riverside town of Kettle Falls, the town was moved a short distance to absorb an existing settlement of Meyer Falls. When the lake covered the falls fishing site, local tribes in funereal dress held a traditional dance of the dead for its loss. The small town is near the northern end of vast Lake Roosevelt and benefits from boating, fishing, and houseboat tourism(see Lake Roosevelt below). Town & Country Days first weekend in June, when the official Grouch also is chosen. www.kettle-falls.com

109

Kettle Falls Interpretive Center, adjacent to the Kettle Falls bridge, was opened in 1992 with pictures and displays of the importance of the falls to Indian life.

Recommended reading about pre-dams Indian life, illustrated. *One Sky Above Us* by M. Gidley (New York: Putnam Sons, 1979). Also *Frank Matsura, Frontier Photographer* by JoAnn Roe (Seattle: Madrona Publishers, 1981). Definitive texts about Northwest Indians in books by Robert Ruby and John Brown.

St. Paul's Mission on the east side of the river near Kettle Falls is one of the oldest churches in Washington. Jesuit Anthony Ravalli encouraged local Indians to build the church. Indian fishing camps and burial grounds were at this site. Below the nearby bluff was Hudson's Bay Company's Fort Colvile (later referred to as Fort *Colville*), now inundated by the Columbia River.

St. Francis Regis Mission became an academy for Indian children, then a B&B, but now is a private residence with no public access.

Fort Spokane is at the Spokane River's junction with the Columbia. After housing a military contingent in pioneer days, the fort has served as a school and medical center, and several buildings remain in use. Spokane was active in early Hudson's Bay Company days as a fur post. See National Park Service. www.nps.gov/laro

East Portal Interpretive Site along Highway 20, west of Kettle Falls, includes a half-mile Log Flume Trail. Learn about logging in the area.

Colville, eight miles east of Kettle Falls, is the home of **Stevens County Historical Museum** with archives available to researchers of the historically important area around Kettle Falls and the Columbia. It was the original site of Fort Colville, the military post. It has a PRCA rodeo in late June and Rendezvous Days the first weekend of August.

Binding together northeast Washington's towns is 150-mile **Lake Roosevelt**, actually the Columbia River backed up from Grand Coulee Dam. Enjoying a warm, sunny climate for all but the winter months, the lake has become a lively destination area for recreational fishing and boating – especially houseboating. Rentals of roomy and well-maintained houseboats are available from Kettle Falls Marina at the north to Keller's Ferry and others to the south. Novices usually are able to operate the boats, since few obstacles threaten along the broad and normally placid waters. The houseboats make delightful vehicles from which families can explore, swim, and fish for 25 species of game fish, including cutthroat and rainbow trout, Dolly Varden trout, and kokanee or the landlocked salmon that reproduces above Grand Coulee as a separate species from the salmon that travel to and from the ocean. Occasionally, one will hook onto a giant sturgeon weighing as much as a half ton. Washington or Tribal fishing licenses are required. Lake Roosevelt Recreational Area. www.nps.gov/laro

By car take Highway 25 south from Kettle Falls to **Gifford-Inchelium Ferry** that accesses the road to **Colville Federated Tribes** tribal center and offices at Nespelem. Proceeding south brings you through hamlets of Hunter's and, near the once-active and dangerous Hellgate Rapids, the old sawmill town of Lincoln. A significant marina and real estate development begun by Win Self is at Seven Bays just north or upstream from Lincoln.

Keller Ferry. Washington State's free ferry crosses the Columbia River. See Lake Roosevelt Recreational Area. Boat and houseboat rentals. The venerable ferry, *Martha S,* operated since 1948, is being replaced by the Washington State Department of Transportation that owns it. The new vessel *Sanpoil* is slated for launching and installation in July 2013. www.wsdot.wa.gov

GRAND COULEE DAM AREA.

Grand Coulee Dam Area Visitor Center is a stand alone building below the dam along Highway 155 with great views of the dam, interactive exhibits, and several films about the area. From Memorial Day weekend to September the free Laser Lights Show, 40 minutes long, has been voted one of the Top 100 Events in North America by the American Bus Association. Water is turned on to run over the dam as a screen for a historical and art show.. Watch from your car (parking is scarce), or the plentiful number of bleachers furnished by the Bureau of Reclamation's Grand Coulee Dam Visitor Center, the deck of Coulee House Inn and Suites (ask first), and other businesses. Exceptional fireworks at Festival of America July 4. That Dam Run 5K, 10K and half marathon May. Great Columbian Triathlon SuperTri in September. PRCA Rodeo May. Several fishing derby events during the season. Numerous other events. www.grandcouleedam.org

Colville Tribal Museum at 515 Birch Street, Coulee Dam, displays native Indian culture and has a quality store of unusual items.

Four Winds Guest House, Grand Coulee, is the converted dormitory for men from construction days. Read the text and capture the historical feel.

Banks Lake is the storage reservoir for excess water that not only awaits power production for Grand Coulee Dam, a small part of the storage, but also provides irrigation water to 670,000 acres of central Washington (Columbia Basin Project). It drowned the former bed of the originally dry (mostly) "Grand Coulee" carved out by the catastrophic Missoula Floods that roared down the course of today's Spokane River-Columbia River and turned south through a series of old faults to reunite with the Columbia and head west. Steamboat Rock and its surrounding area are still above water and have about 100 campsites or RV hookups for visitors. The highway #155 south affords striking views of the sheer bluffs surrounding the lake and leads one to Dry Falls State Park, a heritage site explaining the stupendous falls of the Columbia during the Floods that dwarfed Niagara. *Beware of rattlesnakes if you hike in this area and southward.*

North and West of Grand Coulee Dam is **Nespelem,** the tribal center of the Colville Federated Tribes on the reservation that stretches for miles in three directions from the river. Tribes host a major Pow-Wow of Indians in full regalia in summer that permits visitors to view most events.

Forty miles west of Nespelem on the Okanogan River, a Columbia tributary, the city of Omak holds the annual **Omak Stampede** and **Suicide Race**, both of which include many Indian contestants and a tepee encampment with Indian dancing and games. www.omakstampede.org

Downriver from Grand Coulee the **Chief Joseph Dam** has a visitor center.

Fort Okanogan, at the confluence of the Okanogan and Columbia River, has an interpretive center about the fur trade and the activities of the Hudson's Bay Company, as well as local lore. fortokanogan@communitynet.org

Nothing remains of the old riverboat docks at **Brewster** and **Bridgeport**. The cove at the east end of Brewster, though, was the main site.

Adjacent to **Brewster** and **Pateros** the Columbia makes almost a 90-degree turn to the south and becomes as wide as a lake, backed up from several small dams. It is a good fishing site. The hefty U-bolt used by riverboats to winch themselves upstream is preserved. www.pateros.com

At right angles to the river the highway northwest- leads one through the picturesque **Methow Valley** to the North Cascades Highway (Highway #20) toward the coast. (See Roe, *North Cascades Highway* (Montevista Press). About an hour's drive west is the restored, historic town of **Winthrop** with boardwalks, western shops, and frequent major tourism events – bluegrass, rodeos, barbecue competitions, parades. www.winthropwashington.com

At **Wells Dam** south of Pateros on the Columbia River a large chunk of rock with petroglyphs is exhibited. The Indians used ochre, iron oxide pounded into dust and mixed with an oil, to make their drawings. Adjacent is a fish hatchery.

Lake Chelan Area.

Lake Chelan Chamber of Commerce. http://www.lakechelan.com

The natural Lake Chelan is a very popular and scenic visitor destination. It is one of the world's deepest lakes with an average depth of 400 feet and up to 1,420 feet deep. It thrusts 55 miles into the North Cascades Mountains and is as wide as two miles, lying in a massive gorge carved during the Ice Age by a tributary glacier to the Canadian glaciers that overran today's Northern Washington. At least two major boats make the trip daily to the head of the lake at Stehekin, a town surrounded by formidable mountains and accessible only by water, on foot, or a small plane. This upper lake portion is protected as a Lake Chelan National Recreation Area. A concession for overnighters and a restaurant is available.

The town of Lake Chelan teems with every level of tourist accommodation and attraction yet retains its historic feeling as a small beach town. Landmark **Campbell's Resort** on eight acres of the south lake shore adapts to changing times as needed. Judge Clinton C. Campbell purchased the site in 1900, opening the Chelan Hotel there the same year with a masquerade ball for the locals. By 1947, the success of the Holden Mine up-lake contributed many business visitors. The hotel walls include memorabilia of the past century+. www.campbellsresort. com

Lake Chelan is at an altitude 1200 feet higher than the river channel. It empties into the Columbia through one of the shortest rivers in the country – the Chelan River that rages over a falls somewhat blocked by a small dam that merely creates power for the immediate area. River Walk is a popular site for strollers. **Visitors are warned not to enter the gorge, as one cannot know when water is released from the lake.**

Hang gliders attain unusual heights taking off from lakeshore areas, since the lake is already high and the gorge plus heat creates great thermals.

U.S. Forest Service Information Center downtown has complete information about campgrounds and activities in a broad area near Chelan. www. fs.fed.us

Allison's Interiors at the village of Manson specializes in quality gifts and arts, as well as home interiors. www.allisonsinteriors.com

Several extensive time share resorts are available in the Lake Chelan area, including Wapato Point.

The area now has 21 wineries and major wine events several months of the year. One winery is **Tsillan Cellars** on the south shore. Tsillan is the phonetic Indian word for Chelan. www.tsillancellars.com

Snowmobiles are available for rent and cross-country skiing is popular in this snowy but mild winter climate, where altitudes range from the lake up to serious mountain ranges.

Among the visitor events that occur all year are: Winter Fest Fire and Ice in January, Chelan Century Challenge (bicycling) in June, Chelan Man Triathlon and Bach Fest in July, and others.

WENATCHEE AREA:

Between Brewster and Wenatchee (and farther south) the mighty Columbia runs between steep, dry, rocky bluffs that create a magnificent canyon that rivals those in Utah or Arizona. A side road about halfway between these points leads you to Lake Chelan decribed above. Near Entiat you can see where the 1872 earthquake jarred loose Ribbon Cliff. A good place to view it is from across the river at **Daroga State Park**. This park is delightfully green with RV hookups, tennis courts and striking scenes in every direction. The steep, eroding sand hills on the eastern shore of the river host Lombardy poplar trees, orchards and fields. The western shore cliffs rise up sheer and terrifying, bare of vegetation.

Rocky Reach Dam has a visitor center where one may see exhibits and learn about the grain chutes that went from bluff to river boat. "Gallery of the

Columbia" has photos of sternwheelers, river artifacts rescued before the series of small dams were built for power, pioneer memorabilia, and changing art exhibits. www.chelanpud.org

Mission Ridge Ski Area, 12 miles northwest of Wenatchee, has major ski facilities in lovely powder snow for downhill skiing, base 1,570 feet, peak 6,820 feet, beginner to skilled, chairs and rope tows, cross-country hills, major ski competitions, and overnight facilities –although Wenatchee and other towns are also easy to access.

Wenatchee Valley Conventioon & Visitor Bureau. http://www. wenatcheevalley.org Red Wine & Chocolate mid-February. Special Olympics Winter Games, around March 1. Wenatchee Wine Week mid-March. Renaissance Faire mid-March, Classy Car Parade late April.. Wenatchee River Bluegrass Festival in April. River Run Half-Marathon in September. Other events all year including mountain and ski events.

Wenatchee Valley Museum & Cultural Center. Extensive exhibits on history, archaeology, and pioneer exploration that include the 11,000-year-old and beautiful **Clovis Points from the Richey Clovis Cache** uncovered in a nearby orchard in 1987. Other ancient artifacts. Material on aviator Clyde Pangborn, for whom the Wenatchee airport is named (a plaque honoring him is also there). Pangborn won the Asahi Shimbun prize for flying non-stop from Japan to Wenatchee in 1931. Historical programs, books, extensive archives, gift shop. www.wenatcheewa.gov

Wenatchee Convention Center. A 50,000 square foot center used for major events. www.wenatcheevalley.org or www.wenatcheewa.gov

Wenatchee Riverfront Park is essentially downtown on the Columbia shore, an enlightened use of frontage.

Ohme Gardens, north end of the city, is accessed from near the junction of highways 2 and 97. On a bluff with excellent river views. Original home of Herman and Ruth Ohme, who created the gardens among cedars and pines planted at least 70 years ago. Now operated for the public by Chelan County. www.ohmegardens.com

Washington State Apple Commission has a visitor center, where you can learn about the different kinds of apples and orchard lore. 2900 Euclid Avenue, also near the junction but south. www.bestapples.com

Washington State Apple Blossom Festival is a major parade and festival with a crowned queen presiding over the events, held around May 1 each year. Plan ahead and enjoy the fragrance of apple blossoms permeating the entire area, too. www.appleblossom.org **East Wenatchee** is a well-developed area across the Columbia River from the main city and is an entity of shops and other businesses. See Wenatchee.

Cashmere. Small town west of Wenatchee, home of **Aplets & Cotlets Candy Kitchen**. Also **Chelan County Historical Museum and Pioneer Village**. Archives and several preserved pioneer buildings. Museum has displays of local history and some Columbia River. The Columbia tributary Wenatchee River adjacent to the town and Highway 2 is a popular rafting river. http:// cashmerechamber.org

Leavenworth, Bavarian-style Town, a few miles farther west on the river is a major tourist town with year-round events. Access visitor services directly. www. leavenworth.org

Yakama National Museum at Toppenish a few miles east of the river is an important side trip for comprehensive information about the native tribes along the Columbia River. Restaurant in the museum serves popular Indian fry bread. www.yakamanation.nsn.gov

Suggested entertaining stories about Yakama Indian and pioneer interaction: this book's text, *Kamiakin* by A. J. Splawn (1917, see your library) and *Strangers on the Land* by Click Relander (Toppenish WA: Yakima Indian Nation, 1982).

Some state parks along the Columbia River: Chief Joseph Dam to Vantage: Chief Joseph State Park, five miles from Bridgeport off State Route 173, boat launching and camping. **Fort Okanogan State Park** on State Route 17, picnicking, interpretive center. **Daroga State Park** 18 miles north of East Wenatchee on Highway 97, hookups, boat launching and moorage, trails. **Lincoln Rock State Park** also north of East Wenatchee on Highway 97, RV hookups, boat launching and moorage, amphitheater, monitored swimming beach. **Wenatchee Confluence State Park** Olds Station Road at confluence of Wenatchee River with Columbia River, in city, RV hookups, swimming beach, boat launching, nature trails. **Gingko Petrified Forest Interpretive Center** at Vantage, junction of I-90 and Columbia River has hiking trails in petrified wood area (possible rattlesnakes that are more frightened of you than you are of them – listen for warning). **Gingko/ Wanapum State Park** is south on the west-bank road from Vantage (Wanapum Dam Visitor Center is approached from the east side); Park has hookups and boat launch, fishing is popular.

Vantage itself is a small settlement in a dramatic location. Shops have petrified wood items for sale, as well as nonlocal gems and rocks, and arrowheads native to the site. Learn about the unusual upwellings of lava that formed parts of eastern Washington.

Geology info: Write for "Publications of the Washington Division of Geology and Earth Resources," Olympia WA 98504.

"Music in the Gorge." Major musical groups draw huge audiences to the Gorge Amphitheatre (a lawn terrace type of seating), very scenic and overlooking the Columbia River near the city of George,. Not to be confused

115

with the well-known Columbia Gorge between Oregon and Washington. www.gorgeamphitheatre.net

Ellensburg. A small city west of Vantage that has a major rodeo every Labor Day weekend. Also the site of the John Clymer Museum. Clymer was an internationally recognized western artist born in Ellensburg. Clymer was noted for his Lewis & Clark paintings, in particular. Gallery showings of other western artists, too. www.clymermuseum.com

Crescent Bar Resort on an island in the Columbia near impressive bluffs. Mostly second homes, golf course and other amenities. Ten miles north of Vantage. www.crescentbarresort.com

Desert Aire. On the river shore at Mattawa WA between Vantage and Tri-Cities. A small settlement with restaurants, lodging, gift shop, an airport, and PGA-rated golf course. www.desertairegolf.com

Section III

Tri-Cities and
Down the River

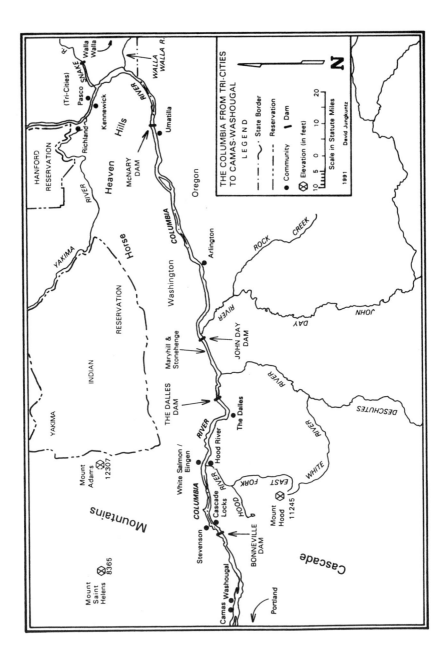

THE COLUMBIA FROM TRI-CITIES
TO CAMAS-WASHOUGAL

LEGEND

State Border

Reservation

Community   Dam

Elevation (in feet)

Dam

Scale in Statute Miles

1991   David Jungkuntz

Chapter 14

Confluence

As the eighteenth century ended, large sections of western America were unexplored. Especially intriguing to English and American governments was the news, verified by Captain Gray and Lieutenant W. R. Broughton, of a vast river entering the Pacific in the Northwest. In Washington, D.C., President Thomas Jefferson pondered the report of explorer Alexander Mackenzie suggesting that Great Britain should set a boundary south of the Columbia and establish settlements to shut out the Americans. British intentions increased the President's determination to send an exploring party into the western lands, a venture that Jefferson had long championed.

In 1803, Jefferson secured the princely sum of $2,500 to finance a westward exploration by Meriwether Lewis, Jefferson's secretary, and William Clark, Lewis' longtime friend and capable military captain. Before they left the junction of the Missouri and Mississippi rivers in 1804, the two learned that Napoleon had sold all of Louisiana Territory to the Americans, a vast French holding that spread to the Rocky Mountains.

The tale of Lewis and Clark's expedition is well related by many writers—the addition of a French-Canadian trapper Charbonneau as interpreter, his wife Sacagawea, the birth of their baby in Mandan country, the coincidence of meeting Sacagawea's own brother, a Shoshone, in the sparsely settled Rockies, the arrival at the Snake River (they called it the Kimooenim) after friendly assistance from Nez Perce tribesmen and the historic arrival at the Columbia River.

Although the scenery was desolate and the climate extreme, the confluence of the Yakima, the Snake and Walla Walla rivers with the Columbia—all within twenty-plus miles—was a natural meeting place. Between the Snake and the Walla Walla were traditional Indian council grounds, where Snake, Yakima, Cayuse and other bands pounded out uneasy alliances. In 1805, the Lewis and Clark expedition used the same grounds for a conference.

The journals of the expedition mention the arrival on October 16, 1805, &t the confluence after the party successfully traversed several lively rapids on the Snake, probably where Ice Harbor Dam now is located.

> The Kimooenim empties itself into the Columbia. We halted above the point of junction on the Kimooenim to confer with the Indians, who had collected in great numbers to receive us. On landing we were met by our two chiefs ... and also the two Indians who had passed us a few days since on horseback; one of whom appeared to be a man of influence. ... After smoking with the Indians, we formed a camp at the point where the two rivers unite. ... A chief came from the Indian camp about a quarter of a mile up the Columbia, at the head of nearly two hundred men: they formed a regular procession, keeping time to the ... music of their drums, which they accompanied with their voices. (Meriwether Lewis, *Lewis and Clark Journals*, Vol. II [New York J.B. Lippincott Company, 1961], 420.)

Much as it is today, the width of the Columbia below the junction was estimated at one to three miles. The junction marked a territorial division between Indian groups, with the Yakima Nation and their kindred on the west side, Nez Perce, Snake and Cayuse on the east and south of the Wallula bend. While the party rested, Captain Clark made a short side trip up the Columbia as far as the Yakima River, where he was greeted cordially by Yakima Indians. Clark commented that they were industrious and their civilization well established, but they suffered from eye disease and blindness, presumed to result from blowing sand and the glare from desert and river.

As the party made its way downriver through the numerous rapids (as many as one hundred existed prior to dams between the Snake and Portland), their encounters continued to be guardedly friendly. The Indians were reassured as to the expedition's peaceful intentions by Sacagawea's presence, for Indians never brought women on a war party. Intensely curious Indians clustered around at every stopping place and particularly delighted in the Americans' violin music and lively dancing of an evening. Of further wonder was York, Lewis's black helper.

Nearing the "Great Falls of the Columbia," or Celilo Falls, the men saw evidences of prior European or American visitors ... brass buttons, kettles, sailors' jackets, and talk of a trader Mr. Haley who lived down river.

Around Celilo Falls the Indians prepared fish to be traded to Indians of the Columbia Gorge, who then sold it to ships calling at the Columbia's mouth. The salmon was dried, then pulverized and placed in a basket of grass and reeds, lined with salmon skin, where it was pressed down firmly and covered with another salmon skin, laced tightly together. Several such baskets were stacked up and encased tightly in porous matting to make a ninety to one hundred pound bundle. The fish remained edible for years.

Confluence

Below Celilo Falls, the expedition encountered still different Indian groups who skillfully manned high prowed canoes that were very seaworthy in rough water. They saw many sea otter from the Gorge to the ocean and ate well on fish and game. The main annoyance was a profusion of fleas. The Indians themselves moved their camps regularly to escape them. The narrator described the joyful end to their voyage on November 7, 1805:

> The river widens into a kind of bay crowded with low islands, subject to be overflowed occasionally by the tide. We had not gone far from this village [of Wahkiakums] when the fog cleared off, and we enjoyed the delightful prospect of ocean; that ocean, the object of all our labours, the reward of all our anxieties. This cheering view exhilarated the spirits of all the party, who were still more delighted on hearing the distant roar of the breakers. (*Ibid.*, 473.)

However, upon encamping, they became dangerously pinned down on a northside beach (Chinook), where the tide rose to inundate their camp, sweeping canoes away. Breakers were so high that they could not dream of crossing the broad estuary to shelter. Moving to a slightly better, but still exposed camp, the party was unable to cross the wild and mighty Columbia for almost three weeks.

Once on the more protected south side of the river, the weary and wet party members built cabins on the Lewis River, some distance from the windy Columbia, in a heavy woods where elk abounded. There they repaired clothing, traveled to the ocean to evaporate sea water for salt, traded what little goods they had with the Indians, and waited for spring and a return east.

When spring came, they were off upstream. Now they discovered the veiled entrance to the Willamette River and explored upstream past Portland's site. After further adventures, the party members were welcomed home by Jefferson. Their grueling but admirably executed trip was a key factor in securing the Columbia River country, the Oregon Territory, for the United States.

Then came the Astorians by sea to build a fort in 1810 near the mouth of the river, and David Thompson of Hudson's Bay was the next explorer to travel the Columbia River to the sea in 1811 , as described earlier.

Among the Astorians was Alexander Ross, possibly the liveliest chronicler of that period, an adventurer who traveled with Thompson, Franchere, Cox and David Stuart. He was stationed at Fort Okanogan, Red River and elsewhere. Astor had sent a party to Astoria by ship and another overland under Wilson Price Hunt. The party was plagued by poor choice of a route, Indian troubles, dissension and deaths. The bedraggled survivors reached Astoria on February 15, 1812.

During their brief stay at Fort Astoria, the Astorians made two mistakes that had far-ranging negative repercussions. During an upriver trading trip, the Astorians had summarily hanged a man for taking a silver goblet from camp. Back at Fort Astoria, an officer sought to impress the Chinooks when he took an empty bottle, shook it and said it contained the smallpox disease—if they did not behave, he would release it. Thereafter, when Indians upriver got the disease by contact with whites, they thought the white man really did release smallpox on purpose.

In 1813 Pierre Dorion, an interpreter for Hunt, and eight other men under John Reed returned to Vale, Oregon, to set up a post. Because the Bannock Indians were so hostile, Reed built a second post on the Snake, where Marie Dorion happened to be on a fateful day. Hearing from a friendly Indian of a plot to kill the trappers, she and her two children rushed through the woods to warn them at the first post, encountering one survivor who told her of the attack, then died. At the post she found everyone dead, scalped and cut to pieces. Madame Dorion and her children spent two agonizing nights in the woods watching to see if Indians returned. It was winter and the youngsters were freezing, yet she was afraid to start a fire.

She told Alexander Ross later that, after dark, she went into the post and found fish scattered about. The provisions kept her and her children from starvation. Madame Dorion set out with her children packed in robes on her one horse, traveling through deep snow and over rocks for nine days. When she and the horse could no longer walk, she made a camp at an overhanging cliff, killed the horse for food and built a hut. After fifty-three lonely and fearful days, they trudged on. Madame Dorion became snow blind and stopped briefly but, fearing starvation, had to continue. Finally she saw smoke. The camp was of friendly Walla Walla Indians. The plucky woman is remembered at Wallula with a plaque at Madame Dorion Memorial Park.

Alexander Ross had his own troubles with Indians in 1814. He traveled from his small outpost (Fort Okanogan) south to buy horses at the big summer encampment around Ellensburg. Ross boldly entered the camp with a few men and two women, one with a child, and sought to exchange trade goods for horses. Perhaps because they had lost relatives to smallpox, the Indians were sullen, jeering at the traders and running off their horses. Ross feigned indifference and went about trading for one horse at a time. Each time he made a purchase, hostiles drove the animal off.

Fearing the seizure of the women and child, Ross spirited them away by night and faced furious warriors the next morning. Matters further deteriorated when an Indian grabbed a sheath knife from the belt of a Canadian. The latter lunged at the thief. Suddenly hushed, the encampment waited. In a brilliant gesture Ross stepped into the fray, holding his own elaborately carved knife, hilt-first, to the Indian, saying that here was a knife for a chief. Suddenly the man smiled and waved the better knife, returning the other to its owner. The Indians then gave the Ross party food and returned all the horses.

Four years later, on the Columbia River north of the Walla Walla River, Alexander Ross and North West Company employees built a trading post, Fort Nez Perces. Ross described the treeless spot as "more like a lake than a river—

with low green hills rising from its distant shore" [the Columbia River]—not very different from its appearance today. The local Indians' chief concern was that the traders would arm their mortal enemies, the Snakes. The strategically placed fort became known as the "Gibraltar of the Columbia," and, renamed Fort Walla Walla after the Hudson's Bay merger, operated until the closure of British-owned posts below the new Canadian-American border.

For the next three decades the fur traders used the river as a highway to supply trading posts thriving from Astoria to farthest British Columbia.

In 1824, George Simpson, governor of Northern Operations for Hudson's Bay Company, arrived at Fort George (as Astoria had been renamed) with John Mcloughlin on a survey of posts, after which Mcloughlin was commissioned to move the Columbia River headquarters to Fort Vancouver across from today's Portland. The move would give the Hudson's Bay Company a fertile farming location in a better climate and escape from Chinook trade domination. Understandably Chief Comcomly viewed the move to Vancouver with dismay.

Under the leadership of Dr. John Mcloughlin, impressive physically as well as mentally, Fort Vancouver became Hudson's Bay Company's anchor on the Columbia River. It rested on a pleasant shelf above the floods (where the city of Vancouver sprawls today), its pickets enclosing a fine factor's home, substantial dwellings for employees, warehouses, a school for employees' children, an Indian trade shop, and other buildings. Outside the palisade were well-tended gardens and orchards, calculated to gladden Sir George Simpson's heart, for he urged forts to become self-sustaining. A lively place, the fort gathered in furs from its district and dispatched supplies outbound as far as today's Kamloops and Prince George.

The post depended entirely on the Columbia River for transportation. Annually a supply ship came around the Horn from England, crossing the dangerous Columbia Bar and sailing upriver. Each spring a fast Express boat left for Hudson's Bay and Red River Settlement (Winnipeg), using the Columbia River as a highway to Boat Encampment, where the men transferred to horses. The return Express brought coveted mail, packets and light supplies, an occasion for fancy dinners at Mcloughlin's home and grog for the voyageurs, those colorful fellows, largely of French or French-Indian ancestry, who manned the oars and knew every nuance of the treacherous Columbia River.

Who else but those voyageurs regularly ran the whole river, rapids and all, for years on end! Short, brawny men, the river navigators often sang cadences to give rhythm to their paddling, ate prodigiously and—off duty—drank the same. Their stories were spellbinding, enlivened by shading the truth a bit. Before arriving at a destination, they changed into their best clothing with colorful sashes, tied bright headbands around their locks, and delivered their Hudson's Bay Company official passengers with a flourish. By contrast, the latter, Scotsmen mostly, often arrived in broadcloth suits and hats.

A contingent of 175 farmers was sent by Hudson's Bay Company in 1841 from Red River Settlement down the Columbia River to work on farms at the Puget Sound Agricultural Company north of Fort Vancouver along the Cowlitz River. Unfortunately for Hudson's Bay Comapny, many farmers soon learned they could own land in Oregon's Willamette Valley and moved there.

The relationships between the Indians and Hudson's Bay Company were easy. Already the powerful Yakima tribe had vast herds of fine horses. Their Chief Kamiakin came to Fort Vancouver in 1840 to purchase the first cattle for ranching, buying more later from immigrants. The Yakima lands extended from the North Cascades Mountains to the Columbia-Snake confluence, including some of the Columbia Plateau and west of the Columbia to the Kittitas Valley (Ellensburg). Good ranchers on ideal grazing grounds, the Yakimas increased their herds dramatically. Indian women gathered camas and herbs in the mountains, and all joined in the fishing and trading at Celilo Falls on the Columbia. The Yakimas engaged in occasional skirmishes with rival Indian bands or raided them to carry off women. This was not uncommon, for Yakimas could marry relatives only beyond the eighth generation. Comparatively content, the Yakimas were north of the main path of westward expansion ... for now.

Chapter 15

The Immigrant Flood Sparks War

It was well into the 1840s before the semifeudal Hudson's Bay Company was seriously challenged on the Columbia River—and then by simple American settlers and religious men, not merchants or soldiers. Despite the adverse political effects for Britain, the Hudson's Bay Company's kindly chief factor John Mcloughlin helped American pilgrims get established in the Willamette Valley, often furnishing supplies on credit or free to destitute and weary families. His openhanded generosity and compassion would get him into difficulty with his penny-pinching boss, Governor George Simpson.

The settlers came in a trickle at first and then in a flood that did not diminish for more than a decade. Interest in "the Ory-gon" was sparked by the publication of explorers' journals and the speeches of missionaries, all denominations, who came to save souls and returned east to gain financing to expand their efforts. Chief among the vocal missionaries was Marcus Whitman. With his wife, Narcissa, a hardheaded business manager William Gray and a substantial party, Whitman founded a mission at Waiilatpu (Walla Walla) in 1836, ministering to the Cayuse Indians and others. On November 30, 1847, wrathful Cayuse parishioners murdered him, Narcissa Whitman and eleven men. The much-admired Hudson's Bay veteran, Peter Skene Ogden, came to negotiate for the release of forty-seven others taken prisoner.

This shocking event scarcely interrupted the tide of westward immigration along the Oregon Trail. Noted author David Lavender in his book, *Land of Giants*, wondered why the immigrants went that far. He pointed out that the majority of Oregon Trail migrants were "mostly family men, prosperous enough to buy substantial outfits." Such farmers could have purchased land in Iowa or Wisconsin at $1.25 an acre, instead of trekking two thousand difficult miles to unknown Oregon. Lavender speculated that the restless urge to see what lay beyond was intriguing to the adventurous, and others thought moving west would stave off the claims of the British to the Northwest. Still others merely were land speculators.

Although smaller parties preceded them, the first major immigration to Oregon had begun with the thousand-person train that left Independence, Missouri, in the spring of 1843. Along the way it dwindled and split, but most of the party arrived in Oregon.

Once at the Columbia River near Umatilla, some immigrants drifted safely downriver, portaging around Celilo Falls. Later parties sometimes trekked along the south shore to The Dalles, arriving weary and hungry, so near and yet so far from the fabled Willamette. The formidable Columbia Gorge with rapids and rain, hostile Indians and barely passable cattle trails awaited them. At The Dalles they dismantled their wagons, placing them on rafts. Appointed drovers followed with the cattle along a haphazard riverside trail on the south shore, laid out by Joel Palmer in 1846. The river travelers soon learned that they must put in to shore before the vicious rapids of the Cascades inexorably swept them away. The portage roads were quagmires, since immigrants usually arrived in fall. They started from the Midwest in spring, in order to cross the mountains during summer, and arrived in Oregon at the rainy season. The six miles of Columbia Gorge Cascades seethed and foamed through an assortment of channels worn through basalt. At some point within the last thousand years a thunderous earthslide from Mount Hood blocked the Columbia and destroyed a natural bridge over the river. The resulting debris and rocks, plus the insistent rush of the river, created a mariner's nightmare of eddies, unpredictable currents and bars. The Cascades were in two main parts. At the Upper Cascades, the whole river was constricted to about 100 to 120 feet, which caused furious rapids to surge for about 100 yards. Then the channel widened but was blocked (the Lower Cascades) for some distance by rocks and shallows, which caused great, dangerous whirlpools and eddies. On the north bank below the Cascades loomed Beacon Rock, 800 feet high, a volcanic remnant.

Since there were no actual falls, the rapids could be run by capable rivermen in stout boats, borne out by the express trips routinely made by Hudson's Bay voyageurs. But the crude rafts and makeshift boats plied by midwest farmers were almost unmanageable. The pioneers took to the land approximately where Bonneville Dam is now located. In chill, howling winds, lashed by rain and sometimes sleet, inadequately clad women and children struggled against fatal hypothermia, their menfolk warmer due to the exertion of carrying everything six miles on the portage road. What was all this about a balmy land where winter never came, as the orator back east had promised!

In 1847 pioneer woman Elizabeth Greer said of the portage road, "I carry my babe and lead, or rather carry, another through snow, mud and water, almost to my knees. ... I was so cold and numb that I could not tell by the feeling that I had any feet at all."

Since the Willamette River Valley was considerably south of the Columbia, some immigrants eyed the mountains around Mount Hood, wondering about an overland route. Among these was Samuel K. Barlow, who arrived at The Dalles in

September 1845. After a cursory examination of the eastern foothills, Barlow and several other families pioneered a trail south of Mount Hood. By late October, it was obvious that snow would kill them if starvation didn't first. Barlow left two men to guard supplies southeast of Mount Hood, while the rest went ahead to the Willamette on foot and with pack horses.

The following year Barlow obtained a franchise to complete a toll road along that original trail and hacked out a barely passable wagon road. Earliest travelers believed him to be a confidence man, because they paid their toll at the eastern end, trekked happily on for four days and came to a wicked stretch of trail over big rocks and along frightening ledges (admittedly the scenery of Mount Hood was spectacular). Then, another day or so west, they encountered seemingly impassable Laurel Hill, where Barlow and his road were cursed roundly, but Barlow himself had gone through. Some immigrants attached trees to their wagons so they would not overrun the teams on the downward plunge; others tied ropes to trees and winched the wagons down. It scarcely seemed an improvement over the terrible Columbia Cascades. Later, a revised trail eased the descent.

Entrepreneurs began to improve the portage trails around rapids. Francis A. Chenoweth, a storekeeper at the upper landing, built a crude two-mile tram by July 1851, just a set of wooden rails and a wagonlike carrier pulled by a disconsolate mule. By 1856, Bradford & Company extended the wooden rails to the downriver end of the Middle Cascades, leaving yet two miles of portaging to the steamer landing below.

Whether despairing of gaining the Willamette or seizing the chance to serve river traffic, some pioneers settled there in the Columbia Gorge; at Hamilton and Bradford Islands; near Lower, Middle and Upper Cascades; and farther up river in the lovely Hood River Valley and the booming trade center, The Dalles.

Not all portions of the Oregon Trail were safe from Indians. On May 19, 1846, U.S. Congress approved $765,500 to staff ten sites with mounted riflemen. By September 1849, a contingent under Brevet-Colonel William W. Loring reached The Dalles. Some troops were sent west along the Barlow Trail, others downriver in makeshift watercraft to set up Fort Vancouver, adjacent to the Hudson's Bay Company post.

Like the other Northwest tribes, except for the aberration at Waiilatpu, the Yakimas accepted (although with growing concern) the few traders, settlers and missionaries. They did not object when early cattleman Ben Snipes ran cattle on their lands. But they became alarmed at Lieutenant George B. McClellan's 1853 expedition to survey a route for the Northern Pacific Railroad through Yakima country.

The great Yakima Chief Kamiakin and Father C. M. Pandosy met McClellan at the Catholic Ahtanum Mission, where Kamiakin demanded to know his intentions. At Kamaikin's request, the Yakima Chief Owhi monitored McClellan's movements in the Wenatchi country and reported back to Kamiakin. Meanwhile,

Isaac Stevens, newly appointed governor of Washington Territory, was surveying from East to West, making treaties with tribes as he went. Ominous news reached the Yakimas that the government was out to buy their land and remove them from it and that, if they refused to go, the soldiers would use force. Governor Stevens met with Chief Owhi in the summer of 1854 to set up a conference in 1855 about land purchase.

Kamiakin vowed the lands would not be surrendered and quietly sent high-level emissaries to all the tribes of eastern Washington and Oregon, and to some west of the mountains, urging a confederacy that would banish the white man forever. A great Indian council was held in 1854 at Grande Ronde Valley; for five days; speeches were made and problems were aired. Most of the Indian chiefs were interested in starting a war, except for Hal-halt-los-sot (commonly dubbed Chief Lawyer for his negotiating abilities) of the Nez Perce and Stic-cas of the Cayuse, who wanted to hear Stevens' proposal first. Kamiakin dramatically stated his opinion: "We wish to be left alone in the lands of our forefathers ... but a paleface stranger ... sends word to us that ... he wants it for the white man. Where can we go? ... Only a single mountain now separates us from the big salt water of the setting sun. .. . Better to die like brave warriors on the battlefield than live among our vanquishers, despised." (A. J. Splawn, *Kamiahin* [Copyright by Mrs. A. J. Splawn, 1917] ,24.)

An unusual union of tribes faced Governor Stevens at the council grounds of Walla Walla the following year, each group arriving in style, possibly four thousand Indians. While preliminary speeches and maneuvering went on, Chief Lawyer went to Governor Stevens and told him that the Cayuse intended to murder them all, that his Nez Perce would move into the Stevens camp to protect them. In so doing, he alienated many of his tribal friends. Conflicting stories spread as to the validity of the threat. Stevens offered two reservations, one for the Nez Perce, another for Yakima, both with their related bands, and later added a third for the Walla Walla, Cayuse and Umatilla. Weary of conversation, Kamiakin and his chiefs made the mark of agreement, yielding twenty-nine thousand square miles of territory in exchange for a protected Yakima Indian Reservation of about 1.37 million acres (over two thousand square miles). The Nez Perce retained a large reservation, including the Wallowa valley for Chief Joseph's band; it was threatened removal of the latter that led to the 1877 Nez Perce war and the now-famous flight of Chief Joseph's people. The Umatilla Reserve was the same as that retained today. For such concessions the tribes received money, implements, and annuities. If the white men kept their promises, it did not appear too bad a deal, under the circumstances. If ... .

Before the ink was dry, and long before the treaties were ratified by the U.S. Senate (four years later), miners brazenly crossed lands from which they were legally banned. There were decent men among the military camps and the governmental officials who sent fruitless appeals to Washington, D.C., for permission to take action against the miners. The army built Fort Walla Walla near the old Whitman Mission as a precaution against war.

War drums began to inflame the tribes. The pretreaty confederacy was largely in place. Kamiakin, a leader respected by both sides, decided to fight. Miners enroute to Okanogan and Colville gold fields were warned not to pass. Qual-chan, Looking Glass, Peu-peu-mox-mox, Quil-ten-e-nock, even Leschi west of the mountains, were talking war. The killing began by disobedient miners, of Indians in retaliation and of the largely respected Yakima indian agent, A. J. Bolon (by three Indians) near The Dalles. The Yakimas turned in two of the three culprits to Captain J. J. Archer of the Ninth Infantry at Fort Simcoe, the third having committed suicide rather than be captured.

More lives were lost between 1855 and 1858. Recognizing that whoever controlled the gorge was master of the territory, the military from Fort Vancouver established a blockhouse (Fort Rains) at the Middle Cascades, just in time.

At 8:30 A.M., March 26, 1856, local Cascade Indians, Yakima warriors and Klickitats attacked the settlement at Upper Cascades, killing one man and wounding several in the first volley. Pandemonium reigned with forty men, women and children making for the stoutly built general store, some killed in the attempt. Late arrivals swam to the riverfront building. Inside, rifles were passed around, defenders shooting back from the store's second story. They watched the Indians loot and burn houses and warehouses. When Indians threw firebrands on the roof of the store, settlers doused the fire with cups of brine drawn from pork barrels.

Meanwhile, the steamer *Wasco* on the Oregon side of the river got away upstream. Just off the Columbia on Mill Creek, the steamer *Mary* managed to get steam going, but Indian bullets hit several crew members and others jumped overboard and drowned in the confusion.

By lying on the floor, Captain Hardin Chenowith steered the boat into the river and with a handful of fugitive settlers that clambered aboard, steamed off to The Dalles.

The Indians simultaneously assaulted Fort Rains, defended by nine troopers. Several nearby families ran to the blockhouse but a man was mortally wounded during the melee. One soldier was captured and cruelly tortured, his screams horrible to the helplessly listening blockhouse troopers. The contingent successfully defended the blockhouse, battering the enemy with their six-pounder cannon. Caught with no water supplies on hand, a man crept to a nearby saloon and raided the liquors to quench the defenders' thirst.

At the lower landing, Indians attacked, but an alarm had given time for everyone to flee in small boats downriver for Vancouver. Enroute they encountered young Lieutenant Phil Sheridan (only three years out of West Point) with forty soldiers aboard the steamer *Belle* and a Hudson's Bay bateau; Sheridan had been warned of the attack by a friendly Indian. No one was killed at the lower Cascades, but the Indians burned all nearby houses and looted or destroyed government stores. When the alarm reached Fort Dalles (which had been established during 1847 and 1850), two hundred men under George Wright and Edward Steptoe arrived on the *Mary*, the *Wasco* and a towed raft at the Upper Cascades on the third day of the battle.

Brevet Lieutenant Colonel Steptoe relieved soldiers and settlers at Fort Rains, and Sheridan's men pursued the Indians near Bradford Island, capturing several warriors and families. Confronted with defeat, the Cascade Indians placed all the blame on the Yakimas and their allies. Colonel Wright arrived shortly from the Upper Cascades, and his officers arrested thirteen men identified as leaders, bringing them to the upper landing. Nine were hanged, including Old Chenowith, the chief. Another was taken to jail in Vancouver, and three escaped to the Yakima camps. Short but vicious, this was the last Indian unrest in the gorge.

Hostilities moved into eastern Washington. In the long run, though, the Indians were outgunned by the army soldiers. The decisive victories led by Colonel George Wright largely quelled further disorders.

While sharply reduced from the territories once controlled, the huge Yakima Nation Reservation extends today roughly from Mount Adams in the North Cascades south to the Columbia River and is embraced by the Yakima River. The Yakimas have a well-organized tribal organization with leaders educated in modern economic ways but holding strongly to their heritage. Showcasing their heritage is the Yakima Tribal Museum in Toppenish, a splendid structure suggesting an Indian headdress. Adjacent to dioramas and archives is an attractive modern restaurant open to the public, serving all types of food. It is only one of the Yakima enterprises

Chapter 16

The Tri-Cities

With Indian resistance largely overcome, miners swarmed northward to Barkerville, Canada, to the international border and—in large numbers—to Idaho. The small community around the Hudson's Bay Company Fort Walla Walla at Wallula became a popular debarkation point for prospectors bound for Idaho after sternwheeler navigation began in 1859. The Chinese were content to sift through the Columbia River's sandbars north of the Tri-Cities.

Walla Walla already was a settlement of sorts, where a medical doctor, Dorsey Syng Baker, ran a store and raised cattle to sell to miners. He needed an outlet to the river at Wallula; so, with minimal capital, Baker and others built a narrow-gauge line using wooden rails strengthened with strap iron, although they used metal rails on curves and steep grades. Popular myth has it that Baker used rawhide instead of strap iron on some rail portions, and that coyotes chewed them off during lean times, causing locals to call it "Baker's Rawhide Railroad." Range cattle were a bigger problem, loafing on the tracks. Baker employed a tough farm dog to ride on the flatcars, jump off and scatter the cows before the train. According to passengers, the train was so slow that the dog had no problem.

Upriver the wind blew dust over the low-lying lands of today's Tri-Cities. It took a railroad, not a river, to spark settlement. In 1879 the Northern Pacific Railroad built a construction town named for J. C. Ainsworth, president of the Oregon Steam Navigation Company, which dominated Columbia River shipping. Ainsworth lay north of the Snake River, as wild and woolly a town as ever arose, inhabited by tough transients seeking transient solace in saloons and brothels. Fueled by drink, they continually fought each other. Ainsworth was not a fashionable address.

A Columbia River steamer, the *Spokane*, brought rails and supplies to a landing on the west bank to serve crews extending tracks westward through Yakima to the coast. A construction camp there, Huson (some called it Hades), soon became platted as Kennewick. The Indian name, "Kin-en-wack," meant "grassy place

131

surrounded with water," an old wintering ground. It also was a tough place, and in 1902, vigilantes moved to expel thirty men considered "riff-raff."

About the same time Pasco was born (partly from buildings moved from Ainsworth). According to best sources, the name "Pasco" was given to the sere town by a Northern Pacific engineer, V. C. Bogue, who compared it to an equally uninviting Peruvian town, Cerro de Pasco, where he lived while building an Andean railroad. Until the bridge across the Snake was finished, Captain William P. Gray skippered the steamer *Frederick K. Billings* to haul freight across the river; the boat later hauled trains across the Columbia from Pasco to Kennewick.

Richland, the third of the Tri-Cities, was originally named Benton in 1905, but was forced to change its name due to postal confusion with Bentson. City fathers offered a town lot free as a prize for the name. When twelve people called it Richland, they drew lots, and the winner was Althea Rosencrance.

Well before Richland was formed, however, small towns along the Columbia River eased into being: Hanford (named for Judge C. H. Hanford of Seattle), White Bluffs, Ringgold. Hanford was a remount station of the United States Cavalry for change of horses enroute between Fort Simcoe and Fort Walla Walla.

The small towns were served by boats, the first of which was the *W. R. Todd*, then the *Mountain Gem* running for four years between Hanford and Pasco, the *Queen City Flyer*, and finally the *Hanford Flyer*, from Pasco and Kennewick until the advent of roads and automobiles.

Above these towns the Columbia was considered unnavigable. But the indomitable mariner, Captain W. P. Gray, challenged the power of Priest and Rock Island rapids in 1888, partly because he had filed a report in 1886 with the Oregon Steam Navigation Company that he felt the rapids could be surmounted. Commercial backers built two boats on the strength of the report, and in 1886, the two tested the waters returning battered with frightened, defeated crews.

Business friends from Ellensburg then persuaded Gray to pilot a new boat, The *City of Ellensburgh*, upstream; feeling responsible for suggesting the original effort, he agreed. Carrying forty-five tons of freight and a handful of passengers, the 120-foot sternwheeler was lined up Priest Rapids without serious difficulty. At Rock Island Rapids the sturdy craft stood motionless against the swift current for about an hour. White-knuckled passengers were convinced they were doomed.

Amidst cheers from crew and shore spectators, Captain Gray permitted the craft to come dangerously close to large rocks to escape the main current and made it through the rapids. He completed his trip into the Okanogan River, and later made four additional trips on the route before low water.

Gray became deeply involved in Pasco's business life. Using kitchen equipment from the *Frederick P. Billings*, he rented a section house from the Northern Pacific and opened a restaurant. He also built a four-bedroom hotel, developed and sold lots as the Gray's Addition, continued as captain of the steamboat, raised hogs, and became land agent for the Northern Pacific. Together with promoter Louis C.

Frey, Gray coined the still-used slogan "Keep Your Eye on Pasco," although many scoffed that there wasn't much there to keep an eye on. The feisty townsmen even made a bid for the State capital in 1890, losing to Olympia.

New settlements sprang up near the railroad. Twelve miles north of Pasco, when heavy rains knocked out a section of the Northern Pacific Railroad, a Cockney workman exclaimed, "There'll be 'ell to pay." A new town at the site arose as "Eltopay," changed to the more discreet "Eltopia" by later settlers. But why not? At Ainsworth there was a school named "I'll Be Damned School," a taxpayer's response when he was asked to pay his school tax.

Water from the Columbia made the Tri-Cities come to life. Verdant crops resulted from a myriad of irrigation plans. Land promoters distributed sensational literature, calling Kennewick "the California of the Northwest," and the sandbars of the Snake "The Italy of the Northwest." A pamphlet of 1912 claimed Kennewick was in a southern climate under northern skies. One settler remarked about the wonderful smell of virgin sagebrush soil after it was broken up by a plough and watered for the first time. It was true that, with water, farmers could raise soft fruits, grains, and vegetables; asparagus and potatoes became winners. In 1905, the parent company of Welch's Grape Juice was formed; it is still operating. The river served the farmers a second time by allowing barge traffic to call at Pasco, taking products to market.

Today new ways of marketing the area's products are appearing—products like pickled asparagus, gourmet vinegar (for all kinds of grapes grow well there), dried cherries encased in chocolate, fancy mustards. Several of the Northwest's finest wines are produced nearby from grapes grown on site.

Early twentieth century farms were remote and life was hard. Rabbits damaged the crops. Dust storms rolled in like tornados, lasting for days. The settlers made their own fun. A pioneer, Otto Olds, told of the fears of children in the treeless desert that Santa could not find them, only to discover presents under a Christmas tree made of sagebrush limbs nailed to a piece of lumber. He recalled walking one day in a canyon with his grandchild, suddenly hearing music. Investigating, they observed Northern Pacific workmen of Italian descent, their train parked on a siding, dressed in their best Easter finery and celebrating the religious holiday with song and dance, accompanied by accordions.

The local Indians were very friendly around Hanford. Storekeepers sometimes "carried" Indian and white families through the winter; one remembered that an Indian man came in one spring to determine the amount he owed, saying, "OK, I go catch wild horses, sell 'em, and be back," and he did. Often in earlier days the Indians came to the river bottoms for wintering.

The river was everyone's lifeblood, not only for water, but for fun. The colorful riverboats *Umatilla* (more or less a workboat), *Twin Cities, Mountain Gem, Inland Empire, T. J. Peel* and the little *Hanford Flyer* were as much household words as Ford or Honda might be today. When the boats were free, they offered excursion trips, especially for special holidays or events. Memorably lively was the celebration at Wallula when the Celilo Canal downriver was opened in 1915, and a boatload of dignitaries came upriver.

One crossed the river on cable ferries where the Columbia was narrow, such as at White Bluffs, Hanford and Wallula. Ice in winter often interfered with their operations, piling up in dangerous floes. The river was too broad for a cable ferry between Kennewick and Pasco; so the pioneers perilously walked across the railway bridge over the Columbia, looking between the ties at the swift-flowing current. Farmers often built log rafts to transport their cattle and horses downriver.

One of the most curious cargos passing through on swift express trains was raw silk from Japan, so perishable and valuable that during fuel and water stops, guards emerged to surround the trains.

Some men acquired enough irrigated land to become wealthy. Pioneer Frank W. Schunemann came from California with six children and two wagons, about all they had, and later held splendid farmland through what is now downtown Pasco, two miles long and a mile wide. Schunemann sold most of his holding to investor James A. Moore of Seattle, who built a pretentious mansion adjacent to the river for his wife, who died before enjoying it. Sold to Thomas Carstens, the property became a cattle ranch and at one time had five miles of Columbia River frontage.

Times changed and the lands were broken up. The Moore mansion became a speakeasy during Prohibition, the best night club in the area and, beautifully restored, a fine restaurant today. The owners keep unraveling the place's history, including discovery of a secret compartment in an attic room, just large enough to hide someone or something. There was an underground passage to the river for receiving illicit liquor, which made a handy septic tank.

Meanwhile, the very aspect that made the Tri-Cities so desolate became an asset—seemingly limitless open space. On April 6, 1926, Varney Air Lines, later a part of the new company called United Air Lines, initiated air mail service from Pasco to Elko, Nevada—somewhat inauspiciously when an incoming Varney airplane had engine failure over Wallula and was forced to land in the desert. However, an enthusiastic crowd watched a stagecoach arrive, symbolically carrying mail from Spokane to be sent to Elko. With much fanfare in 1976,the flight was commemorated in the same kind of airplane, a Swallow biplane.

After the Japanese attacked Pearl Harbor in December of 1941 the United States Nary purchased 2,285 acres north of Pasco for training navy aviators. During the next two years, eight hundred men went through primary flight training without a fatality. In December 1941, the first detachment of WAVES (female naval personnel) ever quartered on a naval station came to Pasco. On the Columbia River southeast of Pasco, the United States Army built a large Holding & Reconsignment Point operated by the Transportation Corps—a sort of way station for outgoing supplies, since seaports were overloaded with activity. Much of the material went to the Soviets as Lend-Lease.

That was only the beginning. Quietly in late 1942, mysterious government men asked strange questions and grimly looked over the half-deserted lands nearby. They were silent as to their objectives, even after February 23, 1943, when the U.S. government started proceedings under the War Powers Act to condemn 193,833 acres in Benton County for the Hanford Atomic Engineering Project. Included within the acreage were the towns of Hanford, White Bluffs and Richland. The following week the government leased an acreage of similar size and put a "hold" on new construction for still another 70,000 acres.

The site had abundant water, electricity from Grand Coulee and Bonneville dams, and remote lands—all required for the mysterious project. Four 6-foot diameter pipelines carried water thirteen miles from the Columbia to a "secret" building being constructed.

Uncommunicative, polite men came to each home, said the owners would receive "adequate compensation" and inventoried every bit of the contents right down to pencils. They went away, and still the residents did not know why they were being moved, only that they must go soon. They were told that, if they knew the reason, they would be proud to cooperate.

Some people called it "The Exodus." Twelve hundred uprooted residents moved, most of them philosophically. A few stunned homeowners received only thirty days of eviction notice, and after the government paid fair compensation for their properties, bulldozers came in and covered up most of the homes. The town of White Bluffs was almost leveled; only a couple of brick buildings and the old cable ferry ramp indicate that it ever existed.

Next came an influx of workers, engineers and scientists, about fifty-thousand of them, also close-mouthed. Across the sagebrush flats south of Saddle Mountain at old Hanford, an enormous camp of trailer houses was established, housing about thirteen thousand people. Newspapers were requested to keep to a minimum any news about the influx of people (the author indeed found the wartime newspapers extraordinarily uninformative). Workers were forbidden to tell their relatives and acquaintances exactly where they were; they could be addressed only at a post office box in Yakima. Since workdays were long and days off limited, workers really could not go anywhere. The wind blew. The dust came. The wind blew. Some workers could not stand the secrecy, isolation and particularly the wind, which came to be known as the "termination wind," causing them to leave the Project.

Surveyors canvassed Tri-Cities area residents to see if they could house "war workers." Restaurants in the Tri-Cities were overwhelmed and ran out of food; one of their biggest headaches was obtaining servers, and government authorities asked women if they could donate two or three hours a day "for the war effort." Pasco had an acute shortage of milk, indeed, a lively black market in milk, caused by a shortage of costly dairy-cattle feed and the appropriation of available milk for government use. Higher wages at the engineering project drew farm workers, and vegetables and fruit rotted in the field, even though the crops were designated for government workers' use.

At tiny Richland the government designed "The Village," with substantial homes and a shopping center, not exactly unattractive, but painted military gray and of forthright design. Before anyone would have believed it possible, people moved in.

The government offered to build one Protestant church and one Catholic church; other religions were on their own. People of various Protestant denominations worshiped together so harmoniously that, even today, they prefer to stay together as Central United Protestant Church.

But the gray buildings housing whatever they contained grew from the sand, and knowing people came and went from the buildings, saying nothing. Under an assumed name, the famed nuclear scientist Enrico Fermi spent time at the facility in consultation. Only after World War II was concluded with the startling explosions of the world's first atomic bombs did most of the workers know, and the Tri-Cities residents and world know what was being researched and produced there.

From 1944 until recent times the process leading to the manufacture of plutonium was performed at the Hanford site. There were two main steps in this process—the irradiation or bombardment of uranium metal in the reactors and the chemical separation processes necessary to recover useful plutonium from the irradiated fuel elements. Eight reactors were built quite close to the Columbia River for easy access to cooling water. Each heavy concrete building had its own cooling building, where the water was circulated, treated and eventually returned to the river. The reactors' end product, the irradiated uranium, was then transferred for chemical treatment. The chemical separation plants were deliberately located high on a plateau near the center of the Hanford site, far above the water table of the Columbia River, because there are admittedly some nasty chemical by-products that must be carefully captured and controlled. No plutonium is being produced at this writing; the ninth and last production reactor was ordered shut down permanently in 1991.

The eight original reactors are deactivated, standing like artifacts from a bygone age, ss indeed they are. Hanford Project workers used to call them "uranium piles," because the buildings look like a pile of concrete. Some say the first Hanford reactor should be declared a National Historic Site. The B Reactor, which produced the first plutonium for the atomic bomb tested at Trinity Site, New Mexico, was declared a National Historical Mechanical Engineering Landmark in 1976, a milestone in the U.S. Atomic Energy program.

The emphasis on this vast reservation now is cleanup of old wastes, not carelessly handled at the time but placed in temporary storage tanks scheduled for more permanent disposal later. Authorities have designated specific soil areas according to the degree of contamination and fenced them off stoutly until they are cleared for use. The chemical separation wastes still containing radioactive material will be solidified in either a glass or thick grouting and left in the ground. Controversy rages on the subject, but the State of Washington and two federal agencies have agreed on a thirty-year "Tri-Party Agreement for Cleanup."

After World War II, much of the government's "hands-on" work at Hanford was assigned under contract to private corporations—Westinghouse Hanford Company, Battelle Memorial Institute, Kaiser Engineers Hanford Company, and the Hanford Environmental Health Foundation. Also having facilities on site are U. S. Ecology and the Washington Public Power Supply System (WPPSS).

During 1972, the WPPSS decided to build five reactors at Hanford to produce electrical power (1n 1992 20 percent of the nation's power came from nuclear plants). Hanford's ninth reactor had produced considerable electricity as a byproduct of plutonium manufacture from the 1960s until 1987. A combination of a recession, costly labor strife, and antagonistic public sentiment after the Three Mile Island nuclear accident caused WPPSS to fail financially in 1983, leaving bondholders unpaid, one of the worst public financial debacles in history. Washingtonians said WPPSS or "Whoops" was a suitable name.

In addition to working on costly but essential cleanup, the private firms at Hanford researched exciting projects: a tiny nuclear reactor for power in space to serve the computers, communications equipment, and so on; better designs for nuclear-powered electrical generating plants; new alloys for longer fuel lifetime in future nuclear energy plants. At the Fast Flux Test Facility, materials testing is carried out, for example, to improve strengths of alloys, to produce isotopes for cancer treatment and to develop spinoff nuclear applications such as luggage inspection at airports.

Visitors would enjoy seeing the Hanford Science Center, the Fast Flux Test Facility and the WPPSS Visitor Center, all open to the public. Since authorities do not want strangers wandering around the Hanford lands—for their own good, as well as fearing terrorists—the grounds are patrolled by boat and helicopter and are off-limits to hunters and hikers.

The presence of such an enormous vacant landmass has attracted elk, several hundred mule deer, coyotes, raptors and waterfowl. Hanford authorities do not interfere with the animals but routinely monitor any dead birds or animals accidentally killed within the surrounding area. The Hanford Reach of the Columbia River, over 50 miles of free-flowing water, is home to blue heron, hatching geese and ducks, curlews, bald and golden eagles and hordes of small birds who favor the myriad deserted islets and marshes of this beautiful section of the Columbia. Water quality of the Columbia is tested frequently, and consistently receives top ratings, according to monitors. Boaters and fishermen enjoy the Hanford Reach.

Hanford is a National Environmental Research Park and has designated a 120-square-mile portion over the Rattlesnake Hills as an Arid Lands Ecology Reserve. Graduate students come from distant universities to study in this outdoor laboratory, still essentially as it was at Lewis and Clark's time. Students can view the natural regenerative processes after a grass fire, or see bobcats, badgers and coyotes having their young. North of Pasco the Columbia's Ringgold Hatchery enhances salmon production.

There is a widely based movement to have the Hanford Reach declared a Wild and Scenic River, prohibiting yet another dam proposed for that last open-river segment. It seems only fair that this one free-flowing, natural section should remain as an outdoor Columbia River Museum. The Reach also teems with spawning fall chinook salmon.

Because of historic floods and the backup of water from McNary Dam, the Corps of Engineers has confined the Columbia River through the Tri-Cities between levees up to 8 feet high. There is talk about persuading the Corps to lower the levees, so residents can have better access to the river—or even see it more easily, now that McNary Dam has largely eliminated flood concerns. To be sure, a handful of hotels and restaurants overlook the river, providing docks for patrons who come by boat of a summer evening. A cruise boat operates locally.

On the Kennewick side, about a quarter-mile-wide shelf of land stretches without levees for about five miles as Columbia Park. Buildings in the park were designed to cope with the probability that they would be inundated from time to time. Here, residents enjoy watching all manner of water events—the Columbia Cup for Unlimited Hydroplanes in July, the Christmas Lights Boat Parade, a big Salmon Derby in September, windsurfing and other spectator sports.

The slack water created behind McNary Dam, Lake Wallula, overran low areas upriver to form ideal wetlands for waterfowl; hundreds of varieties of birds are counted. On Clover Island, a natural island beyond the levees, the Port of Pasco and a few other businesses enjoy a parade of wildlife past their office windows—ducks and ducklings, mink, fish jumping, even a rare spotted sandpiper strolling across the lawn. An elk lives in downtown Kennewick, and deer meander through Pasco's port property, gazing unafraid at the proliferation of barges and tugs that come upriver from Astoria or Portland on the Columbia River.

Chapter 17

Traffic on the Marine Highway

Sternwheelers operated far upriver to the Snake as early as gold rush days. The shallow-draft, narrow-hulled sternwheeler was said to travel on "mists," her paddles hardly biting the water. Captains sometimes backed up narrow channels; they claimed that this made the boat more maneuverable in tight quarters. Sidewheelers required too much channel, and propeller-driven boats too much water.

The first paddlewheel steamer, the Hudson's Bay Company's *Beaver*, came to the Columbia River in 1836. However, Chief Factor John Mcloughlin at Fort Vancouver, was disenchanted with using ships to supply northern posts; he ordered the *Beaver* north into Puget Sound to use Nisqually as a base.

In the mid-1850s a pioneer on the Willamette River, with more verve than grace, designed an odd paddlewheeler powered by six horses on a treadmill aboard ship. The next powered craft to enter the river was a screwdriven steamer, the *Massachusetts*, bringing army troops in May 1849, to staff the new military forts on the river. A year later the Pacific Mail Steamship Company sent the wooden twin-screw steamer *Carolina* to call at Astoria and Portland, more or less the beginning of regular mail service.

But it was the ungainly 90-foot sidewheel steamer *Columbia*, built of odds and ends at Astoria, that charmed Oregonians—for she was all theirs. The boat's shallow draft enabled her to navigate the shallow Willamette River and bring eagerly awaited mail from Astoria directly to Portland. She was the first of many passenger/freight steamers to work the river, followed by boats such as *Lot Whitcomb*, *Belle*, *Wallamet* and *Fashion* ("fashioned" from then-retired Columbia's engines and parts of the *James P. Flint*).

By 1855, one could travel from Astoria to the Snake River, usually changing boats three times: at Portland, the Cascades and The Dalles. There were also short portage roads between boats at the Cascades and The Dalles. From the Cascades to The Dalles, a partnership of Bradford & Company and L. W. Coe offered the *James P. Flint* and the *Mary* (which figured in the Indian war).

Bradford & Coe maintained a freight trail and then a railroad on the less precipitous north shore. On the south shore in October of 1855, army troops built a short portage trail around the Cascades. Soon entrepreneur W. R. Kilborn put teams on the road, in turn eclipsed by construction of the Oregon Portage Railroad by Joseph S. Ruckel and Harrison Olmstead. It had only wooden rails reinforced by iron, the cars pulled by mules. At The Dalles, Orlando Humason operated a fourteen-mile freight wagon portage service over the hills.

Meanwhile, under the leadership of riverboat captain J. C. Ainsworth, the Union Transportation Line was formed, a loose association of boat owners. They ordered a special locomotive to serve a portage railroad being built for The Dalles connection. Until completion of the railroad, the company lent the miniature locomotive to Ruckel for the Cascades. It was scarcely 6 feet tall with a 5-foot boiler and was dubbed the "Pony." On its initial run several formally clad dignitaries insisted on riding in the cab (which had no enclosure) and arrived scarcely recognizable from grime and soot.

Instead of fighting each other, the boat and portage road owners merged, forming a new firm named Oregon Steam Navigation Company (OSN) incorporated in 1860 by Ainsworth, Jacob Kamm (a fine mechanical engineer), D. F. Bradford, L. W. Coe and others. Into the common pot went the chief steamers on the routes and both portage railroads. When a real railroad was finished on the north shore, OSN discontinued Ruckel's railroad and moved the "Pony" to The Dalles.

For decades, the river was securely tied up in this giant monopoly. There were occasional competitors, but OSN either bankrupted them by short-rating for as long as necessary or bought them out. In 1862, for a whopping $10,000 annually, OSN bribed a rival to refrain from competing on the Columbia and ply only the Willamette River.

Columbia River shipping was instantly a profitable business, chiefly because of the gold strikes upriver and in Idaho. High but not outrageous rates were charged; however, a capacity load of five hundred passengers, each paying $23 for passage from Portland to the Walla Walla River port Wallula), amounted to $11,500 per trip! Not to mention a whole deck full of freight. Later, when railroads came, a handsome hotel, the Umatilla House at The Dalles, housed travelers in style. It had two baths for 123 rooms plus a lavatory in the basement. Randall Mills in *Stern-Wheelers Up Columbia* said it was ". . . the best outside of Portland, in spite of its notoriously friendly fleas and occasionally chummy bedbugs and lice. Its fittings were elegant. ... [A guest] would get no single room—if he were lucky he only shared the room with three strangers." (Randall V. Mills, *Stern-Wheelers up Columbia* [Lincoln: University of Nebraska Press, 1947 and 1974], p. 45.)

For years the steamer *Colonel Wright*, built by R. R. Thompson and L. W. Coe in 1858, and initially captained by Leonard White, served the route from Celilo Falls to the Snake River. By 1866, there were other boats: *Nez Perce Chief, Yakima,*

Spray, one of which left Celilo landing every second day at 4:30 A.M.. and arrived at Lewiston two days later. Travelers bound for Salt Lake City and beyond got off at Umatilla, where four stage lines operated.

When the initial stockholders of OSN began to think about retirement, financier Henry Villard bought the whole conglomerate, renaming it Oregon Railway and Navigation Company to reflect the burgeoning railway construction era. Steam navigation would decline in direct proportion to the rise of railway travel in the Northwest.

By 1905 the Union Pacific chuffed along the Oregon side of the river, and in 1908 James J. Hill's Spokane, Portland & Seattle Railway ran along the north bank. Hill granted rights to the Great Northern and Northern Pacific to use his rails, then acquired the Portland-Astoria line. Determined to best archrival E. H. Harriman, financier of Southern Pacific and the Union Pacific, Hill proceeded to buy two ocean vessels and offer train service to San Francisco by placing the cars on the steamers.

The steamboats lasted far into the twentieth century. In their heyday the steamboats were as romantic as the Mississippi riverboats and faced far greater challenges on the treacherous Columbia River. As the nineteenth century wore on, the sternwheeler fleet became more sophisticated, adding vessels with carpets and shiny brassware, filigreed wood accents and polished balustrades. Meals were served on white linen cloths. One main salon boasted a grand piano, and many had gentlemen's salons where the smoke of the best Havanas swirled around the heads of natty businessmen, one foot on the rail as they enjoyed glasses of imported liquor.

Among the most splendid boats, primarily on the lower river between Portland and the Cascades or between Portland and Astoria, were the *Daisy Ainsworth, Wide West, Bailey Gatzert* and *T. J. Potter,* the latter sporting the largest plate glass mirror in the Northwest and a bird's-eye maple grand piano. In a spirit of fun the steamers loved to run impromptu races, the passengers cheering all the way, and no one ever bested the *Telephone* (1885 to 1918).

Sailings were not always smooth. Above the Cascades in 1858, the *Venture,* with forty passengers aboard, cast loose before getting up enough steam and shot through the Cascades rapids stern first, fetching up on a rock. The boat was undamaged, and no one was killed except a hysterical passenger who dove overboard. On the Willamette the *Gatzert's* boiler blew up due to negligence of the attendants, sending cargo and passengers hurtling in all directions. Twenty-eight people died, thirty were injured. The famed *Telephone* caught fire nearing Astoria in 1887; her quick-thinking captain opened the throttle and rammed her at twenty miles per hour into a shallow bank. The passengers were thrown or jumped onto the mud flats to safety (only one man, drunk in his cabin, died), and the Astoria fire crews doused the blaze to save the craft.

The run from Celilo to Wallula was not for the faint-hearted. A succession of rapids challenged the power of sternwheelers. Captains respected the Umatilla Rapids, not the roughest but about three miles long with no relief. Winds then as now howled through the broad canyon of the Columbia, walled by 1,000-foot bluffs near Wallula, where the canyon narrowed to produce a venturi effect. The river could go from flat calm to 5-foot waves within minutes. Dust storms lowered visibility, as settlers plowed the deep silty soils on the bluffs above.

The U.S. Army Corps of Engineers, which had come to build forts and military roads at mid-century, assumed responsibility for maintaining navigation on the Columbia River. J. C. Ainsworth complained to Lieutenant W. H. Heuer of the Corps about the dangers to his boats on Umatilla, Homely and John Day rapids. Heuer responded by surveying the three, and concentrated on removing John Day Rock, completed by 1873, the first permanent change on the Columbia River. As a stage connection, Umatilla was as wild west as any Dodge City. Ranches were springing up in response to the nutritious Oregon bunch grass, cattle and horse operations, not dirt farms, and the cowboys liked to party. Major stock auctions drew crowds, the first operated by Frank Wink at The Dalles. Cattle and sheep were shipped by sternwheelers to market, too.

Arlington once was the largest wool-shipping port in the United States. Sheep trailed through the dusty streets to a sandbar on the river to be held in corrals and sheared, their wool bundled for direct shipment by boat. It also was a place to let off steam. Poker or billiards bets could be a thousand dollars per game.

By 1896 the Cascade Locks were completed at a cost of almost four million dollars to speed transportation. Two locks along a 3,000-foot canal raised the boats 42 feet, eliminating the perils of the Cascades. From the Port of Cascades Locks Marine Park today, one may see the shadowy remains of that busy canal and the locomotive "Pony."

Burgeoning livestock marketing and increasing tonnage of grain spawned the initiation of tug and barge services. By 1908 Shaver Transportation Company used sternwheelers to shove rafts and escort ships; they were fast, tough and maneuverable.

The excursion sternwheeler *Columbia Gorge* operates each summer between Portland and Stevenson, going through the Bonneville Locks on some occasions, and the *Rose* operates on the Willamette. But the last working sternwheeler, the *Portland*, was retired in 1981. Her last captain was Gary Showalter. Former deckhand Kenneth Rea remembered nostalgically, "On a quiet night, moving up the Columbia, I just liked to hear the steam rushing through the stack and the soft whoosh of the paddles."

An ongoing obstacle to navigation was the wild water above The Dalles to Celilo Falls, conquered by installation of the Celilo Canal in 1915, eight and one-half miles long and about 8 to 9 feet deep, skirting the thundering falls frequented by Indian tribes for fishing since time immemorial. Four locks raised boats to the upper river. The canal made it possible to transport entire herds of cattle and sheep to market without the harrowing transfers from boat to boat.

Thus, construction of Bonneville Dam (and the later Dalles Dam) in the Columbia Gorge was not particularly related to a need for better lock-through than Celilo and Cascade Locks already provided. Rather it was in response to the growing need for electrical power, to stem repeatedly devastating floods when the Columbia rampaged, and to provide jobs for needy workers during the Depression. President Franklin D. Roosevelt was a believer in using the nation's rivers "to the utmost," and he was equally adamant about public versus private power.

In September 1933, Congress allocated $250,000 for surveys and $20 million for construction of Bonneville Dam. Since the location then was isolated, a residential village called Bonneville (Oregon) was built in 1934 for key employees involved in construction and later management of the hydroelectric facilities and fish ladders.

As in Grand Coulee, the general labor force was on its own; no facilities were provided except for a few tents with wooden floors. Eventually, a boarding house was built at Bonneville, but until then some workers slept in cars. A restaurant operator converted his three-sided woodshed into a bunkhouse, building four shelves to rent out to workers, three men and one woman. The woman said, "Oh mercy, it was cold! The first guy that got to his shelf was the one that got blankets because you stole them from everybody else. ... You wore your clothes, and shoes and boots."

Dry mesas and bluffs east of The Dalles.

There were very few women on the job, and homely or beautiful, they were sought after. Gambling was common, playing cards on a box or in a car. Poor conditions or not, workers were delighted to have a good-paying job. Some were residents unemployed since the sawmill closed in 1926. Workers would be covered with cement dust, dirty because sanitary facilities were scarce, but they ate well. They built simple homes with kerosene lights and outhouses, using water from the creek. Soon there were five restaurants and several taverns.

Although there are always rumors of men buried in concrete at dams, pouring techniques at Bonneville made this impossible. However, there were accidents from falling objects, and one summer, a repair barge was swept over a Bonneville spillway with three men killed. Reportedly, only nine men died in construction-related accidents. Concrete for the spillways was transported via buckets dangling from a highline across the river, so wide that sometimes the line disappeared into the fog. One brave man rode a bucket to watch operations as a spotter. To fend off cold in winter, he built a little steel stove on a platform in the bucket. Sparks flew all over in the wind.

Tour buses of people came to gawk at the progress of Bonneville Dam; then they would wind uphill to luxurious Cloud Cap Inn on the east face of Mount Hood.

All the time the dam was being built, a fish biologist was on hand to supervise the saving of salmon runs until fish ladders could be completed. A fish ladder is an ascending stairway with pools 16 feet by 40 feet, each 1 foot higher than the last, enabling migrating salmon to pass the dam. There are three ladders at Bonneville and others at all Columbia River dams up to Grand Coulee.

There was considerable controversy about the size of the locks and the wisdom of the construction of the dam, some people calling it a white elephant. Few could foresee the tremendous increase in demand for hydroelectric power, but during World War II the mushrooming industrial plants used all the power that Bonneville and Grand Coulee could put out. The two were and are on a grid that analyzes power needs, adjusting the amount of power generated. Franklin D. Roosevelt was there to dedicate Bonneville Dam's completion on September 28, 1937.

Low wheat prices during the Depression encouraged entrepreneurs to search for lower transportation rates. Veteran working sternwheel owner, Homer Shaver of Vancouver, and Lew Russell formed Shaver Forwarding Company to lease sternwheelers. They moved wheat out of the Horse Heaven Hills of Washington by truck to the river and downriver by barge.

Then the owner of a gasoline distributorship, Spokane businessman Kirk Thompson, sought cheaper delivery of petroleum. His brainchild, the *Mary Gail*, a sturdy 56-foot diesel twin-screw tug, came off the ways in November 1936 and went into service the following year. Under Thompson, Tidewater Barge Lines pioneered river shipping facilities. Elevators received grain at The Dalles,

Arlington, Hogue-Warner (across from Paterson), Umatilla, Port Kelly (for Walla Walla) and Pasco. Ocean-going ships loaded from other elevators downriver at or near Portland.

Fierce competition reigned for several decades. The battle really was between the two tough rivermen, Lew Russell and Slim Lappaluoto, the latter a sinewy, lanky young man working on the *Mary Gail*. When Thompson offered *Tidewater* for sale, Russell outbid Lappaluoto and formed Tidewater-Shaver Barge Lines. Lappaluoto obtained financing and started the competitive Inland Navigation Company. He assisted a colleague, Carl Floten, in developing a dual-purpose barge that could safely transport petroleum upriver and convert to hauling grain downriver.

The two companies engaged in a Columbia River war, no holds barred, in rate-cutting, customer snatching and physical confrontation just short of mayhem. On one occasion a Lappaluoto barge got stuck on a rock above Celilo Falls. Unable to rock it loose, Lappaluoto filed an insurance claim for it. The insurance carrier put salvage up for bids and Lappaluoto put in a low bid, again outbid by Russell, who persuaded Grand Coulee Dam personnel to release three extra feet of water to float it. Russell's men waited below, and as the vessel careened crew-less through the rough Washington channel (the falls are in the middle, Celilo Canal on the Oregon side), they took it under control.

In a complex 1958 sale, Lappaluoto sold to his partners, part of Inland eventually going to Crowley Maritime Corporation, and went into Gulf of Mexico shipping in the 1960s. At meetings of old-time river people, the Sagebrush Sailors, the two old titans—Russell and Lappaluoto—traded good-natured insults.

Meanwhile, Tidewater remained a major force on the river. In 1983, the president and general manager of Tidewater, Ray Hickey, purchased the company from Lew Russell and family, then bought Columbia Marine Lines from Crowley. Today Tidewater Barge Lines holds a premier position on the river, eighteen tugs and one hundred barges operating from Lewiston to Astoria. Shaver Transportation Company and Brix Maritime (formerly Knappton) still run the river (1992) but have added powerful ocean tugs.

Until the addition of the McNary (1953), The Dalles (1957) and John Day (1968) dams, the Columbia River still showed its muscle. The tug captains welcomed the challenges; indeed, most of the old-timers moved on after the dams were built. It just was not exciting enough to work in slack water or ponds.

At mid-century over forty tugs worked between Portland and Lewiston. Loaded barges drew 6-1/2 to 7 feet of water, and many of the worst rapids were less than 6 feet deep; petroleum or freight had to be unloaded to reduce draft. Often, barges scraped bottom or hit rocks in the tortuous channels, even though the U.S. Army Corps of Engineers removed some of the worst channel obstacles. Until dams on the Snake River were built, most shipping stopped at Pasco.

Veteran Captain Keith Rodenbaugh says rapids were hard on engines. "We normally had 3,000 to 5,000 horsepower on the tugs and entered rapids at normal speed. If the load started getting away, we cranked in full power and frequently would blow a piston. We drifted back out and fixed the engine, tried again, and eventually got through."

Tug captains found the exit upstream from Celilo Canal always a thrill. Re-entry to the river was at a 45-degree angle to its flow and the 450-foot procession of tug and two or three barges could not turn until clear of the canal. Finally, with a powerful roar, the tug would manhandle the barges around, but the falls would be alarmingly close astern. "If we ever lost an engine ...

There were no thrusters then, the small boosters on modern supertugs that move the hull sideways, but tugs either had huge sweeps up to eight feet long or three or four rudders across the tug's stern.

"On the tug *Winquatt* we had a big rudder in the middle and another on each side, like a barn door. To grasp the power of these tugs—there were three 1-1/4-inch cables attaching the tug to the barge, and in rapids, if you ever put the rudder hard-over, you would snap those cables like string," said Rodenbaugh.

The worst rapids included Hell Gate, just above Wishram or Celilo, where there were perpendicular bluffs (peppered with Indian drawings—spiders, scorpions, sun dials). There the tug/barge had to make a 180 degree swing. All the while, the entering Deschutes River ran across the Columbia to bounce off the cliffs and roll back in a swirl. Other difficult spots were at the entrance of the rushing John Day River and the lengthy Umatilla Rapids. In the mid-1940s, a terrific storm arose suddenly with blizzard conditions, raising huge waves above Umatilla. Two boats and a barge were wrecked, but no one was hurt.

During spring high water, the Columbia's rampage frequently spread over lowlands and snatched chunks from the cliffs. The Celilo Canal would completely disappear, the masonry under water; so operations had to be suspended. The infamous flood of 1948 shut down shipping for days. Captain Rodenbaugh says the current was so swift the Columbia was crowning in the middle. The same flood completely inundated the town of Vanport. Upstream, south of Wenatchee, the river rose so high it neared the lower face of Rock Island Dam. The turbines ceased to operate, because there was insufficient fall of water to generate power.

Before the creation of pools or slack water by the dams, eastern Washington/Oregon weather was colder. The Columbia frequently froze over solid. In 1884, when snows buried the streets of The Dalles, an unpopular entrepreneur charged twenty-five cents to cross the streets through snow tunnels he had dug. In the 1940s powerful tugs like the *Viking* under Captain Cliff Light acted as icebreakers so The Dalles ferry could run and tugs with barges might move. In 1949, a freak cold snap struck, freezing the Columbia to a depth of 5 to 6 feet and the Celilo Canal totally. The tug *Winquatt* with Rodenbaugh in command was entrapped in ice for days near The Dalles. With the wind-chill factor, the temperature was -25° F.

Like a lion in chains, its waters smoothed by the dams, the Columbia River still storms and swirls. Professional fishing guide Christof Cook of Umatilla was once swamped near dusk by a sudden fifty-mile-per-hour west wind. Before he gained shore in the darkness, he almost gave up swimming. He let his feet sink and touched bottom.

One sudden winter windstorm in the area clocked winds of 102 miles per hour, blowing huge trucks on their sides, and breaking brick walls and windows. Another odd phenomenon on the river is winter fog, dense curtains that lie only 5 or 6 feet deep over the river. Sitting in a boat, one is in fog; standing up, one's head may be in sunshine. For days or weeks the river may be a pleasure, but its moods can change suddenly and violently.

The still-wild shore between The Dalles and Wallula is broken only briefly by a few tiny settlements and the lush, irrigated vineyards of Columbia Crest Vineyards midway. Beaver, muskrat, and otter glide unafraid, and a part of the Pacific Flyway—the Umatilla Wildlife Refuge from Irrigon to Crow Butte—hosts flocks of birds. On the big Blalock Islands in the center of the refuge, the soft rush of wings and the lap of water mark the passage of white pelicans, egrets and sandhill cranes.

Chapter 18

Fishing and Logging

The rapid current of the Columbia, so formidable to mariners, was an attraction for salmon. Some people claimed that the Columbia was the world's richest fishing river. Certainly Northwest Indians along the Columbia River's twelve-hundred-mile length lived comfortably from its bounty. Possibly three-fourths of all the fish taken above Bonneville Dam came from Indian dip-net fishermen at Celilo, before it was stilled in 1957. An Indian not only fed his family but gained enough fish for bartering with other tribes. Latter-day biologists claim that the Indians harvested eighteen million tons of fish per year from the Columbia in the nineteenth century.

The wonderful salmon runs were utterly predictable, the different subgroups arriving at specific times. There were sockeye (called blueback by the Columbia fishermen), silversides, steelhead (a seagoing trout related to salmon), the Chinook (favored by canners) and until Grand Coulee Dam was completed, a splendid June run chinook, huge and prime. Rivermen called them channel fish or June hogs; others dubbed them royal chinook.

The last few hundred miles of the Columbia yield particularly prime salmon. It is early in the spawning run; their stomachs are empty, and their bodies are freed of sea lice by entering fresh water. By the time spawners approach their native streams far upriver, having gone without food for days, they are the "living dead"; indeed, early explorers unwittingly ate them at this stage and became violently ill. Upriver Indians dried such fish or made jerky out of them, which made them edible.

Hudson's Bay Company factors were the first to use salmon as a salable crop, salting them in barrels for export to England or Australia. The fish were reduced to oil, as well. The first American fish merchant did the Columbia no favors; Captain John Dominis of the brig *Owyhee* lightly pickled, salted and transported fifty-three barrels of salmon to Boston in 1830, pronounced almost inedible.

Boston ice merchant Nathaniel J. Wyeth organized the Columbia River Fishing and Trading Company and led two unsuccessful expeditions to the Portland area in 1832 and 1834. He landed on the pleasant island later called Sauvie and founded a farm he called Fort William, but by 1835, he was gone, his failure due to ill luck more than ineptness. The island was settled in 1838 by Laurent Sauvie, who operated a Hudson's Bay Company dairy farm.

Chinook Indians lived on the island, dug camas roots and wapato (which Indian women pried loose with bare toes from beneath the marsh waters), grew tobacco from seeds in wood ashes and fished for salmon. They used cedar bark nets nearly 200 feet long, weighted by rocks to hug the river bottom.

Shipping problems inhibited the fishing industry. The arrival in 1866 at Wahkiakum (north bank) of William and George Hume and Andrew S. Hapgood from California with their crude but effective canning methods initiated an incredible spiral of fishing frenzy, an intensive harvesting of salmon that lasted well into the 1900s. Only the depletion of the numbers of salmon slowed the industry.

By 1876, 450,000 cases (48 one-pound cans per case, totaling 21.6 million pounds) of canned salmon left Astoria or Portland annually for eastern America or foreign ports. This was largely the product of Hume canneries. By comparison, the average commercial catch during 1985 to 1989 was about nine million pounds annually.

Along the broad estuary, nets extended almost to mid-channel, a hard-cussing annoyance to ship captains. It was said the mighty Chinook salmon was dubbed the "channel fish" by upstream fishermen because it got through by following the ship channel.

Sea-hardened Scandinavians, particularly Finns, were attracted to the Columbia River, both for fishing and lumbering, an industry that soared to importance in the early 1900s. They fished in season, logged the balance of the time. With no particular regulation on fishing methods, the men trolled, manned gillnet boats, erected fish traps (particularly in Baker Bay) and set seine nets from shore. The traps collected sediment, too, contributing to the silting in of Baker's Bay.

On any fishing day a stranger arriving at Astoria by schooner was startled to see teams of horses far from shore, up to their bellies in water. On the shallow sand bars near the mouth of the Columbia, men buried a heavy log deep in the sand, attached one end of a seine net to it, then gave it to a waiting doryman. The rowers dragged the net in a large circle, returning to the beginning, where the net was quickly attached to horse teams and pulled swiftly out of the water. Or a team was used at each end of the net.

At The Dalles, where deep water extended to shore, dorymen laid a circle, and on shore, the land crew rushed to attach the lines to "the running team" that literally galloped up the bank to haul in the net before fish escaped. Fish companies had barns for the horses on shore there; at Astoria, they were often on barges. In the 1890s powerful purse-seine boats entered the scene but were soon ruled illegal. Later trollers operated offshore, intercepting the salmon before they could enter the river.

Fishermen considered fishing sites their property, and if anyone planned to drive new fish-trap pilings, he almost needed a marshal to guard him; the gill netters would cast his boat loose or damage the pilings. Trollers carried barbed wire to throw into seine nets.

Territorial feelings ran high, leading to a "war" between Oregon gillnetters and Washington fish-trap men at Sand Island in Baker's Bay. Oregonians claimed their neighbors were taking an undue share of the salmon and, three hundred strong, stormed over to rip out nets. Sixty Washington National Guardsmen came to occupy and keep order at Sand Island, and two weeks later, federal soldiers from Fort Canby ousted the Guard and replaced them on Sand Island to keep order. Washington Guardsmen retreated to Ilwaco. Oregonians were outraged that federal troops had occupied Sand Island, a favorite fishing ground, and sent four hundred Oregon National Guardsmen to Astoria. On both shores, there was more social fervor than battle fever, with grand military balls and outings, parade drill and budding romances. It was the fishermen who were delighted to see the Guardsmen leave, when their respective states said they were costing too much money. That the state line was in the middle of the river was reiterated, and neither state had authority beyond that point.

The original boundary at the middle of the channel proved impractical over the years. Sand Island has moved dramatically from currents and weather; earliest surveys showed it abreast of Point Adams, and by 1868, it was almost halfway across the Columbia's entrance. Today the original wide channel constituting that state border has narrowed to hug the Washington shore in the heavily silted-up Baker's Bay. Yet the state border runs through that same channel, just barely offshore from Washington—causing no end of jurisdictional problems. Furthermore, the main ship channel is much farther south today.

To obtain a fair price for their fish, fishermen formed the Fishermen's Protection Union at Astoria in May 1879; thereafter, officials negotiated a fixed price annually in advance of fishing season. Packers or canneries countered with cooperatives, such as the Columbia River Packers shortly after 1900. Before that, the Humes and Barby of Astoria and Seuferts at The Dalles dominated the industry.

Quite a few fishwheels operated at the Cascades, the first credited to Samuel Wilson in 1879, and the first patented wheel to Thornton Williams. Most Cascades fishermen sold to Warrendale Canneries (started about 1876), six miles west of Bradford Island, or to Rooster Rock Cannery, farther upriver. But few of the Cascades fishwheels were truly effective and some experimental; the swift and myriad channels of the rapids from The Dalles to Celilo Falls were more suitable for them. About twenty fishwheels operated there, either owned outright or controlled through purchase contracts by Seufert Canning Company. Operating from land (reefs or islands in the channel) or from barges, the fishwheel looked something like a waterwheel, only there were buckets instead of blades. The arms on the Seufert wheels usually were 20 feet long. They scooped up fish attracted to the narrow, swift channels and dumped them into fixed containers up to 50 feet deep. Adjustment for depth was critical to intercept the fish. Men had to operate silently lest they alarm the fish. Paint repelled them; so, the wheels remained natural. Most important to success was placement of the device, requiring an astute analysis of the salmon's path upriver —near this bank, by that reef. According to Francis Seufert: "What attracted the salmon to one place over another no one knew. ... These salmon followed definite paths in the river." (Francis Seufert, *Wheels of Fortune* [Oregon Historical Society, 1980], P. 25.)

When volume was low, fishwheel crews sent catches downriver by stringing them on a rope, then fastening the string to an empty barrel. They alerted the cannery downstream to watch for and pick up the catch. Fish pirates became wise to this method and snatched the fish or, in the dark of night, stole fish from operating wheels. Downstream pickup men for Warrendale's once found a naked dead man in the eddy, along with the barrel.

In 1907 Seufert's built cableways from receiving stations on shore to operating fishwheels for transporting caught salmon to the cannery; otherwise, scows with powerful motors picked up fish from the bins.

They had to be strong. The vicious eddies that had drowned Hudson's Bay voyageurs still could swallow, stern or bow first, an entire boat that became caught in a vortex. Whirlpools as wide as 20 feet in diameter were common, and when the whirlpool broke, a huge boil arose, as much as 5 feet higher than the surrounding water. Worse yet, no one could thoroughly predict just where a whirlpool would open.

Celilo Indian fishermen sold most of their catch to Seufert's at the same rate as union fishermen. Some thirty or forty families lived near Celilo permanently, and migrants swelled the population to about one thousand people in fishing season. They built sturdy scaffolds of lashed logs that hung over the boiling cauldron of the river's many-channeled falls. They used no safety ropes (it was considered unmanly), and if they fell in, it was almost certain death. Some must have been relieved when the government required them to use a safety rope. Seufert's built cableways directly to prime sites to enable the Indian to ride out safely to his scaffold and send the fish back. By acquiring shorelands whenever offered for sale, Seufert's soon controlled that part of the river and denied access to fish-buyer competitors coming up from Astoria.

At The Dalles, single transient workers lived in bunkhouses and ate in mess houses. They were an orderly lot, heading to town on their day off for some carousing or conversation.

At Astoria, with more taverns and bawdy houses to choose from, the fishermen/loggers were a pretty raunchy group during their leisure time. Some wound up unwillingly far at sea. Working with unscrupulous tavern operators, ship owners shanghaied men—drugged or drunk, then took them aboard ships as crew. Authorities finally had to step in and sharply curb these practices. As decent women came to Astoria, a close-knit, religious family community of Finns grew up, still cohesive today.

Cannery workers at Astoria and The Dalles were almost always Chinese, because they worked for low wages and also had strong, nimble hands required in butchering and canning fish. The managers contracted with one person called the China Boss, telling him the numbers needed of each specialty, and the crew would materialize. The China Boss also managed the crew on-site. Most of these hard working, first-generation Americans planned to return to China but seldom did.

In 1926 the use of fishwheels was declared illegal in Oregon (and in 1934 in Washington) because they were too efficient, a contention severely attacked by Seufert family members. Gladys Seufert claims the problem was political, not actual, upriver versus downriver, resulting in the taking of more fish by gillnetters and seiners than fishwheels ever did.

Seufert's diversified by canning fruits and vegetables from the Hood RiverValley until it ceased operations in 1954. After 1897, when an irrigation system was installed there, the famous Clark seedling strawberry, apples and pears dominated the area. Some defunct logging firms went into fruit production; today the valley produces over thirty percent of the winter pears in the United States.

The completion of The Dalles Dam in 1957 and subsequent flooding of Celilo Falls was the severe blow that ended Indian fishing. Yakima, Umatilla, Warm Springs and Nez Perce Indians received $23.5 million for their ancestral fishing rights. As water rose behind The Dalles Dam, tearful Indians watched unbelieving as the falls quieted.

According to Gladys Seufert, a diver recently found that the infamous Columbia River silt has covered all but 20 feet of ancient Celilo Falls, formerly 50 feet high in normal water.

Both Seufert's and the Hume canneries processed sturgeon at times. Dwelling sluggishly near the river bottom, sturgeon attain several hundred pounds; indeed, giants of over a half ton have been taken, requiring teams of horses to drag them out. In earlier days eels were numerous around The Dalles, hanging from the banks and the spillways of the Celilo Canal; sturgeon especially bit on hooks baited with decaying eels.

As early as 1878, Astoria's cannery magnate Hume began agitating for salmon management or conservation. A fish commission established in 1891 by the Washington State Legislature urged Alfred E. Houchen and John McGowan to move their Bear River tideland private hatchery, ten years old, over to the Chinook River, where it became the first official state hatchery in 1895. The operation closed in 1935, but in 1969, using volunteers chiefly and especially led by Mel Leback, the hatchery reopened as Sea Resources.

Beginning as early as 1910, Oregon and Washington established a joint committee to work on fish policies. The problem always has been enormously complex, involving escapements (or lack thereof) upstream through dams, divisions between Indians, commercial and sports fishermen, divisions between Canada and the United States and so on. As late as January 1991, a major conference on the subject held at Kennewick, Washington, attempted to air the problems at least—if not the answers.

As mentioned previously, fishermen doubled as loggers. At first, the verdant forest covering both shores of the Columbia River, almost blotting out the sunlight, was considered a nuisance and an impediment to settlement. Portland was first known as "Stump Town," as the giant trees were sawed off with "misery whips" (two-man saws) a few feet off the ground. The stumps were whitewashed so that nighttime carriage travelers would not hit them.

The capital required of a logging firm tended to create large companies, but south of the Columbia in the Hood River Valley, Sterling Hanel founded a family enterprise in 1943, Hanel Lumber Company, that today has nearly three hundred employees, and is the only sawmill in the valley. Hanel's angle is to use small logs for creating dimensional lumber, and even smaller ones for chipping into wood chips to be shipped to market on Columbia River barges.

The pioneers burned forests to clear land, and natural droughts and breathtaking holocausts by Mother Nature destroyed vast areas. Notable was the Yacolt Burn of 1902, burning from the banks of the Columbia River halfway to Puget Sound. Historian Mark Parsons tells of three timbermen caught in the Yacolt Burn, taking refuge in a cave:

> Here they stayed while the night sky turned to screaming orange and reds. The big trees around them caught from the heat and exploded with deafening roars. Wild animals sought shelter with them in the corners of the cave, unaware of each other. ... On the third day they could come out of the cave but they could not walk the hot rocks. ... The countless stark sticks, that were three days ago giants of the woods, were now snags of the dead. (Mark E. Parsons, *Across Rushing Waters* [Camas, Washington: Mark E. Parsons, 1982], p. 56.)

Awesome was the devastation in 1933 of the Tillamook Burn, a super-fire that started accidentally near Glenwood, about twenty-five miles northwest of Portland, and exploded into an inferno that "crowned" (ran through the treetops), destroying 270,000 acres in twenty hours time, slowing somewhat but consuming another 40,000 acres before it was stopped, almost at the Pacific Ocean. Prime timber was reduced to firebrands propelled through the air by a self-generated wind or firestorm.

The flip side of the fire was that the forest was replanted with alacrity, one of the largest restoration projects ever tackled, and today the harvest of prime timber commences once more. Widespread destruction of forestlands came in May 1980, not from fire but from the concussion or blast from the Mount St. Helens eruption.

The earliest lumbering along the Columbia was to provide firewood for the sternwheelers' boilers, reportedly seventy-five cords per day in 1882 at Vancouver alone for boats plus meager settlers'needs.

Willamette settler Ewing Young and Solomon Smith of the Wyeth party built a sawmill in 1836, Hudson's Bay Company at Vancouver had a sawmill, Michael T. Simmons and Jacobo Hansaker each owned a family mill. It took demand from California's gold-rush population (and later, the need for lumber to rebuild fire-torn San Francisco) to spur major investors into lumbering. Some of the world's finest fir trees, rivaling the California redwoods in height, grew in Washington and Oregon. When World War I came, the resilient, tough Sitka spruce was in demand for aircraft.

The Portland *Oregonian*, then owned by Henry L. Pittock, had a hand in the formation of the Columbia River Paper Company at Camas in 1883, because a mill at Oregon City was unable to produce sufficient newsprint for the newspaper. As Georgia Pacific today, the mill manufactures fine papers and tissue, no newsprint. A pioneer company operated until recently at Bridal Veil, across the river from Washougal, sending logs down a flume to the mill below. Large timber companies opened along the Columbia downriver from Portland.

Loggers from Maine or Minnesota forests soon learned to saw the big firs several feet off the ground; when cut nearer the ground, a tree would gush forth with as much as a barrel of pitch. Men worked with hand saws and horse teams, then with oxen on skid roads (smaller tree trunks placed side by side to form a rolling road). The handler or bullwhacker walked beside yokes of five to ten beasts, goading them on profanely. That master of Northwest stories and ex-lumberjack, Stewart Holbrook, said in his book, Holy Old Mackinauw, that, when the bullwhacker swore, the very bark of trees smoked, curled up and fell to the ground. If invective failed to get results, the man was known to walk the backs of the team with his calked boots.

Later came steam engines or donkeys that, attached to cables running over pulleys fixed to a high spar or tree, hoisted logs to the staging area well above the forest floor. At Sedro-Woolley, Washington, a small company, Skagit Steel, adapted a Fordson tractor as a gas-driven "donkey." The company laid down ordinary peeled logs end to end from woods to mill or river port, installed large back wheels on the tractor, and ran the tractor on the log "track" to pull logs out of the woods singly or on cars.

Logs must be moved to mills, and as cutting moved farther back into the hills from the river, timbermen built low dams on small Columbia tributaries, such as the Wind River. They stockpiled logs all summer and fall, and in spring when the river was at flood stage, destroyed the holding dam to send the logs careening down to the Columbia. Woe to the person who happened to be on shore when the torrent came down, but then there were few settlers in the woods. This practice was curtailed by law some years later.

Companies built logging railroads to bring out the logs. Some were of dubious quality, snaking through hills at grades no one would believe possible and creeping over untrustworthy trestles (although the author is not aware of any collapsing with trains).

Typically the loggers sought raucous living on their days off. Portland's August Erikson catered to them with "The Workingman's Club," a night spot as spacious as the mountain forests. It reputedly had the longest bar in the world (684 feet), pipe organ music and the famous free lunch—huge platters of sausages and soft bread, roast beef and the trimmings. The Workingman's Club still operated in 1970, outlasting others such as Fritz's, Blazier's (a family in the logging business), the House of All Nations and the legendary Nancy Boggs who operated a whorehouse on a barge—moving it to a different Columbia or Willamette river location if the police became too heavyhanded.

In addition to the giant logging company pioneers like Frederick Weyerhaeuser and A. B. Hammond, "gyppo" loggers invaded the forests—family operations where mom cooked, dad and the boys did the logging. The gyppo logger's wife tended to be the "go-fer," bumping over rutted roads to get groceries, spare parts for machines, arrange for funds and—all too often—find and drag back home a drunk logger from one of the taverns (the operator obligingly dumped the man into the back of her car).

But all the lumber and fish money was building Columbia River economy in big towns like Vancouver, Washington, and its counterpart, Portland, Oregon. With the wealth of the Willamette Valley's farms to market, the lumber from the flanks of Mount Hood and Mount St. Helens stacked awaiting shipment, and tinned and salted salmon piling up, Portland especially became a busy seaport. Huge lumber schooners of ocean draft could sail right up the Columbia into the Willamette, dredged deeper by the Port of Portland, totally protected from the elements, and connecting to local railroads.

Chapter 19

Travel and Trivia • Tri-Cities and Down the River

Tri-Cities Visitor & Convention Area. At west end of Tri-Cities area. Serves the cities of Pasco, Kennewick, and Richland, as well as smaller nearby communities. Follow signs on I-80. Ask about boat charters and houseboats or sightseeing river cruises. www.visittri-cities.com

Full roster of major events for this lively multi-city area on both sides of the Columbia River. Among popular events are Red Wine and Chocolate February.. Lamb Weston Columbia Cup July (hydroplane race). *Numerous wineries in the area with their own events but:* Spring Barrel late April and Catch the Crush October should be noted. Cinco de Mayo, Christmas Boat Parade, and many other.

Hanford Reach National Monument honors the complex of Hanford, where scientists developed the atom bomb that ended World War II. President Clinton declared the site a monument in 2000. Ever since World War II scientists have worked on (among other challenges) the task of cleaning up the radioactive materials left over from the bomb creation.The Columbia River itself is not contaminated in the area; in fact, one of the cleanest portions of the entire river lies just north of Hanford where a major salmon spawning area thrives today. A portion of the Hanford Monument has never been developed (as a safety barrier) and is the source for study of natural grasses and animals. Visitor information and tours: www.fws.gov/hanfordreach/

Columbia River Journeys. A jet boat takes visitors on a tour of the Columbia River near the Hanford Reservation. Wildlife and scenery. www. columbiariverjourneys.com

History of the Columbia River. The following libraries have archival and other materials to enlighten the seeker more fully about the confluence of the Snake and Columbia River area: Mid-Columbia Regional Library, Kennewick; Franklin County Historical Museum, Pasco; East Benton County Historical Museum, Kennewick; Columbia Basin College library, Pasco.

Columbia River Exhibition of Science, History and Technology. CRESHT Museum for short. Opened in place of Science Museum that closed in 1995. Fine exhibits and programs on topics ranging from space and weather to Lewis & Clark or the Kennewick Man. www.cresht.org

Juniper Dunes Wilderness. As many as 155 species of birds have been noted at Potholes Reservoir north of Pasco and the Dunes, not sites you would expect in Washington.

Clover Island Marina Kennewick, has full facilities for boats and owners. A walking trail affords great views and appreciation of vivid sunsets. http://portofkennewick.org

Moore Mansion. A historical landmark overlooking the Columbia was built by real estate magnate James A. Moore in 1905 as a private home. In the 1920s it became a "speakeasy" with tunnels to the river and other aids to rum-running. In 2013 the home is a frequent venue for weddings and meetings. www.mooremansion.com

Tri-Cities Wine Festival. Since 1979, the annual festival continues to grow in importance with renowned judges and entries from the myriads of wine producers around the Tri-Cities. Early November.

Tri-Cities Bluegrass Festival. One of several eastern Washington venues for bluegrass festivals. This one is held at Sacajawea State Park at the confluence of the Snake and Columbia Rivers in early June. www.mctama.org

Howard Amon Park on the Richland side of the river is good for children. Mini-pool, playground, picnic sites.

Columbia Park. On Kennewick side next to "Blue Bridge" over the Columbia. Biking and walking trails. Boat launch.

Intercity Bridge. The longest cable-stay bridge in North America with a span of 981 feet. In late sun or moonlight it appears as if an ambitious spider erected it.

`Tridec. An organization seeking to assist businesses considering location to Tri-Cities, especially to take advantage of the infrastructure of support at the Hanford site. www.tridec.org

Wallula Gap National Landmark south of Tri-Cities is the site of the ancient break by flowing lava through solid lands to continue to the ocean as the bed for today's Columbia River. Marked by Twin Sisters, two bold rock columns on the east side of the river, as it makes a big curve westward. Picnicking, hiking or playing in the sand.

Ice Harbor Dam on the Snake River above junction with Columbia. Approach from south side. Boat locks on dam.

Whitman Mission National Historical Site and Museum. 55 miles east of the river at Walla Walla on the historic Oregon Trail. Significant Washington history of Marcus and Narcissa Whitman and Indian encounters. www.nps.gov

Umatilla. Historic little town once a stop for barges on the Columbia and a point where covered wagon travelers shifted to river transportation. The townsite moved to higher ground to accommodate plans for the John Day Dam. It was the center of a major U.S. government ordnance facility. Destruction by high temperatures of all ordnance was scheduled for completion by 2012 and closure by 2015 or earlier. A good place to search for antiques. The Old Town portion is on the National Register of Historic Places, because it once was the site of Indian villages. An annual walleye pike derby, usually on Labor Day, and is considered one of the nation's best sites for walleye fishing. www.umatillachamber.org

Columbia Crest Winery on the Washington side of the Columbia west of Umatilla near Paterson is one of several major wineries close to the river. www.columbiacrest.com

Horse Heaven Hills loop northward toward from the Columbia and embrace the wineries above. The wild country was home to large herds of wild horses but now is prime farmland and orchard sites.

Center for Columbia River History. A virtual reality sort of website. Access at www.crch.org

Pendleton Or., just 36 miles south of Umatilla, is the home of the famous Pendleton Woolen Mills, annual major rodeo, and site of underground historic dwellings.

Hermiston is a pleasant small city only seven miles south of the Columbia in Oregon. www.hermistonchamber.org Horse enthusiasts flock there for the Winter and Fall horse sales, from bloodstock to pleasure and cutting horses. The local Bonney family, related to Billy the Kid, is said to be among the founders of the auctions. www.hermistonhorsesale.com

THE DALLES:

At east entrance to the Columbia River Gorge, The Dalles has seen history from Indian days to the present, including Hudson's Bay Company forays, pioneers from the Oregon Trail who chose to travel to the Willamette Valley by raft or boat, rather than take the difficult Barlow Trail – and those preparing for the Barlow Trail. Celilo Falls, 13 miles east of today's city, was a major fishing site for numerous Indian groups who built sturdy but dangerous platforms over the turbulent site to stand on for fishing. Later pioneers built fish traps that were declared illegal. The U.S. government paid local Indians for the right to build the The Dalles Dam, but no monetary payment could assuage the deep sadness that accompanied the silencing of Celilo Falls, the traditional and sacred fishing grounds for most of the area tribes for 10,000 years or more. Even though the falls and rapids frequently claimed lives and boats of both Indians and pioneers through history, The Dalles and Celilo Falls had been a trade center, as well, a peaceful meeting place for native

159

people from the east and west sides of the Cascades Mountain Range to trade coastal products for treasure such as horses and furs, to socialize, and sometimes to obtain brides or bridegrooms from a different tribe.

From the southeastern end of the Columbia Bridge see the now-collapsed Indian Shaker Church and homestead buildings of pioneer Henry Gulick www. thedalleschamber.org Downstream from The Dalles at Columbia River Mile 189.5 is Rock Fort, where Lewis & Clark camped both westbound and eastbound. A plaque commemorates the historical events.

Fort Dalles Museum. Oregon's oldest history museum founded in 1905. Pioneer artifacts and an antique vehicle collection. The only original building standing is the Surgeon's Quarters built in 1856. Fort Dalles Days is a celebration of the area, both past and present, in mid-July involving the entire community of The Dalles. www.fortdallesmuseum.org

The **Dalles Dam.** Tours may be available in summer months; check The Dalles Dam Visitor Center for schedules. Many exhibits about The Dalles, Celilo Falls, fish wheels, etc, Enjoy the view from picnic area. http:///corpslakes.usace. army.mil

Memaloose Island in Memaloose State Park between The Dalles and Hood River was once used as a burial ground by local Indian people. The dead were wrapped tightly and stacked in open log shelters with their possessions. When rising waters created by the Bonneville Dam covered part of the island, designated people respectfully removed the Indian remains.

Columbia Gorge Discovery Center and Wasco County Historical Museum. Well-appointed interpretive center for the Columbia Gorge National Scenic Area, the Columbia River itself, Wasco County history, and the events concerning all of the area. Archives. Programs on diverse topics Lewis and Clark lore, Native American Basketry. Exhibits and info on the river during the Ice Age and the archaeological period of the Missoula Floods, etc. Special information on Birds of Prey (Raptors) and live raptor shows. Books and database on Columbia River history. www.gorgediscovery.org

Wildflowers of the Columbia Gorge. Identify the area's profusion of flowers from this book by Russ Jolley (Portland: Oregon Historical Society Press, 1988).

Learn more about pioneer fishing and fishwheels on the Columbia. **Wheels of Fortune** by Francis Seufert [one of the operators] edited by Thomas Vaughan (Portland: Oregon Historical Society Press, 1980).

The river's sternwheeler history is well portrayed in **Blow for the Landing** by Fritz Timmen (Caldwell, ID: The Caxton Printers, 1973).

Among artists illustrating the Columbia River and Celilo Falls are Steve Ludeman, Anthony Kiser and Laura Ashenbrenner. See Oregon Trail Gallery. Old photographic prints duplicated for framing about Indian fishing over the original Celilo Falls are available at several locations.

Commanding a striking view of the Columbia River from a Washington bluff across from The Dalles is **Maryhill Museum of Art,** an unlikely location for a stunning collection of Auguste Rodin sculptures, Russian icons, traveling art exhibits, Romanian Art that includes Queen Marie of Romania's gilt furniture, and an extensive Native American Collection (especially baskets). Maryhill was built by Samuel Hill, married to railroad magnate James J. Hill's daughter, who took one look at the barren hills and refused to live there. The romantic story is contained in a book, *Sam Hill,* by James Tuhy (Portland: Timber Press, 1983). The mansion sits on 7,000 acres of Hill property. Café on site. Special events year-long. Open March 15 to November 15. www.maryhillmuseum.org.

Nearby the gorge wind whistles through the eerie columns of **Stonehenge**, a partial replica of the original on Salisbury Plains, England. Built by Sam Hill as a memorial to veterans of World War I from Klickitat County.

Arlington on the south side of the river 60 miles east of The Dalles was/ is a port. Early river boats picked up wool from newly shorn sheep and herds of sheep (cattle herds, too) headed for the market. The town was moved to the higher bluff above the river when John Day Dam went into operation.. Stop at the waterside park. Famous trumpeter "Doc" Severinsen was raised at Arlington. www.a2zgorge.info

Travel a segment of the **Barlow Trail** in the Mount Hood National Forest south of the river. Near the junction of highways 35 and 26 is the **Grave of a Pioneer Woman**, dedicated to an unidentified woman who died on the Barlow Trail. www.barlowtrail.org

Timberline Lodge at Mount Hood, a volcanic cone that dominates the south side of the Columbia Gorge, was built in 1937 by Great Depression workers as a ski and hiking shelter. It is now a National Historic Landmark. Worth a side trip. www.timberlinelodge.com.

Columbia River Gorge National Scenic Area. While its offices are at Hood River, the designated Interpretive Center is at the Columbia Gorge Discovery Center at The Dalles, which is where visitors will want to visit unless they have business with the Scenic Area. See above. www.gorgediscovery.org [This section will include commentaries on areas from The Dalles to near Portland. Since items are from both sides of the river, please note OR for Oregon or WA for Washington for many items]

Hood River OR. www.hodriver.org/discover-hood-river On south side of river, it connects by a toll bridge with its twin on the north, White Salmon/ BingenWA. The two charming and accessible towns are the key areas for the extensive windsurfing/kiteboarding/standupboarding crowds that appear during the Gorge's strong winds – a frequent occurrence. The colorful boards skim across the broad Columbia like insects and dot the river all the way to the **Skamania**

County Parks WA. Gorge Windfest OR, the Gorge's oldest wind event, is in late July. Also in July is the Laser Gorge Blow-Out, a sailboat race from Cascade Locks OR to Hood River OR Such events involve both shores, of course. The Gorge SUP [Stand Up Paddlers] Challenge OR is in August. An endurance water-based competition constitutes the Tenacity GamesOR in July. Even swimmers get into the fun in September with a 1.1 mile swim across the river that attracts upward of 500 people. The keen interest in river sports has spawned clothing and equipment specialist manufacturers and dealers to both towns. NO boat rentals are located in the cities because the river is just too rough, but a few professional boat operators host charters. Check www.portofcascadelocks.org/sternwheeler. htm Weather at White Salmon and elsewhere: www.wunderground,com

Ask any information center along the Gorge about interesting places to stay. It is impractical to include such information in this historical book, except for a few; Hood River Inn is literally a few feet from the river and is an icon. The Cloud Cap Inn on the north face of Mount Hood was completed in 1889 and is a Historic Site in a National Historic District but is managed for mountain climbing groups. The Lyle Inn WA is a very small town. Lyle is reputed to be the oldest operating hotel in the Gorge and has gained fame for dining. The venerable and elegant Columbia Gorge Hotel OR was built in 1904 by pioneer Bobby Rand and was sold in 1920 to Portland magnate Simon Benson, then several owners to the present. Portland's Benson Hotel is named after the entrepeur Benson. The Gorge Hotel grounds are lit by 65,000 or more Christmas lights during the season. The Skamania Lodge WA has a magnificent Gorge view and luxury accommodations.

Mt. Hood Railway OR. The century old railroad operates visitor train events, including dinner excursions, all spring and summer. Leaves from Hood River's historic depot. Splendid view of orchards, Mt. Hood, Mt. Adams and parts of the Columbia River. www.mthoodrr.com

Stonehenge replica built by Sam Hill as a memorial to Klickitat County World War I ueterans.

Bridge of the Gods in the Columbia Gorge.

Hood River County History Museum. On Port Marina Drive. Among the artifacts is an American flag made in 1861 by six women and their families, Union supporters. The flag was raised on July 4. www.co.hood-river.or.us

WAAAM in Hood River OR is home to an exciting group of antique, operating aeroplanes, automobiles, and other transportation-related machines. *Note OPERATING.* All are flown or driven. On the second Saturday of each month, the machines that include motorcycles, WWII jeeps, any machine transportation related, are started, driven or flown if weather permits. If not, exhibits are kept inside.. In September a major fly-in of antique aeroplanes. www.waaammuseum. org

Columbia Gorge Festivals. Among the many are Hood River Holidays earliest December, Hood River Harvest Fest mid-October, Hood River Hops Fest late September, Sternwheeler Days in late June at Cascade Locks. Ask nearest visitor center for more.

Dogsledding and other Gorge tours. www.allmounthood.com

Spring Creek National Fish Hatchery. Opened in 1901 at Underwood on the north shore of the Columbia River. Literally millions of fingerlings are released in the spring to travel to the ocean and return 167 miles upstream to spawn at the hatchery. Helps to mitigate Chinook salmon losses due to dam building and other factors. Two miles west of Mount Hood/White Salmon on Highway 14 (Washington).

163

Hood River Valley OR is a verdant agricultural paradise of orchards and farms. Some growers permit tours. Ask local visitors centers. The "Fruit Loop" is a 35-mile loop of vineyards, fruit stands, wineries, lavender fields, nut and berry farms, and alpacas. Canned fruit gift packs are available in local stores. www. hoodriverfruitloop.com

Juanita's Tortilla Factory WA is a minority success story of the Dominguez family that opened the small outlet for farm workers' tortillas and chips in 1977. The business has grown into a corporation that sells products worldwide. www. juanitasfinefoods.com

An immigrant success story was the **Niguma Variety Store** opened in 1905 by a Japanese worker, Taiki Kuma, but today only photos tell the tale at www. discovernikkei.org

U.S. Forest Service. Headquarters website is www.fs.fed.us Covers the Gorge and beyond.

Columbia Gorge Area, continued – West of Hood River to Camas.

Carson Hot Springs Resort WA built in 1901 as St. Martin's Hotel continues as a spa, remodeled hotel, and resort near Stevenson in Skamania County. www. ohwy.com/wa

Ape CavesWA. Longest known lava tube (12,810 feet) in world is 12 miles north of Carson on flanks of Mount St. Helens. www.fs.usda.gov

Mount St. Helens WA can be approached from the Wind River area but most access it from Interstate 5 north of Vancouver.. It sustained a major eruption in 1980.

Wind River Arboretum WA north of Carson in Gifford Pinchot National Forest, is an experimental forestry facility seeking to find the most suitable trees for reforestation. Not set up for general visitation. www.fs.fed.us

Beacon Rock WA, 848 feet high, is a monolith second only to the Rock of Gibralter. It is on the north side of the river and was hailed by Lewis & Clark as a sign they were getting close to salt water. Oregon Trail travelers used it as a beacon that marked the imminent ending of the Gorge. A trail to the top, 4,500 feet long with handrails, is not for the weary as it has a 15% grade but has a matchless view.

Stevenson. Mid-Gorge town on Washington side with basic services and amenities. www.cityofstevenson.com Gorge Blues and Brews Festival late June. Rentals and instructors of sailboards of many types.

Columbia Gorge Interpretive Center Museum WA. The eons old history of the Gorge and Columbia River from the first people to archaeological changes, timber and fishing industries, and the Emory Strong archives of history and artifacts. Very large artifacts include an actual fishwheel, a 1921 Mack truck, and a replica of first people fishing in the falls. A must-see for understanding the Gorge history. At Stevenson near the Skamania Lodge. www.columbiagorge.org

Skamania LodgeWA. Only 20+ years old but in the league of dramatic lodges such as Yosemite or Mount Rainier. Views eastward to the Gorge. Wonderful use of wood in the décor for pillars, ceilings, walls, etc. Golf courses, meeting rooms, all the amenities. Has U.S. Forest Service desk in house. Swimming pool, hot tub, hiking trails, fine dining. www.skamania.com

Bridge of the Gods. A historic auto bridge that marks the site of a Native American story of an ancient natural bridge across the Columbia River, created during a battle between the gods (north and south) of the mountains. Crosses between a point near Stevenson and Cascade Locks. The river here is about 200 feet deep at the foot of the original rapids.

Sternwheeler *Columbia Gorge*. An authentic triple-decker paddlewheeler. Its home port is at Cascade Locks. The venerable and beloved old river cruise boat schedules an assortment of cruises from Portland to Cascade Locks and return for special holidays theme trips, as well as regular cruises. One can book a cruise and learn about the area at the Visitor Center in Marine Park. www.portofcascadelocks. org

Port of Cascade Locks Marine Park. A National Historic Site .Visit the remains of the original locks that assisted upstream travel until the more modern locks at Bonneville Dam were constructed. Italian immigrants did much of the rock work. The location was a a particular hazardous stretch of the river beset by vicious rapids. The original toll building houses three floors of river displays. Statue of Sacajawea. Visitor events. www.portofcascadeslocks.org

Bonneville Dam. Visit both ends of the dam for interpretive material and displays, but the main visitor center is on the south or Oregon side. Watch fish migrating upstream. See text for background information. www.traveloregon.com

Woodie Guthrie. Hired by the Bonneville Power Admministration to write songs about BPA'a achievements in dam building, Guthrie wrote 26 such songs. One of the public's favorites is "This Land is Your Land."

Columbia River Scenic Highway. The original Gorge highway is on the Oregon side, a mostly two-lane, narrow road with turn-outs to see the many beautiful waterfalls that tumble down off Mount Hood to the Columbia River. **Multnomah Falls**, 620 feet high, is particularly dramatic and has its own visitor center, snack bar and shop in a handsome stone building. Occasional winter freezes turn the various falls into ice sculptures of stunning beauty and are worth venturing out in the cold. See maps and visitor centers for details of the highway, which plays hide-and-seek with I-84 from Portland to The Dalles. Ask about the Mt. Hood Columbia Gorge Loop. **Vista House** is as good as its name, high above the river, to provide sweeping views both ways. www.gorgediscovery.org

Parkersville. On the north shore of the river, one of the first incorporated settlements in Washington Territory.

Camas. Home of a major paper mill, it is named after the edible bulb popular with native Americans. Virtually a twin,**Washougal** has a branch of the Pendleton

Woolen Mills. Both towns are adjacent to the much larger city of Vancouver, Washington to the west. Across the river, Troutdale and other communities are a part of the sprawling metropolitan Portland-Vancouver area. Chocolate and wine event first part of February. See major visitor centers and also the text of this book.

Portland/Vancouver to the Sea

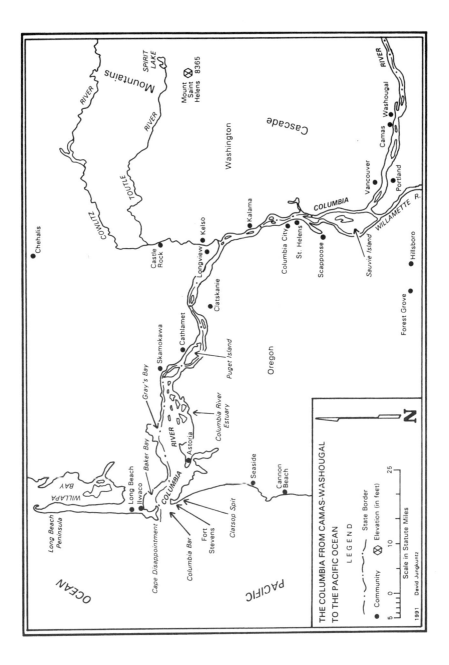

THE COLUMBIA FROM CAMAS-WASHOUGAL
TO THE PACIFIC OCEAN

LEGEND

• Community   ⊗ Elevation (in feet)

——— State Border

Scale in Statute Miles

5   0   10   25

1991   David Jungkuntz

Chapter 20

Cities and Towns Use the River

The lower Columbia River towns and cities were merchant cities born of the need to serve burgeoning businesses—especially fishing and logging, grains and cattle.

Portland, not centering on the Columbia River but always part of its economic area, started as a land claim filed in 1843 by Asa Lovejoy and William Overton. It was a mere clearing in the woods on the Willamette River, for upriver Oregon City, Champoeg and other towns dominated trade with Oregon Trail immigrants in the fertile Willamette Valley. To most immigrants, the Columbia River was more hazard than asset, a wild river to be endured for dangerous passages. But as the produce of the Willamette outstripped local consumption, ways of getting excesses to market became of paramount interest. Until the arrival of railroads in the 1880s, the choice was the Columbia River—either by coastal sailing ship or upriver by sternwheeler. The great falls of the Willamette near Oregon City effectively thwarted any direct access to valley farming communities.

Somewhat of a rover, Overton sold his half of the claim to Francis W. Pettygrove within a year. Both Lovejoy and Pettygrove were of New England merchant stock and recognized the potential of their claim as a future port. They platted a town on the west side of the river, while a handful of others settled east of the river, necessitating a ferry operation, and so it went.

Two key settlers gave impetus to growth—sea captain John H. Couch, filing a claim in 1846, and tanner Daniel Lownsdale, in 1845. Couch touted Portland as the gateway to the sea; Lownsdale laid out a road from Portland to today's Tualitin (Canyon Road) to bring in agricultural products. The road was made mud-proof by laying planks side by side, the Great Plank Road, six miles long. Consequently, instead of transshipping products via Oregon City and boats below the falls, pioneers could haul them directly to the seaport of Portland. The community was off and running. By 1850 the town had 821 people; in 1851 it was incorporated.

The Idaho gold rush gave further impetus to development. Hordes of prospectors clumped through town, transferring from sailing ships to riverboats, buying supplies. Sternwheelers transported cattle, sheep and grain downriver to the "big city" for export or processing. All this activity naturally created a great thirst; Henry Weinhard responded by moving his brewery from its Fort Vancouver location (founded in 1856) to Portland.

Portland became the mail boat's terminus in 1854, mail coming around the Horn on ships from the East Coast. The city developed a distinctly New England feeling as it grew. The ships' captains and mates, Eastern industrialists, and education-oriented settlers founded churches and built fine Victorian or Queen Anne-style homes facing the Willamette with a backdrop of Mount Hood. To show off its riches and beautiful site, citizens chipped in and staged the Lewis & Clark Exposition of 1905. There were statues of Lewis and Clark, photographs of a cigar raft 720 feet long, three hundred Curtis Indian prints, and fruit displays from twenty-four Oregon counties. The biggest hit was the Forestry Building, 100 feet by 200 feet, made of logs as long as 60 feet and 6 feet in diameter.

There was an underbelly to Portland, of course. "Respectable citizens" either closed their eyes or surreptitiously participated in the fun at roistering bars and cribs of the riverfront, traditionally belonging to sailors, loggers and railroad crews bent on spending all their hard-earned money.

When the California and Oregon Railroad (later, the Southern Pacific) was completed to Portland in 1869, and east/west service was assured through Oregon Railway & Navigation Company's Wallula connection to the Northern Pacific in 1883, Portland's preeminence as a commercial port was assured. By 1890 the city was a terminus for fifty-seven steamship lines. As a port, it incurred a disadvantage by being one hundred miles from the sea on a whimsical river of varying depth and current. Its advantage was being one hundred miles closer to landlocked markets. A century later, it boasted 430,000 largely satisfied residents who touted their city as The Rose City, for the flowers planted by Oregon Trail arrivals.

After the Civil War, shipping interests dredged the Willamette, since deeper-draft ships had to unload partially at St. Helens before proceeding to Portland. In 1891 the state created the Port of Portland to dredge and maintain a 25-foot channel from Portland to the ocean.

The city formed the Commission of Public Docks in 1910 to develop waterfront terminals, drydocks and other facilities, merging with the Port in 1970. Under the federal Rivers and Harbors Act of 1912, the Port has been required to keep the Willamette channel dredged to 30 feet, and to assist the U.S. Army Corps of Engineers in maintaining the shipping channel on the Columbia River to the ocean; in 1976 required depth was 40 feet, and further dredging is needed as ships become larger. In the 1920s the Port removed Post Office Bar near the confluence of the Willamette and Columbia, using the dredge materials to fill Swan Island and create Guilds Lake Industrial Park in northwest Portland. Swan Island became the site for Portland's first airport, dedicated by none other than Charles Lindbergh, flying in the *Spirit of St. Louis* only four months after his historic transoceanic flight.

Five generations of the Shaver Transportation Company family have been active on the Portland waterfront, starting with the sternwheeler captain George Shaver. His son, Captain J. W., served on the Port of Portland Commission, and his grandson, Captain George, on the Dock Commission. Fifth generation Mary operated a launch service. Another Columbia/Willamette pioneer dynasty was the Dant family, starting with the Dant and Russell Lumber Company and including the founding of States Line steamship line of thirty-two vessels.

Near the confluence of the two rivers, another scion of Portland, William Leadbetter, willed his 2,000 acres of duck-hunting lands to Willamette University. The Port purchased it in 1964 for multi-purpose use that includes two lakes, where ducklings still waddle behind their mothers every spring.

Across the mighty Columbia, perhaps two thousand Indians and mixed-race families of Hudson's Bay Company employees lived near Fort Vancouver. Americans settled nearby in Columbia City, the area becoming Vancouver in 1853, incorporated in 1857. Privately owned by the British Hudson's Bay Company, Fort Vancouver did not close until the 1860s (it burned down in 1866). Its kindly chief factor, Briton John Mcloughlin, in disfavor with Hudson's Bay Company's Governor Simpson, founded the Imperial Mills after 1846, giving impetus to settlement of Oregon City. He became an American citizen in 1851.

More than agriculture, Vancouver's early growth was gleaned from its forests. Adjacent to the Columbia River, citizens cut wood for riverboats and hewed lumber for homes.

As already described, Indian unrest in eastern Washington and the Columbia Gorge led to the establishment of a small American military post on May 15, 1849—Columbia Barracks, then Fort Vancouver, later Vancouver Barracks, a sub-post to Fort Lewis. It has been home to portions of the Mounted Rifles; the First Artillery; the Fourth, Seventh and Fourteenth infantries; and finally the l04th Training Division of the Army Reserves. In 1917 to 1918, twenty-seven thousand enlisted men were sent to Vancouver Barracks, dispersed among lumber camps and mills to harvest spruce needed for airplanes. The Barracks includes a row of graceful officers' homes where splendid military parties have taken place, facing a broad, grassy parade ground.

Among the luminaries serving at this pleasant post were O. O. Howard and Nelson Miles (central figures in the skirmishes with the Nez Perce), Philip Sheridan of Civil War fame, William Harney (involved in Sioux Indian wars and the laughable "Pig War" at San Juan Island, Washington, when a British pig was shot by an American settler) George Marshall of World War II and Ulysses S. Grant, commander of the Union Army in the Civil War and later, president.

The young officer Grant turned to moonlighting to earn money for transporting his family west. With cohorts he shipped 100 tons of ice to California, but in adverse winds, the schooner took six weeks to make the trip, and Grant lost the cargo. He and a partner planted potatoes, but the Columbia River flooded and reclaimed the field. He even bought chickens and sent them to San Francisco; they died en route. Fortunately, he did better as an army general.

A sturdier version of revered Mother Teresa of the 1980s was Mother Joseph of the late 1800s, an industrious head of the Sisters of Charity of Providence in the Pacific Northwest. Arriving in Vancouver in 1856, Mother Joseph and four other nuns founded the first nonmilitary hospital, orphanage, shelter for the mentally disturbed and home for the aged in Washington Territory. She did the job often with her own two hands, as she was an accomplished carpenter and builder. Mother Joseph is one of two Washington State residents to be honored in the National Statuary Hall in Washington, D.C. The other is Marcus Whitman— illustrious company, indeed.

With a less-protected harbor than the Willamette affords Portland, and without the wealth from its valley, Vancouver never attained the population of Portland but remained a small city depending chiefly upon lumber-related industries. In 1992 it offered anchorage for ten ships and dockside berthing for seven on the Columbia River itself. Around 1855, steamboats had to tie to an exposed river bank, but that year two floating wharves were installed—each with a saloon and store. Soon, permanent docks were built.

The only sandmold brick producer west of the Mississippi, the Hidden Brick Company has manufactured quality building brick in Vancouver from 1871 to the present. A dried prune industry has thrived since the 1880s, and Aluminum Company of America opened a big plant in September 1940. After January 1942, Vancouver was overwhelmed by the influx of workers at the new Kaiser Shipyards right on the Columbia River, a natural location for the industry. Portland also had received two Kaiser yards. Edgar Kaiser, son of magnate Henry Kaiser, managed the shipbuilding companies. He had gained business management experience on the Grand Coulee and Bonneville projects. The shipyards built Liberty ships, aircraft carriers, troop transports and floating drydocks—763 ships in all by war's end.

In December 1943, there were 98,300 employees in the three shipyards, and Kaiser bought 650 acres of land adjacent to the Columbia River in extreme north Portland, built a dike around the property, and established an entire temporary town to house his workers. Chiefly the town consisted of two-story apartment buildings, each containing fourteen apartments, over nine thousand units, making the town Vanport the second largest city in Oregon. The units were furnished and basic; however, residents found them extremely noisy. The mixture of total strangers thrust together led to sociological friction. Kaiser always intended that the buildings should be razed after the war. The Columbia River made the final decision.

Prior to Memorial Day 1948, heavy snows fell along the Columbia's Canadian and U.S. tributaries, followed by unusually warm temperatures and rain. The spring freshet turned into a torrent, causing uncontrollable damage along the entire river system. Grand Coulee and Bonneville Dams were unable to stem the waters. While several feet below the dike's summit, the river broke through a weak spot and poured into Vanport. The water rose swiftly, but with fifteen or twenty minutes time before it grew shoulder height, most residents escaped—the last of them forming a human chain. A few were trapped inside their dwellings or injured, unable to get out. The apartments had been built on supports, which acted like rafts when the water rose; entire buildings floated down river, crashing together and disintegrating; for a time they threatened to topple the Interstate Bridge. With new dams built since then, it is unlikely that the river can attain such monstrous flood levels again.

Kaiser's shipyards were closed when the need ceased, but Vancouver and Portland enjoyed some lasting industrial spin-offs. By the 1970s, Vancouver began to develop as a site for high-tech companies, among them Japanese firms, some introduced to the city by sister city relationships.

In 1980 small children found $5,800 in rotting $20 bills half-buried in the Columbia River sands about five miles northwest of Vancouver. The bills were traced to the loot received by hijacker D. B. Cooper nine years earlier at Seattle. He permitted passengers on Northwest Airlines flight 305 to get off, then demanded to be taken to Mexico. Somewhere over southern Washington, Cooper left the plane in a parachute, never to be seen again despite intensive searches. The town of Ariel, Washington, east of Kalama, still celebrates D. B. Cooper Days after Thanksgiving, cynically enjoying his unusual feat, but many believe he came down in the Columbia River.

Hudson's Bay Company employees often retired along the Columbia River—Tom McKay, stepson of Dr. Mcloughlin, at Scappoose, and James Birnie at Cathlamet. The Chinook leader Casseno, son of Chief Comcomly, made his home near St. Helens. Near the confluence of the Willamette and Columbia in Oregon, St. Helens was founded by Captain H. M. Knighton in 1845 as Plymouth. Here the Charles R. McCormick Company bought a millsite in 1909, dealing in lumber and logging; they later built lumber schooners as St. Helens Shipbuilding Company.

McCormick's first steam schooner, with lines similar to sailing ships, was the *Multnomah*, launched on October 12, 1912, at a gala party. Following were the *Merced, Celilo, City of Portland* and others, the hulls towed to San Francisco for engines and fittings. After the 1930s the shipyard ceased operations, and the lumber site was operated by Boise Cascade. St. Helens is a quiet shadow of its former self, most of it preserved as a Historic Site. On the Willamette waterfront, dozens of small fixed houseboats or apartments rock gently in the wake of freighters passing by on the main navigation channel.

Before steam tugs took over around 1915, the giant lumber schooners around 200 feet long were dubbed the Scandinavian Fleet for their captains. Pope & Talbot Company clung to sailing ships even after most companies had tugs, and the Pacific lumber trade used schooners through World War I. The last wooden steam schooner built was the *Esther Johnson* at Portland in 1923, 208 feet long. The venerable wooden steam schooner *Wapama*, renamed *Tongass*, worked in Alaska until 1947, and in 1948 was purchased for the Maritime Museum on San Francisco's waterfront. She was lucky; some of them wound up hauling garbage or were scrapped.

One of the strangest Columbia Bar wrecks was that of the four-masted lumber schooner *North Bend*. She went solidly aground on Peacock Spit on January 5, 1928, and was abandoned after futile refloating attempts. Weeks later, lighthouse keepers swore the ship had moved. Sure enough, with shifting sand and tidal fluctuations, small pools of water formed and encouraged her progress. In his book *Windjammers of the Pacific Rim* (Seattle: Superior Publishing Company, 1968), Jim Gibbs described it as an "unexplained zeal for life... as if some ghostly hand was guiding her." Thirteen months after she was wrecked, she worked her way clear through the spit and floated into Baker's Bay, her hull still intact.

A few miles above St. Helens, looming like a misplaced moonscape, is the steam-wreathed cooling tower (499 feet high) of the Trojan Nuclear Plant, where swallows incongruously nest around the rim. The power plant, operated by Portland General Electric Company, uses a small fraction of its 634-acre site, donating the rest for public use as picnic sites, hiking trails, a fish hatchery and a small fishing lake. The small plant provides more power than Bonneville Dam and produces about 20 percent of Oregon's electricity. It processes the cooling water to return it to the Columbia River at a temperature less than 1 percent hotter than at the intake point, and has operated for twenty-five years without mishap or any harmful discharges whatever.

As settlers moved onto Oregon shores, some of them fished, others grew peppermint (still do), but lumber fueled most of the growth. At Clatskanie, built then on stilts, pioneers like Simon Benson and James Flippin (an Oregon Trail herdsman for pioneer politician Jesse Applegate) logged the cedar and fir, sending them to the Clatskanie or Columbia River by flumes. Huge cigar rafts were assembled at the confluence of the rivers; the faint outlines of a cradle used to assemble them can be seen yet. The cigar raft had logs laid like a pair of parenthesis meeting at each end, then stacked neatly in between with other logs, and the whole thing lashed securely with chains. The pointed ends rode better than flat booms in the ocean swells, and most lumber was towed down the coast.

As steam power developed, tugs got bigger and stronger; one of the earliest was the 128-foot steel boat *Tatoosh*, operating first as a Columbia Bar tug in 1907. But ocean-capable tugs thereafter towed everything from lumber to barges with Alaska pipeline gear on them, moved ships into berths and wheat barges up and down the Columbia. Chief ocean-tug operators in the late 20th century included Crowley Maritime, Brix Maritime and Shaver Transportation.

In the woods, muscle was giving way to steam, too. At first loggers used ferocious-looking longhorn steers to pull logs. Then, steam tractors took over. One of the log companies painted all its equipment and structures red; even a dance hall facing the Columbia River was painted red. Excursion boats came to mingle with the loggers, and dances often lasted all night. In the camps or towns, boxing matches helped single men work off energy; the matches went on until one participant was knocked out—no TKO's there.

Today major lumber industries still headquarter from Rainier to Wauna— Stimson Lumber Company, James River Corporation and RSG Forest Products, which manufactures cedar fencing. Before modern refrigeration systems for boats, there were fish-buying stations all up and down this section of river shore so that fishermen did not lose time traveling to the canneries. There were horse seiners, too, on the lower Columbia River islands, just as there were on estuary sand bars. During World War II, an army ammunition depot was built at Mayger, present site of a Portland Gas and Electric Company plant.

On the last westerly bend of the Columbia River, the small towns of Kalama and Kelso were settled early—Kelso in 1884, while Kalama's first cabin was built in 1853 by pioneer Ezra Meeker. In 1871 Kalama became the Pacific Coast terminus of the Northern Pacific Railway Company. Population swelled to three or four thousand who thought Kalama would be the chief Columbia River port. The euphoria was temporary because when the railroad was extended to Tacoma in 1873, the headquarters were moved there. Kalama subsided to a whistle stop of perhaps twenty-five families. A bit larger today, its port tenaciously clings to wheat elevator and barge transportation businesses.

Kelso and Longview are virtually one city, but intense civic rivalry has marked their growth. At first, Kelso was the "metropolis," remaining the county seat of historic Cowlitz County, where Hudson's Bay Company tried so heroically to make Puget Sound Agricultural Colony pay. Like Portland, Kelso grew as a river port for farmers and loggers. One entrepreneur scorned traditional farming to take up ostrich raising around 1915 to 1920, giving it up partly because the birds were so hazardous—one good kick could kill a person.

The little town of Monticello predated Kelso, but situated precariously at the mouth of the Cowlitz River, it was decimated by floods. The settlement was founded in December 1849, by the Harry Darby Huntington immigrant party, arriving by canoe. Monticello's brief moment of glory came when, in 1852, a convention was held there by settlers north of the Columbia River to petition Congress for separate territorial status. Oregon Territory was vast, extending from California to Canada and east toward the Rockies. "Washingtonians" were tired of traveling to Oregon City for official business. The forty-four men met in rude summer camplike housing but got the job done. Washington Territory was formed March 3, 1853— "Washington" being second choice; it was almost named "Columbia" Territory.

Kelso was thirty-seven years old, well established, while upstart Longview's site was just a dense forest in 1921—a fateful year. The major lumber firm, Long-Bell Lumber Company, of Missouri and Weed, California, purchased a huge prime timber tract in Cowlitz County and planned a big lumber mill. A new town of Longview was planned—not just any town, either. Idealist as well as businessman, R. A. Long felt that here was an opportunity to build a beautiful, well-planned model city. In a foresighted zoning plan, the architects laid out commercial, industrial, residential and open areas. Landscaping was not overlooked. At first, the city looked a bit peculiar, for buildings were scattered over the large city tract in proper zones—allowing for the spaces to fill in gradually to serve a population estimated at 50,000 (which has never been attained).

With great expense and haste, Longview town sprang out of the forest—not a "Stumptown" as Portland had been, but a real town with a magnificent hotel, the Monticello, paved streets, and flowers. The largest lumber mill in the world opened in 1924, and the town was dedicated with feverish hoopla, including a lively speech by evangelist Billy Sunday and more staid presentations by the governor, senators and congressmen. Although there were alterations over the years to the master plan, Longview still ranks among the most attractive small cities of Washington.

Long-Bell Company is no more, but other lumber corporations thrive to make Longview and its overshadowed neighbor, Kelso, almost entirely lumber-supported towns.

Here on the Cowlitz and Columbia, where Washington Territory was born, an explosion shook the area to its core on May 18, 1980. Thirty-five miles east of Kelso/Longview, Mount St. Helens, pristinely majestic, erupted with such force that more than a thousand feet of its top disappeared, incinerated into a cloud of ash and dust. It sent a cloud 60,000 miles into the atmosphere, perceptibly sprinkling states and provinces far distant. The concussion flattened 250 square miles of mature, sturdy Douglas fir and hemlock, meticulously laying them in rows as orderly as the Great Plank Road. Following the contours of the mountains, the path of the killer wind could be traced easily. The eruptive cloud manufactured its own static electricity.

Ash falling across the Columbia River into eastern Washington was inches deep, plunging towns into darkness. Street lights came on. Cars moved slowly as if in a winter blizzard. Sixty-eight people died, most of them close to the mountain. In the superheated Toutle and Cowlitz rivers, thousands of fish died. On the Cowlitz the terror was not the minimal fallout of ash, but the maelstrom descending from the mountain's northwest side; debris and slurry from melted snow mixed with ground-up rock filled Spirit Lake and overflowed. A wall of destruction surged down the Toutle River, sweeping away bridges and houses, loose lumber and loosened trees, raging into the Cowlitz River and descending through Kelso and Longview to the Columbia. With little warning, residents fled the lowlands, but the river stayed a foot below flood stage at Longview/Kelso.

The following day a ship ran aground on a 20-foot mud bank off the Cowlitz River in the Columbia, a channel then 18 feet, normally 50 feet deep. Longview and Kelso fought to clear their water systems of silt. Twenty-two million cubic yards of silt wound up in the Columbia River.

About fifty ships were marooned upriver, most of them in Portland. Dozens of others milled around the lower river, waiting to get into port, or cancelled their calls. The Port of Portland and the Army Corps of Engineers threw every available dredge into service, deepening the Columbia channel so ships could escape. The deepest draft vessels could not leave the river for more than a month. The fine, easily shifting silt continues to plague the river.

Successive, less catastrophic eruptions left ash sifting onto the Columbia River towns, instead of eastern Washington. A homeowner in Astoria found the ash combining in drainpipes and downspouts to form a solid plug.

Chapter 21

Marriage of River and Ocean

The lower Columbia River is a singular place—glassy smooth at times, dangerous yet mystically gripping in its beauty. The river is filled with islands, large and small, and ever-shifting sand bars. Except for dredging of a ship channel, the river runs wild and free, narrowing to a mile some places, widening to six midway through the estuary. At the infamous bar, the fury of unimaginable tons of fresh water meeting incoming ocean waves, intensified by frequent galeforce winds and towering swells, has been lessened only a little by the addition of jetties. Two thousand vessels have been lost within a fifteen-mile radius of the entrance, with losses of fifteen hundred lives in recorded history.

Yet, along the final hundred miles of the Columbia River, wended the commerce that made possible the prospering of Portland, Vancouver, and small towns and hamlets of romantic-sounding names—Kalama, Kelso, Longview, Cathlamet, Clatskanie, Ilwaco, Skamokawa. Ghostly remnants of others quietly make their claim on the river's history, all but forgotten except for rotting pilings, decayed cannery structures, homes with blackberry bushes growing through the walls.

Fishing and canneries first, lumbering second accounted for most of the defunct towns. They included Pillar Rock near the basalt landmark named by Lieutenant Broughton in 1792; Knappton, a sawmill run by Jim Vaughn and Samuel E. Barr; Altoona, a cannery town also called Hume's Station. Carlton Appelo, local historian, claimed that it was named for Al, a popular fiddler to whom locals said, "Al, tune 'er up."

The steep terrain encouraged creativity. In 1910 the Olson Brothers Logging Company tunneled 650 feet through a hill near Deep River to get logs to water. An enterprising young Finnish immigrant, Helge Saari, delivered milk for twenty-one years, from 1921 to 1942, to river communities by rowboat, timing his arrival to coincide with the tides, for coves were bare at low tide. A Deep River grocery delivered supplies by railroad speeder car. Aging residents remember being isolated by spring freshets, when parts of buildings, uprooted trees and tumbleweeds from eastern Washington swept by to the sea.

Retired in Cathlamet, tugboat captain (Smith Tug & Barge, Rainier) Stanley Everman estimated that he has towed 5,600 log rafts with his 60-foot tug *Ajax*. Rafts typically were 750 feet by 55 feet. Logging companies stored logs in the sloughs among the myriad islands, particularly Carroll Channel, Rainierson Slough and Cathlamet Channel.

River men frequently were on the scene of wrecks. Everman rescued the crew of an Italian vessel, sunk to the superstructure on a dark and rainy night above Rainier. During the rare freezes of the river, tugs were used to break ice and bring supplies to small communities, encountering trouble themselves because ice would clog the water intake (cooling). Everman sees wildlife (including black bears, elk, deer) on the increase along the river, especially harbor seals and sea lions, which voraciously consume salmon.

On Tenasillihe Island there is a refuge for Columbia white-tailed deer, which, along with huge flocks of birds, inhabit the island and nearby Lewis and Clark Refuge, a group of islands partly under water at high tide. Kelso tug operator Michael Johnson has the unusual task of moving cattle to and from Tenasillihe Island to eat down the grass, for the deer prefer grass about two inches high.

Storms and accidents are routine hazards of the river, but hardly "tidal waves," yet in January 1965, a big chunk of earth, formerly a viewpoint, slid thunderously into the Columbia west of Rainier, sending a giant wave onto nearby Puget Island.

A re-creation of Fort Clatsop, the wintering place of Lewis and Clark. Near Astoria.

It wrenched loose a water front home, washed it 200 yards inland, and flung it over the dike, but the elderly occupant escaped unharmed. Another home was crushed along with its owner.

While Vancouver was the oldest Washington settlement, the grandfather of all in Oregon Territory was Astoria, beginning in 1811 as Fort Astoria, Astor's fur post. While the area was still under joint jurisdiction of Britain and the United States, Solomon Smith, a member of the Nathaniel Wyeth party, became the first to take up property at Clatsop Plains in 1840, marrying a daughter of Clatsop Chief Cobaway and opening a store. He was there to help the chilled survivors of the beautiful U.S. sloop of war, *Peacock*, when she struck the sands beneath frowning Cape Disappointment on July 18, 1841.

The *Peacock's* captain, Lieutenant William Hudson, was under orders from surveyor Lieutenant Charles Wilkes to chart the Columbia River. Acting on notes given him by a Captain Spaulding, veteran of several Columbia River entries, Hudson attempted to enter the channel in low visibility. When he saw a breaking sea, he concluded he was too far south and turned away; instead, he was too far north and turned into the sands near Cape Disappointment. The ship broke up in high swells that slammed her repeatedly onto the spit, and the crew abandoned ship, their unfortunate adventure giving the name "Peacock Spit" to the sands around today's north jetty. The ship was neither the first nor the last to end her days near the treacherous Columbia entrance.

Despite its vagaries, the river was a creator. Carrying tons of silt and sand, the Columbia's current swirled northward to build Long Beach, the long spit embracing Willapa Bay. In fact, it continues to add to this, the longest continuous straight beach in the world. Cottages built on the shore in 1900 are a quarter-mile inland today. To compete with Oregon's Seaside and Cannon Beach, which attracted tourists from Portland, sternwheelers braved the turbulent estuary to transport beach-goers from rail's end at Astoria to Ilwaco on the Washington shore. One of the sturdier boats in 1865 was the *U. S. Grant*, under Clinton Kelley and later John H. D. Gray (relative of pioneer mariner W. P. Gray). At first, tourists were met at Baker's Bay by a horse-drawn stage driven by Louis Loomis, a rollicking ride for sure. With no roads on the spit, Loomis mostly drove the hard beach sands all the way to Nahcotta on Willapa Bay. Occasional waves swirled around the horses' feet, and a rogue breaker once briefly floated stage, horses and all.

In 1874, a wharf was built at Ilwaco, and the 110-foot *General Canby* furrowed through the broad reach from Astoria. To keep afloat, owners of Ilwaco Steam Navigation Company also hauled troops and supplies to army posts Fort Stevens (Oregon) and Fort Canby (Washington). Shortly afterward, the Oregon Railroad & Steam Navigation Company initiated a direct run from Portland to Ilwaco, but the swells overwhelmed its boat, and it had to be towed in. Thereafter, the federal government banned sternwheelers west of Smith's Point near Astoria.

The stages, though colorful and adventurous, were phased out in favor of a narrow-gauge railroad up Long Beach spit. Tracks were laid onto the wharf so that trains could back out close to the steamer. The first train left Ilwaco for Nahcotta on May 29, 1889, operating daily with canopied flatcars giving passengers splendid ocean views. Brisk freight traffic from Willapa Bay to Columbia River, chiefly oysters, helped finances.

The delightful, long-lasting little "Clamshell Railroad," stopped anywhere, taking several hours to travel the route. The versatile railway even hauled rescue crews to wreck sites, since ships frequently got into trouble near the Columbia Bar. During major storms train schedules were interrupted by huge breakers raging far inland!

The monopolistic river firm, Oregon Railway & Steam Navigation, acquired the railroad and Ilwaco's docks and buildings in 1900 and put on a direct Portland-Ilwaco steamer, the *T. J. Potter*. The firm added revenue by hauling logs from Willapa Bay to the Columbia, then laid tracks to Megler near Point Ellice (Washington end of Astoria Bridge) in protected, deep water, abandoning Ilwaco. Gradually automobiles replaced the charming Clamshell Railroad after 1930. A ferry ran between Megler and Astoria until 1966, when the trans-river Astoria Bridge was completed, 4.1 miles long with a shipping span 1,070 feet wide and almost 200 feet high. Ilwaco developed a charter-boat fishing industry; it is home to commercial fishermen and still is a gateway to Long Beach tourism.

Across the Columbia River, usually heaving with ocean swells, the camps of the Corps of Engineers, Upper Astoria, and the cannery workers' dwellings, Lower Astoria, became one. Entire fleets of small boats dotted the river, dubbed the "butterfly fleet" because the unique boat design has two sails on one mast. Once a year the sailor-fishermen competed in the Astoria Regatta. In 1915, almost three thousand gillnetters, three hundred trap owners and fifty seiners using horses were plying the lower river. Tuna fishing in the ocean began in 1938, the last tuna boats quitting about 1980. There was Uniontown, where most of the fishermen and logger Finns lived; a large Chinatown of cannery workers; Swill Town where those of questionable moral activity reigned; and the scenic hillsides where ship captains, bar pilots, cannery owners and shopkeepers built modest and a few pretentious homes. Perhaps a third of Astoria's seven thousand residents were Chinese.

The 1900s concert hall—called The Louvre—built by August Erickson dominated the social life, not a rough place like his bar in Portland, but a gorgeous, three-story hall with rooms for games, concerts, two tasteful bars and no "monkey business."

Tourists came to Oregon beaches. In 1888 the Astoria and South Coast Railroad Company line to Seaside made travel faster, if not easier, as the passengers traveled on flatcars with "porch" rails and hard benches. D. K. Warren, for whom Warrenton on Clatsop Spit is named, was its president. Following the demise of bankrupt competitor companies, a group headed by A. B. Hammond completed the Astoria and Columbia River Railroad, building tracks from Astoria to Goble, leasing Northern Pacific's rails on into Portland. The first train left Astoria on May 16, 1898, to a din of whistles and bells from boats, churches and government buildings as it eased out over the Tongue Point trestle.

A broad highway to the interior, the Columbia River necessarily had to be fortified against potential enemies before the days of electronic detection. Cape Disappointment, the formidable headland north of the entrance, was a natural fortification, commanding a clear view of the Columbia River, the jetties and the Pacific Ocean for a score of miles. The government established a military reservation in 1852 on the site of Pacific City, moving away seventy buildings, most of them to Ilwaco, and built Fort Canby.

In 1856, the Cape Disappointment Lighthouse began beaming the way to the entrance, today the oldest lighthouse in use on the west coast. Its companion, North Head Lighthouse, was built in 1898. Fort Canby's fortifications and batteries were expanded and improved, and were manned until after World War II when new technology made them obsolete. The site became a state park that encompasses Peacock Spit, a beach below North Head whimsically called Waikiki Beach, and sandy camping areas.

At this striking location the Lewis and Clark Interpretive Center has opened with fine exhibits about the Expedition and also displays of lifesaving methods, shipwrecks and lighthouses.

On the storm-swept shore east of Ilwaco, where the Chinook Indians once made their home, the United States constructed Fort Columbia between 1896 and 1904. It was staffed by military services until after World War II. Fort Columbia's batteries never fired a shot in anger, and the facilities and grounds today are a state park.

On the Oregon shore at Clatsop Spit, Fort Stevens (built during the Civil War) guarded against incoming hostile ships. It became the largest of the forts by far, staffed by 2,500 troops during World War II. Soldiers from the fort mined the entrance to the Columbia River off and on from 1898 through World War II. Fort buildings were camouflaged with artificial trees, and a battery was installed on the ocean sands west of the fort.

A Japanese submarine actually fired on Fort Stevens on June 21, 1942, the shell landing 300 yards from Battery Russell, the only military installation in the continental United States fired upon by a foreign power later than the War of 1812. Japanese submarines also sank or fired on freighters and tankers off the mouth of the river and sent thousands of tiny incendiary devices floating over coastal Oregon, hoping to set devastating forest fires. In the rain, the efforts failed. Today Fort Stevens Military Museum, Interpretive Center, and grounds comprising 3,800 acres are open to the public. On the ocean beach the remains of the wreck *Peter Iredale* may be seen, and one can walk out a way on the jetty (although signs sternly warn of the dangers, since sneaker waves wash sightseers off the jetties almost every year).

With breaking swells visible almost continuously along the Columbia Bar, no wonder early explorers thought a solid beach existed there. However, jetties built by the Army Corps of Engineers tamed the entry so that wrecks of larger ships are infrequent today. The south jetty was finished in 1895, the north in 1917; secondary jetties inside the entry seek to control silting. To transport rock to the south jetty, engineers built a railroad in conjunction with the jetty as they went. One stormy night the four-masted schooner *Admiral* struck foul ground in a seventy-mile-per-hour wind and was hammered against the jetty, coming to rest on the rocks and rail trestle pilings. The fractured rails whipped like tentacles in the winds, helping to damage the ship. Five survivors managed to struggle up to the railway trestle, where alerted rescue crews cautiously crept through the night toward the wreck, the seas sending scud against the locomotive to create clouds of steam. They rescued the five. The Point Adams Life Crew saved seven others, using a breeches buoy. The ocean battered the *Admiral* to pieces, wreckage drifting across the bar, according to Jim Gibbs in his book *Pacific Graveyard*.

Astorians assumed their city would be the large maritime center, situated just inside the river entrance; however, lack of rail connections to interior markets until 1898 permitted Portland and Vancouver to upstage Astoria. In 1913 the Port of Astoria was incorporated, not recognizing defeat. Believing the town would be another San Francisco, the Port built three docks and 26 acres of warehouses (Astoria had only ten thousand residents), urging shipping companies to save the long haul upriver. But after World War I, the government dumped thousands of steamships on the market dirt cheap, and shipping companies steamed right on past Astoria, unconcerned about any small savings. Increased trucking also hurt the location.

The next blow was that, during the market crash of 1929, New York financiers defaulted on their bonds, leaving Astoria's port financially desperate. Instead of being a major port, Astoria remains a fishing port with three small pleasure-cruise companies calling, more than a hundred log ships annually, Canadian ships with newsprint for the Oregonian, and an occasional Russian ship—offshore cannery ships giving their sailors shore leave.

From the beginning, ships have depended on Astoria bar pilots to guide them safely through the meeting of Columbia River and Pacific Ocean, and upon the United States Coast Guardsmen from Ilwaco and Astoria to rescue them when they were in trouble.

Chinook Chief Comcomly is credited with being the first bar pilot, for seventeen years paid with trinkets to guide Hudson's Bay Company ships safely across the bar. Three ship captains, James Johnson, William Mouatt and James Scarborough, guided Hudson's Bay Company ships for a time after Comcomly's death in 1830. In August of 1846 a deserter from the *Peacock* (one James deSaule), who operated a trans-river canoe service, attempted his first and only pilotage; he brought the sloop-of-war *Shark* solidly aground on Clatsop Spit.

On December 16, 1848, the Oregon Territorial Legislature passed an act creating a State Pilot Board, authorizing it to employ a state bar pilot. Selah Reeves was the first. Unfortunately, he piled up his first two boats, too, the Hudson's Bay Company barque *Vancouuer* and the whaler *Maine*, whereupon he was fired. The next pair, Geer and Alexander, used the boat to sell liquor to the Indians. Irate Clatsop tribal elders dragged them to the beach and repeatedly dunked them in the Columbia River, half-drowning them as a warning. Jackson Hustler was a capable pilot for a year or two, but not until the advent of George Flavel with his 64-foot schooner *California*, did the Columbia get a long-staying and reliable pilot.

Flavel was a tall, lean man with piercing blue eyes and a manner that earned him the nickname of "Hawk" behind his back. In his first two years on the bar, Captain Flavel also lost two ships. One must remember that a pilot is not the "lord," for the seas can overcome anyone. On January 29, 1852, Flavel was outbound aboard the small grain-loaded steamer *General Warren*, wallowing heavily in wind-whipped waves and snow. The creaky ship began to leak, and under orders from her captain, Flavel deliberately put the ship onto Clatsop Spit, where all night she was battered by foaming breakers. About 3:00 A.M. Flavel obtained nine volunteers and set off in the long boat under oars and managed to make Astoria harbor. Rescuers returned to the spit to find no one alive. The *General Warren* had disintegrated in the surf, and only bodies came ashore to be buried in a common grave.

The second accident involved the barque *Oriole*. At a crucial point when the *Oriole* was crossing the shallows, the wind stopped, leaving the barque at the mercy of currents. She, too, hit the Clatsop Spit, but all the crew members were saved.

Crucial to successful pilotage was obtaining a rugged boat to intercept ships outside the bar. Sometimes in the 1800s a pilot traveled with an outbound ship to San Francisco, where he picked up another scheduled for the Columbia River. Flavel's *California* proved equal to the tasks required, and his pilotage business grew, with four additional pilots hired to assist him. Rates for guiding vessels across the bar were from $10 to $12 a foot, and as commerce grew, so did Flavel's income. He branched out into partnership in a sawmill, operation of a trans-river ferry by sloop, a grocery, was county treasurer for a time, and in 1883, became president of the First National Bank of Astoria.

When marine engines became more reliable, the Oregon State Legislature of 1868 authorized subsidy of a steam tug of no less than 50 tons for a three-year period. Guess who was the first to get his name on the contract? Flavel, of course. He promptly ordered construction of the 101-foot tug *Astoria*, which was replaced by a new *Astoria* in 1887, the same year he finally retired from pilotage to his handsomely appointed home, now a museum, across from the county courthouse. He is credited with helping Astoria become a recognized seaport.

Today the bar pilots include a brave and extraordinarily capable cadre of about twenty-five men, many former ship captains or Coast Guardsmen with Master's Certificates. (Customarily but not necessarily there is only one bar pilot organization to a port.) The privately organized firm works under federal regulations, owning two boats—the *Columbia* for fair weather, the *Peacock* for foul—to transport the pilots to their rendezvous seventeen miles away.

The *Peacock* is of an unusual design: at the sharply defined stern is a sort of "way," where a smaller boat, called the daughter boat slides onto the larger one. This is launched when necessary to transport the pilot to or from a vessel. Imagine yourself poised at the brink of a tall wave, waiting for just the right moment to plummet forward and find the narrow niche of the mother boat! Piloting is not for the fainthearted; indeed, these transfers outside the bar between two wildly rolling ships have taken the lives of bar pilots.

Despite the improvements made by the Army Corps of Engineers, the sands still shift, currents are unreliable depending on the river's height, and breakers always approach the bar from a new angle. A bar pilot undergoes at least two years of specific training, no matter how experienced he was in his prior commands.

The same is true of the river pilots, who take over from the bar pilots just off the Astoria docks. The River Pilots Association, also a private enterprise, is based in Portland. With the Columbia's ship channel monitored by the Corps of Engineers and thoroughly marked with navigation guides, ships still require local knowledge of shifting channels and changing currents. A pilot says he literally can feel the changes by the behavior of a ship; and to permit a ship to slide sidewise of the river could be a life-threatening disaster or initiate a collision. That is why a river pilot cannot be absent from the river more than sixty days, or he has to undergo a re-familiarization period with another pilot. He knows the minutest details of currents and depths around the different berths for docking, and learns to work with foreign ship crews with minimal language skills.

Serious weather is relatively rare during Pacific Northwest summers; for days at a time even the Columbia Bar can be almost flat, allowing pleasure and fishing boats easy transition. But when weather is bad, the bar is dangerous; winter weather is especially fickle. Here is where the U.S. Coast Guard comes in. Headquarters are at Astoria Airport, where especially equipped rescue helicopters are located. The Aids to Navigation Team at Tongue Point maintains buoys, lights, dayboards, etc. Tucked behind Cape Disappointment are two large Coast Guard cutters, plus several smaller but very special rescue boats—incredible craft that can roll entirely over in the surf and right themselves.

The Fort Canby Lifesaving Service was funded and established in 1877, with a nine-man rowboat and a beach wagon pulled by men or horses for rescues near shore. The men shot a line by cannon to the stricken vessel, then used a breeches buoy to get people off. In 1883 crews managed to get 175 passengers off the *Queen of the Pacific* when, in low visibility from forest fire smoke, she went on Clatsop

Spit. The first lightship *Columbia* (No. 50) was stationed off the mouth of the river on April 11, 1892, and the last *Columbia* (No. 604) was replaced in 1979 by an electronic navigational buoy. During World War II, the Coast Guard patrolled beaches with dogs and horses.

Equipment continued to improve. In 1961 because of the enormous surf assailing the Columbia Bar, Cape Disappointment's lifesaving station was chosen to test a new 44-foot motorboat, a self-righting one. To train American and foreign personnel, the National Motor Lifeboat School was established there in 1968. Trainees must first hold grade E3 or better in the Coast Guard and have six prior months of experience in motor lifeboat units. Training under actual bar conditions and on rescues is not for the timid; it takes steel nerves to choke down panic when the boat takes a 360-degree roll while you are head down in the water, strapped to the boat, for what seems like hours but is only seconds. A still more sophisticated and seaworthy 47-foot aluminum craft was introduced in 1991.

From Base Astoria, airborne patrols search for illicit activities, aided by the 200-foot cutter *Resolute*. In 1978 the Coast Guard captured a 167-foot freighter with 10 tons of marijuana aboard. Helicopter patrols check the Columbia River for oil spills, including marina checks for clandestine dumping by pleasure boats. The helicopter often removes people from a distressed vessel by basket on a lowered cable, or drops rescue swimmers to help people into the basket; if injured, they are placed on a litter first. Mostly in summer there are calls to rescue swimmers swept seaward by the strong undertow or swept off the jetties by high swells.

A Coast Guard officer says that the fishermen and crabbers working outside the bar seldom are careless; the ocean warrants too much respect for that. However, engines fail, rudders or controls break, and the radius offshore from the Columbia is no place to lose control.

A few years ago an Air National Guard F-4 airplane failed, and the pilot ejected forty miles offshore in bad weather and high seas. Using sophisticated communications, a CG helicopter located the pilot, put a rescue swimmer overboard and rescued the severely injured pilot. He was so dangerously hypothermic that one helicopter pilot crawled into the bag with the F4 victim to add body warmth. The effort saved the man's life, even though he endured many surgical procedures afterward.

One of the worst disasters was on May 4, 1880, when the sea was flat and most of the fishing fleet was in the ocean. A freak wind over one hundred miles per hour arose suddenly, whipping the ocean into huge waves. In an article in *Western Boatman* (May/June 1984), Don Marshall debunks a popular, ever-expanding myth that 240 boats and 300 people were lost in that catastrophe. The toll was bad enough in fact, thirteen dead and a couple dozen capsized boats.

Shipwreck and rescue stories are endless on this dangerous coast of two thousand wrecks. One of the strangest and most riveting tales unfolded on January 12, 1991, while the author was on research in Astoria. To understand what happened that day, we must first review the dramatic events of January 12, 1961, thirty years earlier.

On that day, the Cape Disappointment Lifeboat Station received a distress call from the fishing craft *Mermaid* of Ilwaco, which had lost its rudder and was drifting into the surf near North Head. While the Coast Guard responded with a 36-foot self-righting boat and a standard 40-foot patrol boat, the weather—already terrible—worsened. In low visibility, the Coast Guard had difficulty finding the *Mermaid*. Dusk came.

Taking the boat in tow, the 40-foot Coast Guard boat under Petty Officer Darrell Murray labored into the swells toward the entrance, monitored by the 36-footer nearby. Murray asked the two fishermen aboard the *Mermaid* if they would transfer to the Coast Guard boat. When they refused, he radioed Point Adams for help from the 52-foot Triumph. In gale force winds now, the latter could not reach the other boats at Buoy 1 for two hours but then took the *Mermaid's* tow from Murray.

In the following sea, the double-ender 36-footer rode reasonably well, but the 40-footer took a series of 25-foot and higher swells, slid down a huge wave and turned over. The crew of three surfaced and climbed aboard the hull. Meanwhile, the 36-footer sustained damage, too, and—knowing it could not negotiate the roiling bar—the coxswain Larry Edwards turned toward the lightship *Columbia* seven miles out to sea. As he turned, he saw Murray's boat upside down.

Edwards edged up to the hull and snatched the men off, but in the process severely smashed his own hull. With the stern awash, the engine room half-filled with water and minimal rudder control, Edwards made it to the lightship (escorted by the pilot boat *Peacock* which had responded to the disaster), but the Coast Guard boat sank after all were taken off. During the transfer one member of Edwards' crew was swept off the ladder, only to be plucked from a succeeding wave by the lightship's engineer.

Meanwhile, the big 52-foot Coast Guard *Triumph* was in trouble, too. The towline to the foundering fishing boat *Mermaid* broke in or near the breakers, and while the *Triumph* sought to retrieve the line, the Coast Guard craft rolled over. A crewman from the *Triumph* was picked up by the *Mermaid* somehow, but then it, too, was claimed by the sea. On the *Triumph*, Gordon Huggins emerged on deck from a watertight compartment fifteen minutes later when the boat righted itself to find the other five crewmen missing. The boat rolled again, throwing him into the sea; amazingly, he was cast up on shore.

The disaster was one of the worst tragedies played out on the bar—seven men and four boats lost, two survivors from the overturned boats (plus the plucky crew of the 36-foot boat that later sank).

Now, on this morning of January 12, 1991, exactly thirty years later, the survivors and participants of that terrible disaster gathered in Astoria to mourn, to remember and to be healed of their memories. On this anniversary day, an almost identical rescue attempt ended disastrously. Early that morning a 75-foot trawler, the *Sea King*, radioed that it had taken on dangerous amounts of water in the lazarette. The engine room then flooded, and the vessel was wallowing, with the pumps unable to cope.

The Coast Guard sent its 52-foot boat, the *Triumph* (namesake of the one lost thirty years earlier) to take the boat in tow. Off Peacock Spit and North Head once again, the drama continued. The Coast Guard helicopter came to lower men from the *Triumph* to assist with pumping on the *Sea King*. In the process of removing an injured man, a basket cable broke, spilling the man back on deck. The helicopter was in danger of winding the flapping cable in its rotor, and returned to base. Matters seemed stable enough to await flood tide, rather than attempting to tow against strong ebb currents. However, winds were heavy and the vessel unwieldy; when the tow commenced, the *Sea King* suddenly broached and slid below the surface, the *Triumph* crew cutting the tow line. Six men were pulled from the water, another was missing, and two died at the scene. One of them was a Coast Guardsman unable to escape the sinking boat.

Coast Guard mariners are required to respond to every distress call, no matter what the conditions. Their motto is, "You have to go out, you don't have to come back."

Chapter 22

The Columbia, Scenic and Economic Treasure

So ends this river, Columbia's River, a fitting and defiant termination of a stream of multiple personality and mood. A river that gives life to the drylands of Washington and takes away the crumbling debris of earth from its eroding canyons and pulverized mountains. A freeway for ships and a highway for salmon. The thoroughfare on which man traveled to visit his neighbor and the killer that claimed his children in its swift rapids.

Along its tortuous 1,214 miles are diverse images. Bubbling water chattering across the gravel of its birth. The raucous cries of birds on the marshes of the birth valley. Snow and a stillness of the wild on Kinbasket Lake. Grizzly bears swinging their massive heads beside giant man-made dams. The reflections of bluff and forest on the lonely stretches of lake above Revelstoke. Happy cries of children swimming in the Arrow Lakes, and the splash of kokanee in distant coves. The growl of chain saws in the nearby forests and the puffs of steam from factories turning trees into paper for this book to be written on. Frightening giant whirlpools waiting to swallow up boats or people. Tiny fingerlings waiting to be loosed in the blue reaches of Lake Roosevelt that disappear into the distance.

The whine of turbines at Grand Coulee, Bonneville and lesser dams as they turn out electricity to light and heat our homes and run businesses, and the shrieks of seagulls as they wheel and dive to gobble up salmon trying to travel upstream. Cowboys silhouetted in still waters, their herds driven before them in scenes as old as America. The prehistoric cliffs looming above and reflected in the pools above Wenatchee. Arid lands that pant for water and reward one with greenery if they get it. Squat buildings seemingly from another land at Hanford, and the serene, reflective reaches beside them where the only sounds are bird calls and the soft plunk of jumping fish.

Straining to see across the glassy waters where Lewis and Clark delighted in their discovery of the River of the West at the Snake. A claustrophobic recognition of the danger of barren cliffs and rough waters below Wallula Gap. The echo of oxen and wagons lying ghostly and tangibly near Umatilla, where the Oregon Trail pioneers came to the river. Roaring Celilo Falls, now lying beneath still waters, but remembering the shouts of Indian fishermen and the slap of huge salmon.

The still awe-inspiring canyons and drowned rapids of the Columbia Gorge, with its snow-covered sentinels of Mount Hood and Mount St. Helens on either shore. Fleet sailboards skipping across the windswept river, challenging the swooping birds. Commerce and bustle of airplanes, automobiles and ships at Vancouver and Portland. The sky darkened with birds from refuges adjacent to urban centers, wildlife and people living amicably together. Losing oneself in the channels of the islands to imagine that no one else exists. Tramping the ragged shores teeming with reminders of rural past. Columbia's River, broad and swollen, spreading into bays and coves, then narrowing, gathering itself for its final thrust into the sea.

What lies ahead? The questions that are asked have complex answers. The questions include:

Under the Columbia Treaty, Americans' purchase of power from Canada expires thirty years after each project goes on line. The treaties will expire within a decade. How will this affect them?

How are salmon runs to be maintained without destroying our need for inexpensive power sources?

The shipping channels need dredging; where will the material be placed? Will land-use laws prevent filling river banks for industrial sites?

Can the life-taking Columbia Bar be yet improved to minimize its dangers? Should it be?

What is a just distribution of water rights among Indian people, ranchers, power makers, fishermen?

How can the Indian nations be assisted in making transitions to modern life? Practically, they cannot go back to a total salmon economy.

With management of wildlife, lopsided populations of sea lions, harbor seals, and birds are destroying more salmon than hatcheries can produce. What is an equitable solution?

How are recreational sports on the river and commercial shipping to coexist without harm to either?

Factories once seriously polluted the river, and individuals threw every kind of offal and garbage into it. Largely we have remedied these matters. How can we continue to clean up decades of neglect? What is the plan for dealing with an oil spill?

We think we have flooding under control, but what are the contingency plans for a flood of the magnitude of 1894 or 1948?

Northwest residents love their river dearly. Can we work together to create justice for all users?

The Willamette River (tributary) that runs through Portland.

Chapter 23

Travel and Trivia • Portland/Vancouver to the Sea

PORTLAND AREA.

Portland is a large cosmopolitan city with numerous attractions and historical points, as well as annual events of interest, all too numerous to mention in this book. Please acquire a comprehensive travel book to peruse them. Frommer's Guide is one popular edition. However, here are a few special notes pertinent to this book's text. www.travelportland.com

Portland Rose Festival. A major international festival today held in May-June. C.E.S. Wood, a soldier quoted in this book for his description of an Indian encampment, became a painter and poet of Portland later. He suggested holding an annual rose show. More than 60 events, a stunning parade, and celebrities. www.rosefestival.org

World Forestry Center. Its location on Southwest Canyon Road is on the route of Portland's original Plank Road. A remarkable museum for learning about the logging and lumbering world with large displays and exhibits. The center also maintains an outdoor learning center, Magness Memorial Tree Farm near Sherwood, Oregon, that includes a demonstration forest, forestry classes, summer camps, and such. The World Forestry Center is privately funded and not part of the U.S. Forest Service. www.worldforestry.org

Oregon Zoo, formerly named Washington Park Zoo, is near the World Forestry Center on 67 acres in southwest Portland, an area called West Hills. In the words of one zoo employee, animals are from Uganda to Alaska and from pinhead size to elephants. www.oregonzoo.org

Oregon Museum of Science and Industry often known as just OMSI. On Southeast Water Street near the Marquam Bridge across the Willamette River. Omnimax, five large auditoriums, planetarium, and major exhibits, light show. www. www.omsi.edu

Tom McCall Waterfront Park. A walking park of 36.59 acres along both sides of the Willamette River in downtown Portland named for Oregon's governor 1967-75. Obtain map from visitor centers or other.

Oregon Historical Society. The downtown, several-story building is one of the most active historical societies in the nation. Displays of Oregon and Columbia River history, extensive archives, library, and comprehensive book shop. The society publishes books, has a speakers bureau, and educational service department. Lecture series. Television series in conjunction with Oregon Public Broadcasting. www.ohs.org

Oregon Maritime Museum. Especially important to Columbia River history buffs. Has large archives. Walk through the commerciaol sternwheeler *Portland*. It is the last steam-powered sternwheel tugboat built in the United States and is entered in the National Register of Historic Places. At least two other large craft are moored there, too, a barge and a fishing boat. www.oregonmaritimemuseum. org

Benson Hotel. Lumber magnate Simon Benson built the hotel in 1913, still operating in style downtown. Benson contributed water fountains to the city in hopes that his off-duty loggers would drink water, not booze. Perhaps some did…. www.bensonhotel.com

Heathman Hotel. Another historic hotel (1920s) in downtown noted for its afternoon tea. www.heathmanhotel.com

Champoeg Historical Pageant. Champoeg State Park near Oregon City is considered the birthplace of Oregon. It was a meeting place for Oregon Trail pioneers, Indians, fur traders, and adventurers. Stories about early Oregon are told. National End of the Trail Museum. Dr. John McLoughlin's (HBC friend of settlers) house. Other historical events. Friends of Historic Champoeg. www. champoeg.org

Oregonian. Newspaper still the voice of the area was started in 1860 by Henry L. Pittock. When he started work, it is said he slept on a shelf below the counter, and it was so cold that he poured boiling water on the composing stones to melt the ice. Today it is a sophisticated big city publisher of the newspaper and other publications.

Henry Weinhard's Brewery, founded in 1862 and considered the west's oldest, continuously operated brewery, still brews popular beers. www. henryweinhards.com

Port of Portland. Oveersees maritime traffic on the Columbia and Willamette rivers, real estate, dredging, aviation and who knows what else along the rivers. A major port for ships plying the Pacific Ocean and beyond and, of course, Columbia River craft. Several cruise ships, many docked near Jantzen Beach crossing (which formerly had an amusement park), have five-day, six-night cruises up the Columbia and Snake rivers as far as Lewiston, Idaho. There are ships that take passengers from Portland to Puget Sound and Victoria. Popular riverside hotels have been and are Red Lion on the River at Jantzen Beach, Portland, and Red Lion at the Quay near I-5, Vancouver WA. www.portofportland.com www.redlion.com

Vancouver, WA. Across the river from Portland in Washington State.

Vancouver is smaller than the Portland metropolis and developed differently from Portland historically. When the Americans increasingly moved into Oregon, the English Hudson's Bay Company moved from the mouth of the Columbia River to a larger site at Vancouver. Called Fort Vancouver, it was not necessarily built for military purposes but as a center for HBC's far north fur dealings. Supply ships came from the ocean to Vancouver, after which the supplies and messages were sent by fast courier boats up the Columbia and its northerly tributaries to the fur posts, with the reverse trip bringing furs to Vancouver to be sent to Britain and elsewhere. After the departure of the British into Canada at Fort Langley, Vancouver was a maritime port, a lumber and logging center, and also a military post. See text. As always, today its fortunes are tied inexorably to the Columbia River and adjacent mountains. Gateway to Mount St. Helens and information about the 1980 eruption. Helicopter rides over the crater. Riverside restaurants to watch boats. Mountain hiking trails. Lantern-lit tours of Fort Vancouver early January to mid-February. Annual bonsai conference September. www.visitvancouverusa.com

Fort Vancouver National Historic Site. One can almost hear the joyous song of the voyageurs as they swept up to the docks to deliver furs and messages. Chief Factor Loughlin's home. Palings surround the site. They were not to repel attacks, but to prevent robbers from stealing the substantial supplies at the fort. Research library, book shop, film presentations, Brigade Encampment in mid-July features fur trapper stories. Giant fireworks on 4th of July. www.fortvan.org

Vancouver Barracks. A sub-post to Fort Lewis, the military camp was established on May 15, 1849, and served as home to several military groups including the Fourth, Seventh and Fourteenth Infantries. It was the first military post in the Northwest. The Barracks gradually is being transferred to the National Park Service. Still standing is a row of graceful homes that housed top brass such as Nelson Miles, Philip Sheridan, and Ulysses S. Grant.

Pearson Air Museum at Pearson Air Park. Most of the airplanes at the museum were built before or during World War II. Aviation memorabilia. Has a flight simulator station where visitors can try flying the old birds. The airport was formerly a military airport associated with Vancouver Barracks, and the Barracks, Pearson and Fort Vancouver all are listed as a National Historic Site. Local pioneer flyer made the first crossing of the Columbia River from Portland to Vancouver Barracks (Pearson) in a dirigible. In 1937 two intrepid Soviet aviators landed there after the first ever trans-polar flight. www.visitvancouverusa.com

Chelatchie Prairie Railroad, aka Lewis & Clark Railway. Popular 10-mile ride from town of Battleground, north of the river, to get Christmas trees at

Moulton Falls, site of huge sawmill, near Yacolt, center of devastating1902 fire that swept all the way to the Pacific. www.bycx.com

Christmas Parade of Boats. Find a dining spot on either side of the Columbia River to watch the annual parade. A lifetime memory.

Pomeroy Living History Farm. Yacolt educational museum especially popular with children. Farm life of the 1920s. Steam Logging Show early June. Staff dressed in 1920s clothes. Hayrides, cider pressing, theme teas, sometimes muzzle loader groups. www.pomeroyfarm.org

Ridgefield National Wildlife Refuge, on Columbia's shore 10 miles west of Vancouver on 5,218 acres. Reserve of Columbia River floodplain lands for habitat, especially winter refuge, for thousands of songbirds and other birds from sandhill cranes to Canadian geese. Lesser number of animals includes coyotes, black-tailed deer, brush rabbits, otter, etc. A replica of a Chinook Indian cedar plankhouse. Hiking trails. www.fws.gov

Hidden House. Now a restaurant the home was that of successful businessman, Lowell Hidden, and has the original stained glass, door knobs, and woodwork. Hidden's Brick Factory provided the bricks in 1871 to build Mother Joseph's Providence Academy. See text. www.touchofathens.com

Pioneer Mother Statue. In Esther Short Park, the statue honors the women who settled Oregon Territory.

Clark County Historical Museum. Memorabilia about pioneers such as Mother Joseph, Esther Short, Lowell Hidden, and more. Archives and extensive Clark County photograph collection. Kaiser Shipyards information. www.cchmuseum.org

Cedar Creek Grist Mill. North of Vancouver at confluence of Lewis River with Columbia, the mill is the only operating 19th century grist mill in Washington. Includes a log flume. Tours and description of how a grist mill served early pioneer's needs. From May-September the mill's volunteers help visitors cook up typical pioneer foods containing materials processed by the grist mill or turn wool into yarn. www.cedarcreekgristmill.com

TOWARD THE ESTUARY.

Fort William and Sauvie Island. Nathaniel Wyeth had some shortcoming as an explorer, but he recognized pleasant country when he founded the fort on Sauvie Island, accessed only from a bridge off U.S. Highway 30. Superb bird-watching at the north end at the wildlife refuge. From Reeder Beach on Multnomah Channel you can almost touch passing ships. This was once a riverboat stop. Fishing, hunting, houseboat dwellers, RVs, camping. http://sauvieisland.org

Trojan Nuclear Plant. The massive installation produced nuclear power from 1976 to 1993.It was the largest pressure water reactor built. Power was not as inexpensive as anticipated, and the plant was under siege the entire time by antinuclear activists. During the decommissioning period, in 2001 the massive reactor was encased in shrink-wrap plastic and foam and barged to Hanford, where it was buried in a 45-foot deep pit and covered with six inches of gravel. The cooling tower was demolished by dynamite in 2008, and all that remains of the site next to the Columbia are several buildings.

St. Helens. The small town is not the burgeoning metropolis on the Columbia that it once was but a charming place to visit with historic buildings and homes wandering over the hills. Old Towne, a Nationally Registered Historic Site, is 10 blocks of historic buildings that include old shipbuilding and loggers' sites. The town once had a major basalt quarry and was an important river town. St. Helens is still the county seat of Columbia County. Tours of the homes and sites during Historic Days late May. Klondike Restaurant still operates in what was one wing of the St. Helens Hotel, with the rest having been demolished in 1954. Has original 28-foot bar. Columbia River Fest in mid-August. The Chamber of Commerce is in the historic train station. www.ci.st-helens.or.us

Tom Flippen Home, town of Clatskanie on south shore of Columbia, is a "Castle" and open to visitors. Flippen was a successful lumberman. Simon Benson once had a home here, too-.

Kelso and Longview. The towns are separate but essentially run together. Kelso is known as the "Smelt Capital of the World" for the small, silvery fish that appear suddenly in January and February and leave as quickly. Dipping for smelt ia popular in the river. The Cowlitz County Museum has exhibits and information on the Hudson's Bay Company farming efforts in the Cowlitz area during the 1800s and other lore. At Woodland near the river's course are the Hulda Klager Gardens featuring new varieties of lilacs. Kelso honors its namesake in Scotland with an annual Highlander Festival in early September. www.kelsolongviewchamber.org

Longview was/is the center of extensive lumbering activity, Businessmen congregated at the Monticello Hotel for social talks and events. It was built and given in the 1920s to the community by city founder R.A. Long. Mounted on the imposing lobby walls are 46 oil portraits by artist Joe Knowles. Many pertain to Columbia River history, including works about Robert Gray, John J. Astor. Chief Joseph, wreck of the ship *Peacock*, and such. He made national headlines by spending two months in the wild stark naked with no supplies to prove man could survive in nature. www.themonticello.net

Here the Columbia River makes a significant turn to flow purposefully toward the Pacific. It winds through gem-like small islands scattered across the lower Columbia River. To commemorate the 1992 Bicentennial of Captain Gray's discovery of the Columbia River, the Oregon Historical Society created in 1991 the **Columbia River Heritage Canoe Trail** that begins at Clatskanie and ends near the junction of the John Day River into the Columbia near Astoria. Because of the islands, it is a peaceful, bucolic, and beautiful 45-mile paddle through Julia Butler Hansen National Wildlife Refuge for the White-tailed Deer and the Lewis &

Clark National Wildlife Refuge that was part of Lewis & Clark's original pathway to the ocean. www.trails.com

Westport and Cathlamet. On opposite sides of the river, the two hamlets are connected by a small ferry. Both towns were/are closely associated with the maritime commerce toward Astoria and the Pacific – tugboats, salmon runs, salmon canneries, Each is a charming settlement with old, well-kept buildings. Cathlamet's historic importance is as the site for HBC employee James Birnie's fur trading post. The Wahkiakum Courthouse (named after the Indian groups originally settled in that area) was built in 1921 and still in use. Cathlamet was home to Congresswoman Julia Hansen Butler. Find her book *Singing Paddles*. Bald Eagle Days in July celebrates the selection of the bald eagle as a national symbol. Gray's River Covered Bridge west of Cathlamet is a century-old structure still in fine shape with its own historical celebration in October. www.cathlametchamber.com

Skamakowa. The tiny settlement once was a steamboat port, now on the National Register of Historic Places reincarnated as the Inn at Skamakowa Landing on pilings over the river. Redmen Hall is a restored pioneer schoolhouse atop a steep hill and is now a local small museum. The entire shores on the Washington side were sites for numerous salmon canneries, most of which have completely disappeared or are broken-down wrecks. Several B&Bs and inns have taken advantage of the bluffs of this scenic shore for ship-watching and rural charm. See text. Also see Carlton Appelo's books on the small shore settlements. www.welcometowahkiakum.com.

Elochman Slough Marina, Cathlamet, is a popular base for a few hundred boats that use the Columbia River estuary often. Yurt camping. www.cathlametmarina.org

Julia Hansen Butler National Wildlife Refuge. Mentioned in text and above several times. www.fws.gov

Lewis & Clark National Wildlife Refuge. www.fws.gov

Astoria Megler Bridge was opened in 1966 from Astoria to Point Ellice near Megler across the Columbia River, which sharply widens near the entry to the ocean. The 4.1 mile bridge is the longest continuous three-span-through-truss bridge in the world. The ship channel portion is more than a thousand feet wide and rises 200 feet high. Huge ocean liners and freighters pass under the bridge with no problem, fun to watch from seashore restaurants. Read more about the bridge on Internet sites. One site is www.oldoregon.com In mid-October you can run across during the Great Columbia Crossing event, Accidents are infrequent but, in 2012, an empty semi-truck was blown onto its side during a 101 MPH gust. It did not fall into the river. www.greatcolumbiacrossing.com

Chinook beyond the bridge toward the Pacific is the approximate refuge of Lewis & Clark before they were able to cross the broad Columbia. A plaque near Highway 101 between bridge and Chinook marks the spot.

Sea Resources is a historic salmon hatchery in the area.

LONG BEACH PENINSULA AREA

Warning: The parks and towns of this area post warnings. Be sure to heed them. Each year visitors are swept out to sea from jetties or beaches. Rogue waves occur here, and breakers are far higher than the average at times.

Long Beach Peninsula Visitors Bureau. See text. www.northcoast.com Long Beach Peninsula is a national sliver of land that stretches for 23+ miles north of the Columbia Bar. It is a natural formation but has been widened by the building of the breakwaters and natural sands build-up. It has always been a major destination for Columbia River and Pacific Coast visitors, who provide the peninsula's primary industry. The bluffs and lands around Cape Disappointment spawned several sites discussed below. The peninsula largely has visitor amenities and events including the International Kite Festival in late August. Visitors should also visit the World Kite Museum and Hall of Fame.. At the north end of the peninsula is Willapa National Wildlife Refuge with a pristine 274-acre cedar grove. Oysterville has a jazz festival in August.

http://funbeach.com is the address for most little towns along the peninsula.

Ilwaco. http://ilwacowashington.com Riverside town and home town for about 1,000 people who include the staff and brave mariners at the **National Motor Lifeboat School** and **Coast Guard Cape Disappointment Station.** www.uscg.mil The latter responds to emergencies by vessels crossing the once-notorious and still dangerous Columbia Bar, the entrance of the river to the ocean. See text. The CG has 50 on staff and uses one 52-foot vessel, two 47-foot vessels, three 25-foot boars and utility vessels for its needs. The 52 and 47-foot boats are especially designed for surf and breaker use, and can be rolled over without damage under worst situations. Often helicopter assistance is rendered from the Astoria Airport.

Columbia Pacific Heritage Museum. In earlier days a narrow-gauge railroad ran the length of the Peninsula, sometimes dampened by the tides. Dubbed the Clamshell Railroad it was popular with weekenders. Clamshell Railroad Days in mid-July. Peninsula Quilt Guild show in mid-March. Loyalty Day Children's Parade and Blessing of the Fleet after which the 52-foot CG boat is on display at the Ilwaco dock, early May. http://columbiapacificheritagemuseum.org

Lewis & Clark Interpretive Center. Atop Cape Disappointment. Large murals about the L & C expedition. Glassed-in viewing areas offer dramatic views of the Columbia Bar, the modern jetty and coasts. Shipwrecks and lifesaving exhibition. Short film presentations. Maritime and river displays. Open all year. www.parks.wa.gov See text also.

Cape Disappointment State Park (formerly Fort Canby State Park). Extends along the ocean for two miles from the Bar. Hiking, beach combing and adjacent towns of Ilwaco and Long Beach and its peninsula to explore. Fort Canby at the Cape was a military garrison to protect the mouth of the Columbia beginning in 1852 with actual construction in 1863, spurred partly by the Civil War. The garrison had a barracks, a few buildings, and operated as many as four 12-inch mortars and five 6-inch guns. The park includes the Lewis & Clark Interpretive Center and the North Head Lighthouse. A machine gun installation originally was below the Cape on the seashore. The fort served until 1945 or after the end of WWII, along with Fort Columbia, located more easterly of the Cape along today's Highway 101 in Chinook Point National Landmark with eight guns. Fort Stevens in Oregon completed the original defenses of the mouth of the Columbia River. **Fort Columbia** still has remains of about 30 buildigs, barracks, and old batteries (gunnery installations). Walk the coastal trail through Fort Canby State Park among giant Sitka spruce trees and wildflowers in season. www.parks.wa.gov

The Shelburne Country Inn. Most of the Long Beach Peninsula is devoted to tourism but The Shelburne Country Inn (has restaurant) merits mention as a historic gem built in 1895 and still going strong. Art, antiques, stained glass, views. www.shelburneinn.com

You can drive your car on the hard-packed sand of the Peninsula. Watch the tides and waves, though.

Lady Washington, 72-foot replica of Captain Robert Gray's second ship (the first was the *Columbia Rediviva*) was faithfully created and moored at Gray's Harvor, north of the Columbia River. It was launched in 1989, eventually became the official State Ship of Washington, and continues each year to host groups at ports in Puget Sound, the Strait of Georgia, and elsewhere in the Pacific Northwest. www.historicalseaport.org

Astoria. The major historical town in Oregon that fronts on the Columbia River and Baker Bay, part of the broad waters that exist just before the river forces its way into the Pacific Ocean. Connected to Washington by a 4.1 mile bridge (above) and a road along the river from Portland to the rest of the world. Ride the Astoria Trolley along the river shore downtown. Scandinavian Midsummer Festival mid-June, Astoria Festival of Music early July. Maritime art in many galleries is special due to setting. See text for history. www.astoria.or.us www.oldoregon.com (Visitors Bureau and Welcome Center).

Columbia River Maritime Museum. The riverside building may be one of the world's greatest. Exhibits, galleries, and archives deal with the HBC fur trade and exploration period, fishing, sailing, and steam vessels, river fleet. Displays of the "butterfly fleet" and other vessels. Moored outside is the lightship *Columbia*. Today's big ships pass by from ocean to Portland very close to the museum. Wrecks on the Bar. Rescue equipment. Archives. Everything nautical. It was the site of the celebration of the 200th anniversary of Captain Gray's discovery of the river. Author JoAnn Roe was invited to sign the 1991 version of *The Columbia River* at the Bicentennial celebration in the plaza of the Maritime Museum. One buyer was Robert Gray, the Captain's namesake and direct descendant. The text you are reading is roughly the same but the Travel & Trivia sections are totally different. *Caxton Press.* www.crmm.org

Fort Clatsop. Lewis and Clark spent the winter about five miles from Astoria in a wooded area on the Lewis & Clark River. Recreated low buildings, walkway to the L&C dock. Interpretive center. At times live models in period clothing. Special events include matters such as firing muzzle loaders. www.nps.gov or www.ohs. org

Heritage Center Museum. Also **Flavel House.** Local and region history of this important river area. Wrecks, including artifacts from the ship, *Peter Iredale,* that went aground on the Bar with remains above water and sand that lasted for years and now are almost gone. Bar pilots including George Flavel, long-time pioneer pilot. Indian artifacts. Info on many old historic homes of the area. 10,000 catalogued historical photographs. Books. www.oldoregon.com

Astoria Column. Built in 1926, the column sits on a 600-foot bluff, Coxcomb Hill. It is 125 feet tall, providing a sweeping view of the mouth of the Columbia River and 360 degrees far beyond. You will climb 162 steps to the top. The Column was built by the Great Northern Railway and grandson of John Jacob Astor, Vincent, to honor the family's participation in Astoria's beginnings and growth. Murals around the Column tell of Oregon's history. www.astoriacolumn. org www.oldoregon.com

Astor Public Library has unusually complete historical collections.

Fort Astoria. At 15th and Exchange Streets is a bastion representing the original fort. Also nearby is a monument inscribed in English and Japanese to honor **Ranald MacDonald,** grandson of Chief Comcomly and son of Archiband McDonald, HBC factor and Comcomly's daughter. MacDonald was raised as any other HBC offspring, well-educated. He went off to sea and eventually became the first teacher of English in Japan to 14 Japanese, one (possibly two) of whom greeted Admiral Perry's fleet in Tokyo Bay. See *Ranald MacDonald, Pacific Rim Adventurer* (WSU Press, by JoAnn Roe).

Fort Stevens. Third leg of the three forts protecting the mouth of the Columbia River (Canby and Columbia in WA, Stevens in OR) Over the years since WWII the fort properties have grown to be 4,200-acre State Park. Military museum that includes an underground gun battery almost a century old and samples of mines removed from the Columbia River following wars. Details about the little-known attack on the fort by a WWII Japanese submarine. Remains of the old trestle for the railroad that brought rock to the river entrance to build the jetty. Walk the long Clatsop Spit that reaches to the south edge of the entrance to the Columbia River. A tower exists to enhance viewing the surroundings. Remains of the ship *Peter Iredale* are almost gone. Numerous ships and boats have been wrecked on the spit. While walking, be aware of changing tides and wave heights. www.oregonstateparks.org www.nwcwc.org www.oldoregon.com

Books about the sea and coast by Jim Gibbs (some out of print) include *Oregon's Salty Coast* and *West Coast Windjammers*, both by Superior Publishing Company.

Charter boats abound. Take one on the broad reaches of the Columbia River before it meets the Pacific or on the Pacific itself. Fishing or sightseeing.

Scenic flights from Astoria Airport. Whale watching or sightseeing.

Twilight Eagle Sanctuary. East of Astoria on Highway 30, turn on Burnside just past mile market 88, drive one-half mile. Viewing platform and interpretive signs. Bald eagles.

Selected Bibliography

The complete bibliography has been filed with the Columbia Gorge Interpretive Center in Stevenson, Washington, where it is available for perusal. Of approximately two hundred books and manuscripts consulted, the following were particularly useful:

"A Salute to Timber," special section, *White Salmon Enterprise, The Dalles Weekly Reminder, and Hood River News*, November 7-9, 1989.

Cross, Francis E., and Parkin, Charles M., Jr. *Sea Venture*. St. Petersburg, FL: Valkyrie Publishing House, Inc., 1981.

Dark, Russell. "History of Bar Pilots," unpublished manuscript in Astor Public Library, Astoria, OR.

Downs, Art. *Paddlewheels on the Frontier*. Sidtrey, BC: Gray's Publishing Ltd., 1972.

Feagans, Raymond J. *The Railroad that Ran By the Tide*. Berkeley, CA; Howell-NorthBooks, 1972.

Freeman, Lewis R. *Down the Columbia*. New York: Dodd, Mead and Company, 1921.

From Pioneers to Power. Grand Coulee, WA: Bicentennial Association Committee, 1965.

Gibbs, Jim. *Windjammers of the Pacific Rim*. Seattle: Superior Publishing Company, 1968.

Golden Memories. Golden, BC: Golden and District Historical Society, 1982.

Gray, W. H. *A History of Oregon*. Portland, OR: W. H. Gray, 1870.

Green, William Spotswood. *Among the Selkirk Glaciers*. London and New York: Macmillan and Co., 1890.

History of Skamania County. Stevenson, WA: Skamania Historical Society, 1958 [?].

Holbrook, Stewart. *Holy Old Mackinaw*. New York: The Macmillan Company, 1956.

Howay, Frederick W. *Voyages of the "Columbia."* Boston: The Massachusetts Historical Society, 1941.

Kerr, Charles C. "The World of the World," anthology of newspaper articles 1905-80, *Wenatchee Daily World.*

Kosachova, N. G. "The Doukhobors," in *Russian Canadians.* Ottawa: Borealis Press, 1983.

Lawrence, M. J. *The Columbia Unveiled.* Los Angeles: The Times-Mirror Press.

_____.*Lewis and Clark's Journals.* New York: A. S. Barnes and Company, 1904.

Lewis, Meriwether. Introduction by Archibald Hanna. *Lewis and Clark Expedition*, 3 vols. Philadelphia and New York: J. B. Lippincott, 1961.

Lockley, Fred. *History of the Columbia River Valley.* Chicago: The S. J. Clarke Publishing Company, 1928.

Lyman, William Denison. *The Columbia River.* New York and London: G.P. Putnam's Sons, 1917.

McClelland, John M., Jr. *Longview.* Portland, OR: Binfords & Mort, 1949.

Maben, Manly. *Vanport.* Portland, OR: Oregon Historical Society Press, 1987.

Marshall, Don. *Oregon Shipwrecks.* Portlaild, OR: Binfords & Mort, 1984.

Miller, Emma Gene. *Clatsop County Oregon.* Portland, OR: Binfords & Mort, 1958.

Purdy, Ruby Fay. *The Rose City of the World.* Portland, OR: Binfords & Mort, 1947.

The Quarterdeck, selected editions. Columbia Maritime Museum, Astoria, OR.

"Rainshadow," historial pamphlet prepared by Royal City High School (WA) Social Studies Class. Wanapum Dam Visitors Center.

Raufer, Sister Maria. O. P. *Black Robes and Indians.* Milwaukee: The Bruce Publishing Company, 1966.

Ross, Alexander, edited by Thwaites, Reuben Gold. *Adventures of the First Settlers of the Oregon or Columbia River.* Cleveland: The Arthur H. Clark Company, 1904.

Ruby, Robert H., and Brown, John A. *Half-Sun on the Columbia.* Norman: University of Oklahoma Press, 1965.

_____.*The Spokane Indians.* Norman: University of Oklahoma Press, 1970.

Seufert, Francis. *Wheels of Fortune.* Edited by Thomas Vaughan. Portland, OR: Oregon Historical Society, 1980.

Splawn, A. J. *Ka-mi-akin* Mrs. A. J. Splawn, 1917. [Bellingham Public Library, Washington.]

"The Story of the Columbia Basin Project." Washington, D.C.: U.S. Government Printing Office.

Turner, Robert D. *Sternwheelers and Steam Tugs.* Victoria, BC: Sono Nis Press, 1984.

Tyrrell, J.B., editor. *David Thompson's Narrative.* Toronto: The Champlain Society, 1916.

Van Arsdol, Ted. *Vancouver.* Northridge, CA: Windsor Publications, l986.

Wheeler, A. O. *The Selkirk Range.* Ottawa: Government Printing Bureau, 1905.

White, Derryll. *Fort Steele.* Surrey, BC: Heritage House Publishing Company Ltd., 1988.

Index

Index

OTHER TITLES ABOUT
THE WEST
FROM
CAXTON PRESS

The Pony Express Trail
Yesterday and Today
by William Hill
ISBN 978-0-87004-476-2, 302 pages, paper, $18.95

The Lewis and Clark Trail
Yesterday and Today
by William Hill
ISBN 978-0-87004-439-7, 300 pages, paper, $16.95

A Fate Worse Than Death
Indian Captivities in the West
by William Hill
ISBN 0-87004-xxx-x, xxx pages, paper, $18.95

The Deadliest Indian War in the West
The Snake Conflict 1864-1868
by Gregory Michno
ISBN 978-0-87004-460-1, 450 pages, paper, $18.95

Massacre Along the Medicine Road
The Indian War of 1864 in Nebraska
by Ronald Becher
ISBN 0-87004-289-7, 500 pages, cloth, $32.95
ISBN 0-87004-387-0, 500 pages, paper, $22.95

For a free catalog of Caxton titles write to:

Caxton Press
312 Main Street
Caldwell, Idaho 83605-3299

or

Visit our Internet web site:

www.caxtonpress.com

*Caxton Pres*s is a division of The Caxton Printers, Ltd.